MAVERICK
VOICES

Logos
Perspectives on Modern Society and Culture
Michael J. Thompson, Series Editor

The books in the Logos series examine modern society, politics and culture, emphasizing the connections between these spheres rather than their academic separateness. Skeptical of what current intellectual trends call "interdisciplinary," titles in this series explore the ways that politics, economics, and culture inform one another, overlap, and weave the complex fabric of modern life in a global context. By putting forth bold ideas written to appeal to a broad range of interests, the series situates itself within the long tradition of intelligent social critique.

Islam and the West
Critical Perspectives on Modernity
Edited by Michael J. Thompson

Maverick Voices
Conversations with Political and Cultural Rebels
Kurt Jacobsen

Forthcoming
Planetary Politics
Human Rights, Terror, and Global Society
Edited by Stephen Eric Bronner

MAVERICK VOICES

Conversations with Political and Cultural Rebels

Kurt Jacobsen

ROWMAN & LITTLEFIELD PUBLISHERS, INC.

Lanham • Boulder • New York • Toronto • Oxford

ROWMAN & LITTLEFIELD PUBLISHERS, INC.

Published in the United States of America
by Rowman & Littlefield Publishers, Inc.
A wholly owned subsidiary of The Rowman & Littlefield Publishing Group, Inc.
4501 Forbes Boulevard, Suite 200, Lanham, Maryland 20706
www.rowmanlittlefield.com

PO Box 317
Oxford
OX2 9RU, UK

Copyright © 2004 by Rowman & Littlefield Publishers, Inc.

British Library Cataloguing in Publication Information Available

Library of Congress Cataloging-in-Publication Data

Maverick voices : conversations with political and cultural rebels /
[edited by] Kurt Jacobsen.
    p. cm. — (Logos)
  Includes bibliographical references and index.
  ISBN 0-7425-3395-6 (hardcover : alk. paper)—ISBN 0-7425-3396-4 (pbk. : alk. paper)
  1. Biography. 2. Interviews. I. Jacobsen, Kurt, 1949–. II. Series: Logos
(Rowman & Littlefield, Inc.)
  CT105.M385 2004
  920'.009'04—dc22

                                                          2003026835

Printed in the United States of America

∞™ The paper used in this publication meets the minimum requirements of
American National Standard for Information Sciences—Permanence of Paper
for Printed Library Materials, ANSI/NISO Z39.48-1992.

In memory of Nell Wendler,
and for Jack

CONTENTS

INTRODUCTION

Mavericks may not make this infuriating world go around, but they do make it an infinitely more interesting place. Of course, every now and then these intrepidly independent souls spur the resistant societies surrounding them to lurch forward, ever so grudgingly, along a path toward a slightly more decent (or less ruthless), slightly more open (or less bigoted), and slightly wiser (or less gullible) society. But their subversive influence is more likely to build over time, as a slow accumulation of eye-opening gibes that the wider world absorbs until, as W. H. Auden wrote of Sigmund Freud, a fierce maverick in his own era, their hitherto heretical views constitute a "whole climate of opinion." And then? New mavericks come along. It's just insidious.

Maverick Voices offers seventeen interviews with, or about, daring and determined artists, writers, filmmakers, psychotherapists, and activists who, despite the odds, succeeded in their chosen fields and gained some, or even a lot of, recognition. Mavericks usually do not fare so well in the way of rewards, which are bestowed by establishment entities, because they either are systematically stymied or don't angle adequately for them.[1] "Prominent iconoclast" is nearly oxymoronic; the two words rarely pair up. Many a preening "maverick" celebrated today is little more than a shrewd self-advertiser or pure studio creation who very carefully ventures only within sight of the jagged edge of conventionality, lest he or she suffer unpopularity or even spark reprisals.

Aspiring hotshots realize that one way to get ahead is to glom on to a risky but intriguing perspective and then tame it to suit the authorities' bottom line. So the music producer seeks a white who sounds just like a talented black; the scholar reshapes radical views into a neutered form that wary gatekeepers in the profession will welcome; the brash film-maker, rocker, or writer dabbles at rebelliousness while aching all the while to settle chummily into the lucrative mainstream. A lip-curling collagenic sneer, a double-nose-coned bustier, wraparound designer shades, or scads of Spanish leather, alas, are no assurance of authenticity. Once inside the cozy throne room, they find that the scantily clad emperor starts to look remarkably well attired after all. Few such folk could conceive that anyone would ever do anything except play the odds. "Survival at the top," Colin Powell remarked, "is pragmatics," as is reaching it.[2] Real mavericks are not cult or club members—or, at least, not for long. There is no such thing as a school of mavericks; if anything, they shoo away disciples. Mavericks may strike poses too, but they can back them up. If they somehow inspire a new school (e.g., psychoanalysis, surrealism, and even Marxism), it is usually rather unfair to blame the innovators for the rigid routinizers that their alleged disciples often become.[3]

Every emperor remains stark naked—and not just when it is to the maverick's advantage to notice. Why do supremely talented people take this difficult road, the one so dishearteningly less traveled by? What drives them to go against the tide? Is it principles or prejudices (into which principles easily can degenerate) or defective genes or Oedipal mischief or sheer cantankerousness? One doubts that there is a ready-made formula. Noam Chomsky, a notable (and thus widely derided) maverick himself, speculated that "because of the unique linguistic capacities of the human species," there may be an inborn basis for freedom, for an unruly tendency to venture beyond cultural and material boundaries—which may be a stronger yen in some folks than in others, depending on luck and circumstance.[4]

The outsider role often is simply forced on people by minority status. So one perforce becomes the "stranger," or marginal figure, who sees the culture in all its hidden facets unhindered by the approved blinders everyone else wears, or pretends to wear. A maverick is distinguished from a meritorious misfit by willfully becoming a thorn in the side of the trendsetters and the powerholders. A maverick deliberately veers off the well-plotted course, heading way out where there be dragons. The alluring *terra incognita* exerts an irresistible pull. The stance of outsider is where every true artist or writer winds up anyway. To an unquantifiable and untraceable degree, the maverick tendency probably stems from an indefinable gut revulsion against dull-wittedness, greed, and inhumanity.

Why is it so rare for an investigative journalist to intrude into an arms bazaar to put dumbfounded salesmen on the spot by asking what their bright shining products do to human beings within shredding range?[5] Many news editors would be as dumbfounded as the arms peddlers and would spike the resulting article. But some wouldn't. So do not assume that mavericks always operate alone; it's still an interdependent world. Even mavericks require confederates, enablers, and closet mavericks within staid organizations to smuggle anything out into the public realm. Perhaps mavericks aren't unique deviants; perhaps they come in all sorts of disconcerting shapes, sizes, and apparel.

A maverick, says *Webster's*, is a "refractory or recalcitrant member of a political party who bolts at will and sets an independent course, or an intellectual or a member of a social upper class or any other group who refuses to conform and takes an unorthodox stand."[6] Both venerable species of mavericks make ample appearances in these pages. Artist Ad Reinhardt, a stubborn visionary, liked to recycle the wonderfully rueful wisecrack (attributed to many wits, including Mark Twain and Will Rogers) that "It ain't what people don't know that brings them trouble so much as what people know that just ain't so." Every maverick, in this sense, is a dedicated enemy of images and notions that just ain't so.

Restive people buck the status quo because there are powerful interests who do well from things as they are and who aim to keep it that way. The right compliant images and messages keep the machinery humming: the almighty market, peace through strength, defending the Fatherland (or lately the creepily Germanic-sounding Homeland). An abiding problem for the gadfly ever since Socrates is how to stir up change, even inadvertently, without inciting what C. Wright Mills called the power elites to rub them out, or in wealthier and more smoothly administered societies, starve them out. Mavericks may express their disgruntlement (their "Great Refusal," as Herbert Marcuse termed it) on a strictly personal and private plane, but these rascals set a worrisome bad example anyway. The maverick is unlikely to brandish a program or manifesto, just an urgent recognition that rhetorical balloons full of piping-hot air badly need popping

An iconoclast, according to *Webster's*, is one who attacks "established beliefs, ideals, customs, or institutions." The *Oxford Dictionary* defines an iconoclast as anyone "who attacks cherished beliefs."[7] Everyone likes to believe that the creeds of people in the other country, county, or coffeehouse are fair game while their own views are impeccably sound. Many a thin-skinned critic—a perennial comic figure—launches furious assaults at miscreant outsiders on behalf of utterly unexamined and unproven beliefs of their own. The red carpet is seldom rolled out for folks with corrosively skeptical dispositions, mercurial intellects, and lack of a hearty appetite for cant. These barbaric spoilsports are shunted aside as long as possible, so it is all the more remarkable when talents who refuse to "go along to get along" break through anyway. Indeed, most mavericks are never heard from or only are appreciated in small professional circles, as is still the case with several interviewees.

It's hard going. So novelist J. P. Donleavy recounts listening, slackjawed, to a refined New York publisher explaining that *The Ginger Man* was the finest work to come across the transom in many years, but the publishing house would decline it anyway because it was, according to the tight-laced standards of 1950s America, too risqué. Studs Terkel was blacklisted in that same scurrilously repressive McCarthy era, of which post-9/11 America is getting a fresh foul whiff.[8] Dr. Noel Browne, who in a stunning stint as Irish minister of health wiped out the scourge of TB, endured decades in the political wilderness, and near penury, in his (and his wife's) unflagging quest to nudge that little nation, long mired in pettiness and begrudgery, toward more progressive policies and humane attitudes.

In genial counterpoint, sculptor and novelist Desmond MacNamara trains his effervescent intellect (and near-total recall) on the changing Irish scene as a witness, participant, and perpetrator. Only the cognoscenti really know Mac, and one hopes that this interview will in some tiny way help to remedy that situation. Readers also meet a Welshborn British Para (paratrooper) turned radical documentary filmmaker, whose fierce reputation is as yet contained within professional circles. At the other end of the spectrum is the former "party girl," acclaimed for her exotic beauty and her celebrity marriage, who by dint of hard work and passionate commitment emerged as a powerful spokeswoman for human rights. Celebrities are supposed to prefer plastic surgery to politics.

Mavericks do not reckon that life would change "if the czar only knew" (because czars of all descriptions either know or else don't care). The citizenry, those without vast investment portfolios, need to know what the schemers are up to, even if many are too frightened to admit that their own leaders are louts. Daniel Ellsberg, once a devout Cold Warrior, helped to expose colossal governmental deceit, and his revelations improved American democracy as a result. Everyone is encouraged to believe that their own shining nation, unlike all others, primly pursues noble causes and just wars. It would be amazing if it were otherwise, since elites everywhere are quite anxious to secure consent for their back-room deals with as little public muss or fuss as possible.

But writers such as Larry Heinemann beg, most unhumbly, to disagree. Heinemann left working-class Chicago—a generation or two removed from Nelson Algren and James Farrell—for Vietnam, which became his crucible and his forever-smoldering topic. The savvy, sick-at-heart soldier saw, heard, felt, smelled, and tasted imperious power up close as it incinerated vast swathes of Southeast Asia, for nothing. The corporate media incessantly bleats the Chamber of Commerce refrain of the "magic of the marketplace," but writer John Nichols, especially in *The Magic Journey*, and director Dusan Makavejev pierced the mumbo-jumbo to detect the "psychotic ingredient" in the idolatry of markets—markets crafted for the sake of well-placed groups. John Kenneth Galbraith, a wonderfully wry maverick economist (and regrettably not included here), has long pointed out what a rigged arrangement the modern market is.

The French were blissfully content with the soothing myth of widespread resistance to German occupation during World War II, but documentary filmmaker Marcel Ophuls demolished that pretty illusion with *The Sorrow and the Pity*.[9] Ophuls's acrid documentaries, such as his Oscar-winning *Hotel Terminus* (1988), demonstrated that other nations are far from morally superior entities and that, for example, Western intelligence agencies have more in common with authoritarian counterparts than with democratic forces inside their own societies. Woody Allen may be a household name on every continent, but his box office numbers say otherwise. Spike Lee shoots television commercials for the likes of Nike (lampooned and harpooned elsewhere by the redoubtable Michael Moore) but consistently takes admirable cinematic chances. Maverick still seems an apt label.

Writing about mavericks raises the question of what they are mavericks in response to, what the backdrop is. What's wrong with wanting to fit in anyway? Well, Erich Fromm, for one, charted and lamented the nasty proliferation of "good Germans" during the Nazi ascent: "It seems nothing is more difficult for the average man to bear than the feeling of not being identified with a larger group. However much a German citizen may be opposed to the principles of Nazism, if he has to choose between being alone and feeling that he belongs to Germany, most persons will chose the latter."[10] It's a bad fit, no matter how you do it.

Lest Americans believe they are divinely immunized, Dr. Stanley Milgram's so-called Eichmann experiments at Yale distilled a hard lesson when an embarrassingly high percentage of Americans became "willing executioners" so long as an authoritative guy in a clean white lab coat took responsibility for any harm they inflicted by electroshock of a screened-off subject.[11] Those who had the temerity to refuse were a minority—only one in three heeded conscience over authorities' suave blandishments or bullying. The lesson for Milgram, and any maverick, was mighty clear: "If we accept the alternatives that authorities give us, we are doomed."

Interviewed in Studs Terkel's oral history masterpiece *The Good War*, Telford Taylor, a prosecutor at the Nuremberg trial of Nazi war criminals, delivered a downbeat assessment of how Americans would behave under conditions similar to those Germans experienced.[12]

> People most of them are followers. Moral standards are easily obliterated.
> . . . They so easily fall into the pattern that their superiors set up for them,
> because that's the safe way. They may be loving husbands, nice to their
> children, fond of music. They have become accustomed to moral stan-
> dards prescribed from above by an authoritarian regime. The safe way to
> be comfortable in life is that way, following orders.

Americans, brought up in a ballyhooed tradition of fierce individualism, are, as Alexis de Tocqueville and other perceptive outsiders observed, historically hardcore conformists and not so far behind the joked-about Germans and Japanese as they fancy.[13] Perusing a recent exemplary book set in the contemporary American West, for example, one meets rugged Marlboro Man cowpokes aplenty who nonetheless are careful to keep themselves and every other community member within the corral of local pieties, which include casual racism, Klan loyalties, sexism, and other hoary homespun values.[14] Yet Fromm is surely incorrect when he says that a strong tendency toward obedience applies only to the "average" person.

The social world that Ellsberg defied was a highly privileged one whose denizens, dominated by intellectual inertia and status hunger, could not bring themselves to rat on an atrocious war built on a Rube Goldberg structure of lies.[15] No one likes having the whistle blown inside their comfortable aerie. So how dare Ellsberg inform the public about devious and illegitimate schemes hatched in these upper realms? How dare he betray employers who betrayed the American public who employed them? In one of Studs Terkel's priceless "memory books," as he calls them, a police chief finds that the physical courage that cops commonly display is hardly ever matched by the moral courage to face down the ridicule or disapproval of their peers, even if they think it right to do so.[16] Moral courage is a rare commodity in every social strata, although perhaps rarest at the top where scruples are nothing more than nuisances for cynics who dicker in realpolitik and global finance.

Bona fide mavericks typically and sometimes gladly (or masochistically) suffer the slings and arrows of outrageous career misfortunes, financial hardships, whispering campaigns, blacklists, and relegation of their work to fringe outlets, or no outlets at all. It's the price you pay for doing or seeing things a tad too differently. The eternally world-weary fact is that most plum posts are grabbed, or insinuated into, by those who arduously tailor themselves to serve the whims of the coveted institutions. Odious outsiders will be studiously ignored as long as possible. Yet sometimes the cumulative and potent body of work breaks through in an arena jammed with rivals who compromised and scrambled all their lives to get where they are and don't enjoy the reproachful presence of anyone who did not.[17] Success for a maverick is always an affront, a lèse-majesté against the success-at-any-cost ethos that fuels market bubbles, breeds official apologists, and engenders Enrons. Nonetheless, many people admire and even envy these renegades, if only from afar.

Still, mavericks aren't much use if they aren't motivated by principles that serve someone other than themselves. Disputation for disputation's sake can be awfully tiresome. To be out of step does not mean you are always right. A compulsive kind of dissent is only the flip side of mindless obedience. So a maverick needs a wee bit of discretion, an intuitive ability to judge whether the issue is worth the trouble of disputing here and now. No one in this volume is a maverick for the sheer Sid Vicious sake of contrariness—although being a contrarian is no bad thing, especially if you don't mind confronting self-styled contrarians too.[18] There is no room here for pseudo-Nietzschean supermen. To be different from the crowd is one thing; to feel innately superior to the herd is quite another.

When success arrives, it often comes wrapped obligatorily in bright and brittle denigration. I recall, soon after interviewing Terkel, a middle-aged suburban professional woman prattling to me about Terkel's "old fashioned" New Deal and pro-labor ideas. Her critique was exquisitely ironic, considering that the "new" ideas she championed stemmed from disinterred eighteenth-century market platitudes, a robust recycling of which she was wholly unaware.[19] Mavericks bang up against inverted logic and bad history all the time. So do other people, of course, but mavericks don't keep quiet about it.

Donleavy may well be grousing but nonetheless is quite right that many critics express only those opinions that they reckon can be "safely reinforced." I recall a noted film critic, a few years before the fall of the Berlin Wall, telling me confidently after seeing the astonishing Soviet World War II film *Come and See* that the brutal Nazis in it were caricatures. I later asked a survivor of the Eastern Front atrocities portrayed on screen if a caricature were even possible. "The Nazis were worse," she replied. "No movie can imagine it." But in the Reagan era one had better not depict anything to do with the Soviet Union as faintly admirable, even in relation to the Nazis whom they did play the major role in crushing.

How many mavericks can a society afford? Perhaps there is only a certain number of disorderly influences that a society can withstand. Jules Henry, a rogue anthropologist, noted the perennial tension in societies between phalanxes of obedient plodders and disparate crews of insolent innovators.[20] In a ruefully post-Platonic way, Henry saw both sorts as necessary. A world made up wholly of mavericks may seem a disturbing vision, what with all the chaos and tumult it supposedly implies. Indeed, a notable political scientist long ago approvingly saw that "it may be said that society depends upon a certain amount of pathology, in the sense that society does not [encourage] the free criticism of social life, but [establishes] taboos upon reflective thinking about its own presuppositions."[21]

Yet it always has been the unduly orderly societies—societies that make a dark fetish of order—that are the most murderous ones. It's neither madmen nor misfits nor maniacs who slaughtered tens of millions in the twentieth century, as R. D. Laing observed; rather, it was what we are pleased to call "normal" people who maimed and killed at so massive a scale.[22] In a BBC documentary on atrocities in the Pacific Theater in World War II, the producer/director found that the perpetrators of innumerable hideous acts were "not the 'criminal' outcasts I had been expecting to meet, but the ambitious achievers at the centre of their societies who wanted to rise in their careers. It was hardly surprising therefore that they seemed normal when one met them."[23] Perhaps it is ambitious achievers, not mavericks, that societies have to keep their eye on.

Maverick Voices assembles the most memorable of hundreds of interviews conducted with rebels of all sorts over twenty-five years. I would have added more, or gone looking for more of them, but space forbids. The interviewees cover politics (Ellsberg, Browne, Jagger), literature (Donleavy, Nichols, Heinemann), art (MacNamara), cinema (Makavejev, Lee, Ophuls, Allen, Davies), and psychotherapy, especially in appraising the controversial case of Bruno Bettelheim (Bergman, Elliot, Janowitz, Coles). The chats usually took place on the occasion of the release of a new film or book, but often enough they were simply a matter of seizing an opportune moment in their travels (or mine) to sit down for a reflective debriefing. The original interviews appeared in outlets such as *The Guardian* (UK), *The Sunday Tribune* (Ireland), *Film Comment*, *Logos: A Journal of Modern Culture & Society, Left Curve, Lettre Internationale, The Progressive*, and *The Journal of Irish Literature*.

The common threads that entwine almost all of them are an articulate inner voice well vocalized, a judicious distrust of authorities, an impatience with ill-thought-out morals and manners, a skepticism that does not exclude their own work, and an overriding purpose, a purpose beyond a commercial quest for product differentiation for the sake of filling store shelves. They mostly appreciate that a theatrically surly attitude is no substitute for hard-eyed analysis. Their skeptical bents and irreverent stances are worth savoring, especially at this post-9/11 juncture when citizens are force-fed the usual scoundrels' plea that it is supremely patriotic to blot out all the myopic idiocies and selfish schemes that leaders, elected and unelected, can cook up. I felt fortunate to cross paths with this varied batch of iconoclasts and in most cases thoroughly enjoyed their company, as will, I trust, readers.

Mavericks are anything but an endangered species. MacNamara may well be correct in saying that the level of civilization, and the standards of human decency, are rising, even if ever so slowly, even glacially (although that somewhat cheery observation says nothing about how far and swiftly people will backslide when placed under acute pressure). It's difficult to say, though, whether adversity or hospitality is the better breeding ground. Brendan Behan, the raucous and brilliant Irish playwright, liked to say that there was a liberated "fifth race"—a noncolored, nongenetic, non-physically distinguishable group of human beings scattered worldwide whom "you could talk to, who would have understanding," people who happily stray beyond the more mindless strictures of society (courtesy is not a mindless stricture) and recognize one another when they meet. It may not take one to know one, but it may well take one to fully appreciate another one, as the concluding set of reflections on the much-maligned Bruno Bettelheim demonstrate. Mavericks shake things up and enliven our existences, whether we like it or not. They're the ones who tell Milgram's experimenters to get lost. And I daresay there seem to be more of them today than forty or fifty years ago. Perhaps there really is a maverick inside everyone trying, as best as it can, to get out.

NOTES

1. On courtiers and the fine art of angling for rewards see Lewis Lapham, *Waiting for the Barbarians* (New York: Verso, 1998), 111–17.
2. Quoted in Bob Woodward, *Bush at War,* rev. ed. (London: Pocket Books, 2003), 14.
3. "Just as Marx used to say about the French Marxists of the late seventies: 'All I know is that I am not a Marxist,'" wrote Frederick Engels in a letter to Conrad Schmidt dated August 3, 1890, in Karl Marx and Frederick Engels, *Selected Correspondence, 1846–1895*, trans. Dona Torr (Moscow: Foreign Language Publishing House, 1959), 472.
4. See Noam Chomsky, *Power and Prospects: Reflections on Human Nature and the Social Order* (London: Pluto Press, 1996), 53, 70–93.
5. John Pilger, *Hidden Agendas* (London: Vintage, 1998), 116–17.

At the Paris arms fair, I asked a salesman to describe the working of a cluster grenade the size of a grapefruit. Bending over a glass case, as one does when inspecting something precious, he said, "This is wonderful. It is state of the art, unique. What it does is discharge copper dust, very, very fine dust so that particles saturate the objective. . . ."
"What objective?" I asked.
He looked incredulous. "Whatever it may be," he replied.
"People?"
"Well, er, if you like."

6. *Webster's Third New International Dictionary* (Springfield, Mass.: G & C Merriam, 1964), 1395.
7. *The Concise Oxford Dictionary of Current English,* 7th ed. (Oxford: Clarendon Press, 1983), 494.
8. McCarthyism was an exaggeration, but only a modest one, of underlying conformist and xenophobic trends in American culture and politics. See, for example, Ellen Schrecker, *Many Are the Crimes: McCarthyism in America* (Boston: Little, Brown, 1998).
9. See Ian Ousby, *Occupation: The Ordeal of France 1940–1944* (New York: St. Martin's Press, 1998).
10. Erich Fromm, *Escape from Freedom* (New York: Avon, 1969), 180–82.

11. See Stanley Milgram, *Obedience to Authority: An Experimental View* (New York: Harper and Row, 1974). Also see Thomas Blass, ed., *Obedience to Authority: Current Perspectives on the Milgram Experiment* (Mahwah, N.J.: Lawrence Erlbaum Associates, 2000).

12. Studs Terkel, *"The Good War": An Oral History of World War II* (New York: Pantheon, 1984), 464. After the Nuremberg trials, Telford Taylor addressed the membership of a Jewish synagogue in Brooklyn: "'The idea that the Nazis of the holocaust are all a bunch of abnormal sadists is not so. Most of them are ordinary people like you and me.' You should have heard the uproar that went up from that audience. The same thing happened to me last spring. I told the rabbi that my views were a bit clinical and might not be the right thing for his congregation. He said 'it's a very sophisticated group.' Exactly the same thing happened."

13. Alexis de Toqueville, *Democracy in America* (London: Everyman's Library, 1994), bk. 1, 263.

I know of no country in which there is so little independence of mind and real freedom of discussion as in America. . . . In America the majority raises formidable barriers around the liberty of opinions; within these barriers the author may write what he pleases, but woe to him if he goes beyond that. Not that he is in danger of an auto-da-fe, but he is exposed to continued obloquy and persecution. His political career is closed forever, since he has offended the only authority that is able to open it. Every sort of compensation, even that of celebrity, is refused to him. Before making public his opinions he thought he had sympathizers; now it seems to him that he has none any more since he has revealed himself to everyone; then those who blame him criticize loudly and those who think as he does keep quiet and move away without courage. He yields at length, overcome by the daily effort which he has to make, and subsides into silence, as if he felt remorse for having spoken the truth.

14. Annie Proulx, *That Old Ace in the Hole* (New York: Scribner, 2002).

15. See Daniel Ellsberg, *Secrets: A Memoir of Vietnam and the Pentagon Papers* (New York: Viking, 2002).

16. Studs Terkel, *The Great Divide* (New York: Pantheon, 1988), 348.

17. See Peter Loewenberg, *Decoding the Past: The Psychohistorical Approach* (Berkeley: University of California, 1985), 70–71.

18. Christopher Hitchens, *Letters to a Young Contrarian* (New York: Basic Books, 2002).

19. See Thomas Franks, *One Market under God* (London: Secker & Warburg, 2001).

20. Jules Henry, *On Sham, Vulnerability, and Other Forms of Self-Destruction* (New York: Vintage, 1973), 178–79.

21. Harold D. Lasswell, *Psychopathology and Politics* (1930; reprint, New York: Viking Press, 1960), 200.

22. R. D. Laing, *The Politics of Experience* (New York: Pantheon, 1967).

23. Laurence Rees, *Horror in the East* (London: BBC Books, 2001), 152.

1

DANIEL ELLSBERG

activist and author

Daniel Ellsberg is as good a candidate as any for the role of patron saint of whistle-blowers. In the spring of 1971, Ellsberg and Rand Corporation colleague Anthony Russo released a 47-volume internal Defense Department review chronicling 30 years of systematic deception of the American public regarding the Vietnam debacle. Nixon, who saw everything in conspiratorial terms, rapidly unraveled his own administration in the frantic course of harassing Ellsberg and anyone else who might inform the citizenry or Congress of anything the imperial president didn't want known. Nixon's infamous "plumbers" rifled the office files of Ellsberg's psychiatrist long before they exercised their bumbling burglary skills at the Watergate Hotel. The White House tapes on the day of publication of excerpts in the *New York Times* reveal chief aide H. R. Haldemann commiserating with Nixon about this heinous act, which ruined the "infallibility" of the president—a hitherto handy thing to wield. They were grieving over the grave of public gullibility, which the George W. Bush administration has tried so hard to resurrect.

Ellsberg was born in Chicago in 1926 and earned a doctorate in economics at Harvard. Not many hawkish intellectuals today can say that they began Marine Corps boot camp the day after defending their Ph.D. thesis. After three years of service, he joined the Rand Corporation think tank in 1958 as a specialist studying ways of averting accidental nuclear war. In 1964, he became special aide to Assistant Secretary of Defense

John McNaughton, whose brief happened to include Southeast Asia. Ellsberg went to Vietnam as a civilian State Department employee over 1966 and 1967, where he came to realize the futility of a "mistaken" intervention. He concluded that the war was an immoral enterprise only when he joined the Pentagon Papers project, commissioned by Secretary of Defense Robert McNamara, and read an uncensored history of a skein of indefensible decisions. The public, he believed, had a right to know. After winning acquittal at his 1973 trial, where it was revealed that the government had tapped his lawyers and tried to bribe the judge, Ellsberg participated avidly in antinuclear and anti-interventionist movements, accumulating a very long rap sheet.

The conversation took place in September 2002 as Ellsberg was preparing a book tour for *Secrets: A Memoir of Vietnam and the Pentagon Papers*. The book ranges well beyond the Pentagon Papers episode, including intriguing, unsparing, and often-surprising portraits of key figures. For example, Ellsberg's account of superspook Edward Lansdale, the model for the naively malevolent advisor in Graham Greene's classic *The Quiet American*, raises the piquant question whether Greene was gulled by the country-boy pose Lansdale liked to strike. Apart from the book, we talked about his disturbing sensation of déjà vu as he beholds George W. Bush.

Secrets describes a bright, red-blooded, john wayne–loving American shedding all the nice lies that he was taught to believe, but not all his ideals. A lot of Americans who grew up in the 1960s especially can relate to that.

I grew up during the Second World War with the notion that we were fighting aggression. We were unquestionably the good guys, believing in the ideals in the Atlantic Charter. At my trial in 1973, Howard Zinn quoted words from the Atlantic Charter about self-determination, and tears came to my eyes. I was crying at the thought of [what had happened to] what we believed in. There was a kind of innocence then. That is what I thought we were fighting for. We could have avoided Vietnam if we only had been true to that Wilsonian ideal of self-determination, which of course Wilson ignored when Ho Chi Minh raised it in 1919 at Versailles. Certainly the British, Churchill, never meant what they said about self-determination for British colonies. So FDR did not carry through on self-determination for French colonies lest that be a bad precedent for

British colonies. There we go back to 1945. But then I believed what our government was saying about the Soviet Union and became very anti-communist. The fallacy there was equating Stalin to Hitler.

WHY IS IT A FALLACY?

All these people—Stalin, Mao, Saddam—are quite comparable to Hitler in ruthlessness, and conceivably in megalomania. But Hitler was very different in his reckless military pursuit of his megalomania. Hitler could not be deterred, and it was not productive to negotiate with him. The equation that Stalin can't be contained either is the argument for preventive war. Still, our leaders did on the whole understand that there was a difference from Hitler and that containment and deterrence were not only possible but preferable to preventive war. The military chiefs toyed with the idea of preventive war more than we knew.

HOW SECURE ARE SECRETS? YOU SAY THAT THE GLIB BROMIDE THAT WASHINGTON CAN'T KEEP SIGNIFICANT SECRETS FOR LONG IS WRONG. IS THIS AN OLIVER STONE UNIVERSE WE ARE PEEKING INTO?

Secrecy enabled governments to carry out neo-imperial and colonial policies without opposition. The American public thinks of itself as anti-imperial. Most Americans assent to this image of ourselves, to the proposition that we stand above all for freedom and independence everywhere. The idea that we placed high priority on democracy in underdeveloped countries—the plantations of the world, in effect, where what we wanted was natural resources or cheap labor—has always been a fraud. It was not just that we put up with dictatorship instead of communism. We chose dictatorship rather than liberal regimes or social democratic regimes or welfare regimes or anything that put any restraint on our economic control.

A MOTIVATED RESEARCHER CAN FIND THESE SORDID FACTS IN A PUBLIC LIBRARY. WHAT ABOUT SECRETS ONLY THE CHOSEN FEW KNOW?

I'll give a current example. George W. Bush and Dick Cheney rely on the image of Saddam as a brutal dictator, which he is. He conducted chemical warfare and can be counted on to do it again. They refer to its use against Iran but particularly against the Kurds, who allied with Iran in that area in 1988. Only secrecy enabled them to conceal the fact, until the *Times* revealed it [in August 2002], that Rumsfeld and others, while in

Reagan's administration, were reopening diplomatic relations with Iraq in 1984–1985, supplying them with the chemical research for weapons, and covertly giving them satellite coordinates and reconnaissance photos when we knew they were using this information to make chemical attacks. Those were, to all effect, American attacks, American-supported attacks. Saddam was extremely ruthless. Our leaders covertly were just as ruthless. We continued to give trade credits to them—in some cases illegally—and to turn a blind eye to their nuclear program. What it illustrates is that our leaders by virtue of widespread discipline on secrecy have made allies of some of the worst dictators for reasons that have nothing whatever to do with anticommunism and to do this very consistently in Guatemala, Iran, Indonesia, Vietnam, around the world.

HOW DO YOU SIFT PERSONAL INTEREST FROM NATIONAL INTEREST WHEN DECIDING WHAT IS WORTH KEEPING SECRET? WHOSE PURPOSE DOES SECRECY SERVE?

It's certainly not purposes they are willing to expose for open debate as to whether these are truly in the national interest. In terms of what they perceive as the American interests, and in terms of their sense of what means are allowed so long as they can be secret, our leaders don't yield anything to anyone in terms of ruthlessness. I'd like to believe that they couldn't get away with some of this stuff if it had been in the open.

ANOTHER THEME IS THAT DOMESTIC DEMOCRACY AND AN AUTOCRATIC FOREIGN POLICY CANNOT COEXIST.

If you want to run a large part of the world, and these people do, they think it cannot be done without military means and threats that the public would reject in terms of dangers and values. If you want the empire, you have to protect these operations from democracy, and secrecy is the way you do it. George W. Bush knows that he has to make up reasons for this war. He has to manipulate, has to deceive. His blatant reasons are not the real reasons. That was the case for Vietnam, and that is the case now in Iraq.

Here are some questions I learned to ask from my experience. When was the Patriot Act, this several-hundred-page document, put together? Was it after September 11th? I think it was a matter of waiting for the appropriate moment to be enacted. We've learned that they had every reason to expect major acts of terrorism from Osama bin Laden. I assume that they did not know exactly when and exactly where. All we are told they did about it is to have John Ashcroft stay off commercial airlines. Which is kind of a minimal reaction. I think they did more than that. They drafted the Patriot Act and had in writing the enabling legislation that they passed on September 14—a broad resolution passed by Congress to do whatever needed to be done, which the president tried to say was enough to authorize an invasion of Iraq, which is blatant but not more than Lyndon Johnson did. The analogy to the Tonkin Gulf Resolution is very close. I am sure there is planning right now for going farther than the Patriot Act and for exploiting the next terrorist act if there should be one. The president will make use of that to get an authorization out of Congress, a blank check, as Johnson consciously did to use the Tonkin Gulf incidents, especially the second Gulf incident, to get the Tonkin Gulf Resolution. They'll follow that analogy to the letter. My experience of the government leads me to assume that they are preparing themselves for that and with very positive expectations of pulling it off.

WHAT DO YOU THINK OF THE RECENT FRENCH BOOK ALLEGING THAT U.S. AGENCIES WERE BEHIND THE SEPTEMBER 11TH ATTACKS? COULD THIS CONCEIVABLY BE CONCEALED? HOW MUCH CAN THESE AGENCIES PULL OFF?

That is a degree of competency that I don't really give them. I have to say I would be amazed if we have a government agency that is capable of doing that. There was an incident in the Vietnam War just before the election between Ky and Thieu in 1967. One helicopter supposedly misfired a rocket that went into a room in Cholon and knocked out six or seven of General Ky's major supporters in the port authority and dope trade. Every Vietnamese assumed the CIA had done it to destroy Ky as a rival to Thieu. I was still in Vietnam and gave no credence to the idea that the CIA could accomplish that, knowing precisely when those people would be there and hitting them with one rocket. It didn't make sense with the level at which we operated. I just don't see us pulling off the collapse of the World Trade Center. But might we be capable of knowing that something like that is going to be done and letting it happen because we feel it would be useful to us? Possibly.

YOU HOOKED UP IN VIETNAM WITH JOHN PAUL VANN, WHO NEIL SHEEHAN USED AS AN ICONIC FIGURE IN HIS BOOK A BRIGHT SHINING LIE.[1] WHEN DID YOU BEGIN TO DISAGREE WITH VANN?

Where we did disagree on a major premise is that by 1968 or 1969 he continued to believe that it would be very damaging to our credibility if we suffered defeat in Vietnam. He did not believe we could win, but he did believe we could keep going at much less cost by building up ARVN[2] and so forth and that it was worth doing. That's where I, more or less, was at up to 1965. Once we committed air power and ground troops there, I went through about a year of believing we had to try very hard to make something out of this. By 1967, I no longer felt that the cost of this [intervention] in human lives was justified even by those objectives.

How did Vann stack up to Sheehan's portrait?

The book is a masterpiece in many ways. I admire it, especially his description of the early years. Sheehan was about twenty years younger and didn't know Vann very well. He started on the book after Vann died. Vann as a person did not come through. John was a very funny guy. From the book, you might think he was a humorless fanatic. But he was a terrific companion, a very good friend, and very generous. Remember, although unlike Vann, I had a brief military background, three years, and some limited combat experience only while in Vietnam, my idea of Vietnam initially had been shaped by that. I was not a pacifist. I believed in just wars, that the cause was just and the means proportionate—until it became clear to me that the thing got way out of control. Vann continued to believe in it because of the notion that the United States had to be a central pillar of world order. He was a Cold Warrior who had to serve in a just cause, justly conducted. You have to consider soldiers who don't want a war of aggression, a war against women and children.

That's how we want to believe American soldiers behave, as if they are concerned with decency and justice.

A lot of American soldiers are. I'm extremely critical of Bob Kerrey not just for what he did [in the Mekong Delta village slaughter in 1969] but for implying that that was what all soldiers did. What Kerrey was part of at that time was an operation called "Speedy Express," which was part of the Phoenix program. John was totally critical of the Phoenix program. He recommended that these things be stopped, although there was not a chance. He saw no justification. He was against the use of air power and artillery and the "reconnaissance by fire"—90 percent of it unjustified—that killed civilians.

WAS THERE A SOLID RATIONALE FOR AFGHANISTAN?

My own view has changed a bit. My first impression was that al-Qaeda paid a kind of ransom or bribe to the Taliban to operate there. Peter Dale Scott showed me some evidence that the Taliban government was providing an operational base and was collaborating very strongly. So that there was more of a rationale for attacking the Taliban than I perceived.

SO YOU APPROVED OF THE AFGHAN CAMPAIGN?

No, strictly speaking, I did not approve of it. In retrospect, it was not necessarily the best thing to do but there was a rationale for it that does not exist in the case of Iraq. Even though the attack on Afghanistan was conducted more prudently and in a more limited way than I foresaw, I still say that the risks involved in carrying out that war were unjustified even though the risks were not entirely realized. But an attack on Iraq is in great competition with the war against terrorism. It's close to abandoning the unified coalitional struggle against terrorism, just as the war on Afghanistan amounted to abandoning the war on drugs: it led directly to a vast increase in opium production there. The war on drugs has been thrown overboard. Look at Colombia. That's another part of it. We are backing the major drug traffickers because they are going against the so-called revolutionary forces there. We are exacerbating the cocaine problem by our policies, not lessening it.

DID YOU IMAGINE IT WOULD BE A NEW VIETNAM?

I was very worried. What little I did know suggested that at the time the administration intended to send a large number of troops to the occupation of Afghanistan. You have to give this administration credit for stopping short of that, and pretty much where the Russians ended up, in mainly occupying the cities. So Afghanistan did not turn out as badly as I thought it would. Afghanistan was an exceptional case. There is very little scope for military action. What you need is a climate for cooperative measures among governments against terrorism. Both our Israeli policy in Palestine and this impending war against Iraq, separately and especially together, are likely to make it impossible for Arab states and Muslim states in the Philippines and Indonesia and so forth to cooperate with us in the face of public outrage at what we're doing. I thought the Gulf War would be more costly to the Americans because I expected that they would move on to Baghdad. George Bush had turned against it with the advice of Powell; I give Powell credit and I do not agree that he should have gone on. So what we are facing now is that the very people who believed it was a mistake then, including Cheney, are in power and proposing to correct what they see as his father's error, even cowardice, in having been bound by the UN and by the coalition objectives and by public opinion.

DO YOU SEE A PARALLEL HERE TO YOUR VIETNAM SCENARIO OF ESCA-LATION GOING NUCLEAR?

George Bush kept that thread open a dozen years ago with the threat of nuclear weapons against chemical or biological attack. The very refusal to rule out nuclear weapons constituted a threat and so constituted a use of the weapon. You use a weapon when you point it at somebody, whether you pull the trigger or not. Moreover, they feel that threat was effective, and it encourages them to use it again. George W. Bush absorbed that lesson and has shown a greater willingness to use the threat of nuclear weapons than we have seen since Nixon. Nixon did it covertly.

THIS SOUNDS LIKE A THROWBACK TO THE CHEERFUL NUCLEAR-WEAPON THEORIZING OF HERMAN KAHN—THINKING ABOUT THE UNTHINKABLE.[3]

Herman Kahn was a Rand Corporation consultant who wrote from the outside, but he was elaborating what the secretary of state was doing with massive retaliation policies from 1953, which is relying on nuclear brinksmanship. Unfortunately, it led to a generation of Joint Chiefs who based a lot of planning on it. Now we've got a president who is a throwback to that era of openly threatening nuclear war. There is less public resistance than there would have been fifteen years ago because of the ending of the Cold War. People no longer see that threat as leading to an all-out nuclear war with the Soviets. They're a lot more tolerant.

YOU STRESS THAT THE HIGHEST POLICY CIRCLES KNEW THE CONSE-QUENCES OF GETTING INTO VIETNAM. MIGHT WE ASSUME THAT GEORGE W. BUSH KNOWS THE NEGATIVES TOO? IS THIS DÉJÀ VU?

I do have the feeling that our country is reliving the situation in 1964 and 1965. We have a president who is determined, for reasons of his own, in engaging in an aggressive war that the country as a whole does not see as necessary. He will make every effort to manipulate Congress, the public, and UN opinion so as to get a minimal degree of support. He is moving toward a renewed Tonkin Gulf Resolution, a broad blank check, a delegation of power from both Congress and the UN. I never thought I would be feeling thankful to House speaker Richard Armey. But I have to admit he is saying the right things: it will be unconstitutional, unwise, and an aggressive war. These, by the way, are phrases that were almost never used about Vietnam, except by Senator [Wayne] Morse.[4] On the Democratic side, there is scarcely more opposition than there was under Morse and Gruening. So I can't say I rely on Congress to save us, though it will be what I'll be trying to achieve by adding my voice to whatever else is happening. I expect to be using my book tour as much as possible for showing the analogy between then and now and trying to prevent another Tonkin Gulf Resolution.

ONE DIFFERENCE NOW IS THAT GEORGE W. BUSH IS BEHAVING AS IF HE CAN DO WHATEVER HE LIKES.

Nixon and Johnson believed they were entitled to do that, but George W. Bush is more open about acting as an emperor than any president that I can remember. He pays less lip service to democracy or to constitutional constraints, let alone to the UN. Has he acknowledged even one international commitment that he likes or feels bound by? Yet now with Iraq Bush wants to revise basic principles of international order, which Chirac describes as desirable and as only a few rules, a few principles, a few laws.

IN TANDEM WITH A WAR ON TERRORISM IS AN ATTACK ON THE HOME FRONT. IT SEEMS CLEAR THAT THE ILLEGAL ACTIVITIES THE NIXON BOYS PERFORMED AGAINST YOU CAN BE GOTTEN AWAY WITH TODAY: BREAKING INTO YOUR PSYCHIATRIST'S OFFICE, WIRETAPPING YOUR LAWYERS, EVEN ARRANGING TO HAVE YOU ASSAULTED.

Surely. George W. Bush is in the process of removing all those constraints. The things that were done against me I suspect are pretty much happening right now. It hasn't all been tested much, legally. He's maintaining the idea of secret courts, of detention without charges, without even releasing the names. We are moving in the direction of a police state now. I don't want to overstate how bad it is. We're not there yet. He's removed the freedoms he wants, but it's mainly been against Middle Easterners and so made other people pretty passive about it. People are passive about it just as with AIDS, which they thought only affected the gays, but it ain't gonna stop there. It can get a great deal worse.

DO YOU SEE ANY RAYS OF LIGHT?

There is much more leaking than any time during the Vietnam War. A big difference from the Pentagon Papers time is that virtually all the military are opposed to this operation. There's a handful of civilians who think defeating Iraq will be as easy as deposing the Taliban or as cracking the Iraqi draftees in Kuwait. The military are not so confident and are worried about what he would do if attacked, and rightfully so. It is not so likely now as in 1991 that Saddam, under mortal threat, would be deterred from using chemical and biological weapons. His ability to constrain himself, to be deterred, already has been tested in a way no other power ever has. No other power that possessed weapons of mass destruction, as he did, has been bombed for over six weeks and refrained from using those weapons. The idea that he would impulsively use those weapons when he is not being attacked is ridiculous. Our military also are not counting on the Revolutionary Guard divisions to collapse in the way the divisions invading Iraq collapsed. And they are not counting on this being an easy pacification program or occupation. So they are leaking in a way like nobody did at the time of Vietnam, and that's a good sign. There should be more of it.

DO YOU SEE THE "VIETNAM SYNDROME" OPERATING HERE: THAT IS, THAT WE DON'T INTERVENE WITHOUT CLEAR OBJECTIVES, PUBLIC SUPPORT, AND AN EXIT STRATEGY?

All that is operating, and there are some tones of one further thing that was part of the Vietnam syndrome. The usual critical questions are: Can we succeed? What will the cost be? Is it really worthwhile? The question that was rarely raised at the time was: Did we have a right to succeed? One big difference today outside the administration, and which certainly is affecting our allies, is that this would be seen as clear-cut aggression in a way that Vietnam was not perceived by most people. As I describe in my book, I did not perceive it as an aggressive war either when I was at the Pentagon or was in Vietnam. It was reading the history that changed my thinking. Of course, I already had felt we should get out, that the war was hopeless, and so forth. But in 1969, I went beyond that by reading this history to see that the notion that this was a legitimate, though perhaps doomed, effort was wrong. That we re-

ally were engaged in an aggressive war, a colonial war that was not jus-
tifiable in terms of our values.

In *Secrets* you remark to an American soldier in Vietnam, "Do
you ever feel like you are a redcoat?" and he says he sure does.

Exactly. This is clearly looming as an aggressive war. People can see
that. Preemptive is the word the military uses for action against an attack about to be launched. But what he is talking about is not imminent
attack; it is a preventive war, it is about a speculative possibility. That is
what the UN Charter prevents. The question of aggression is being
raised more now than during Vietnam. We were effectively confused by
the bullshit put out by [Secretary of State Dean] Rusk and the generals.

And the empire is always striking back.

You see articles now by people like Tom Friedman in the *New York
Times* about what is to be said for the good side of empire. They are acting with more self-awareness and less apology. They're making the case
that the world needs an empire, and, if not us, who? The argument for
this Iraq operation is the case made for empire, for the good countries
of the world to exert leadership and bring enlightenment and order to
the world. At least there is a good deal of skepticism. I think the fact that
there is as much criticism as there is, and it is growing, could induce
George W. Bush to move more quickly. Cheney has said that time is not
on our side. He thinks opinion is going against him, and it gives him lots
of incentive to do what he can. So Bush is announcing that we are what
any other nation will be perfectly fair in describing as a rogue superpower. We don't feel bound by anything, really. All this stuff about the
weather is not right and it takes longer to prepare disinformation to confuse the Iraqis and catch them by surprise. I and a lot of other people
will do what we can to avert that. I think there is a chance of averting it
by drawing on valid analogies and what memories there are of Vietnam.

As a thought experiment, let's compare Powell in regard to
the stance you took when placing loyalty to country over loyalty to a boss.

Powell is in the position that McNamara was in early 1966. By then,
McNamara felt that our policy was not only hopeless but wrong and
that it should end. But he didn't choose to get out then. I suspect

Powell's inclination is to act very much as McNamara did. Others had that temptation, like George Ball in 1964 and 1965, feeling that they might at a critical moment influence the president in the right direction. I didn't have that positive incentive to keep my mouth shut. I believe McNamara thought of himself as protecting the country from what the Joint Chiefs of Staff then wanted to do. Powell may be staying in for a similar reason. Not to protect us from the Joint Chiefs, who probably agree with him very closely, and he was chairman of the JCS himself, but to protect us from civilian militarists who are far more reckless and unconstrained than the military. So in a way, the position of civilians and the military have reversed since the Vietnam War. The Joint Chiefs then were pressing for a larger and bloodier and more dangerous war than we saw. I think that the public to this day has underestimated how dangerous that situation was. That perception from the inside—and everything I have seen since has confirmed it—was driving me [in the Pentagon Papers episode].

I WAS SURPRISED TO FIND THAT LBJ SAID HE WOULD HAVE GIVEN WESTMORELAND 200,000 MORE TROOPS IN 1968 BUT FOR THE LEAKS.

I wasn't entirely sure where LBJ stood in 1968. I did learn from [scholar] Paul Joseph, who interviewed Westmoreland and Wheeler, that he was very open to enlarging the war, more than I realized. I did fear that this polity would go in that direction. I believe we now have a secretary of state who really does not want to go into Iraq, but I see very strong signs that he may be drawn into serving as the rationalizer and legitimizer of this attack. I do think, just like McNamara, that he could prevent this war. His prestige is such that if he resigned, the resignation alone might have a great effect, although of course there's no guarantee. If he honorably got up and did what [Weapons Inspector] Scott Ritter, a former marine colonel, did in speaking out about what he knew as an insider.

He could do what McNamara should have done, and that was to testify before Congress with documents as to what the facts were. If McNamara did it in closed session with Fulbright in February of 1966, but let it leak out, I believe he could have ended the war. It would have been at the cost of any further executive appointment and membership of the establishment. The advantage would be saving forty to fifty thousand American lives and several million Vietnamese lives. That is what he would have had to weigh. The same is true of Powell. We are looking at horrendous things that may happen in terms of a real nuclear war resulting from this, and even short of that, enormous Iraqi casualties and perhaps significant American casualties if city fighting does result. And a wave of hatred in the Arab and Muslim world that poses a concrete cost to terrorism in this country.

Aren't there real dangers of nuclear terrorism?

There are real dangers, but the war against Iraq is a diversion. The fear is that Saddam will give the weapons to al-Qaeda. Now that would be making a case for preventive war. It is important to keep al-Qaeda from getting nuclear weapons. But the notion that they would get them from Saddam is close to ridiculous. The notion that al-Qaeda would get them from Pakistan is not ridiculous at all. The notion that they would get them from Russia is not crazy either—not by Russian state action, not from Putin, but by buying or stealing or hijacking them. That is a real danger, and there is no one in the world I'd less rather have them than Osama bin Laden. How do you deal with that? You deal with that by helping the Russians with security for their weapons. You deal with it by dealing with Pakistan in a number of ways that are not improved by attacking Iraq. The nuclear weapons would be safer from al-Qaeda if Saddam weren't attacked than they would be in Russia or Pakistan. So that is a total hoax.

Is speaking truth to power ever enough?

During the Vietnam War, a major theme of a Quaker activist group I knew of was telling truth to power, which was exemplified by literally going into the Pentagon or White House and speaking frankly in a dialogue with them. I don't at all want to say that that is worthless, but there is a difference in values and priorities there. These people are not going to be reached by that. There is an expression in Congress that "they may not see the light, but they'll feel the heat." What people in power need is to have their own power undermined by exposure of their wrongly held secrets and their pretensions to legitimacy and their concealment of what their real politics are. They need to be confronted by generating counterpower through Congress, the courts, the unions, the universities, and the press. None of which did very well in the Vietnam War. Still, without all of them in motion, it would have gone on a lot longer and it would have gotten a lot worse. So I think an important lesson of the book is that I was inspired by Randy Keeler and others who stood in the doorway of the Oakland induction center and were in demonstrations and who were not simply speaking the truth behind closed doors to power. They were inspiring people to join in a movement that challenged that power. I was convinced then and I am all the more convinced now that this has to be done nonviolently.

Violence simply plays into the hands of the violent institutions. It legitimizes their means and legitimizes their use of them, and it justifies repression. It makes it easier for them. Given a nonviolent philosophy, the personal risk-taking that's involved in telling the truth that the boss does not want told can be effective, although there's no guarantee of it. If Powell stays in office, I suspect it will be partly in the tradition of a McNamara, who says to himself that nothing he does as an individual against the will of the president will have any effect. I've known so many people who tell themselves that "nothing I do can possibly have any effect." Well, actually a number of people took the risks and Nixon through his own reaction did things that brought him down. You can have an effect.

NOTES

1. Neil Sheehan, *A Bright Shining Lie: John Paul Vann and America in Vietnam* (New York: Random House, 1988).

2. The ARVN is the Army of the Republic of Vietnam, that is, the South Vietnamese Army.

3. Herman Kahn was a Strangelovian character, an establishment researcher who published books with rather arresting titles such as *On Escalation: Metaphors and Scenarios* (New York: Praeger, 1965), *On Thermonuclear War* (Princeton, N.J.: Princeton University Press, 1960), and *Thinking about the Unthinkable* (New York: Horizon Press, 1962). He lightheartedly labeled the escalatory stage of full-scale nuclear war as "war-gasm."

4. Senators Wayne Morse and Ernest Gruening were the only dissenting voices against the Tonkin Gulf Resolution in 1964.

2

LARRY HEINEMANN

novelist

When I accompanied novelist Larry Heinemann, and companions, to meet Daniel Ellsberg on a book-tour stop in Chicago, Heinemann made a point of thanking Ellsberg for exposing the lies underpinning Vietnam: "A great, brave thing you did, sir." Heinemann is a stocky five foot ten with a graying beard and twinkling eyes. He is a lifelong Chicagoan (four generations in the same North Side neighborhood and five, he points out, if you count his kids) who was drafted in 1966. During 1967–1968 he served in the 25th Division in Vietnam, where he saw action in Cu Chi, Dau Tieng, Tay Ninh, and the "Iron Triangle" region northwest of Saigon. After a stint as the surliest bus driver in Chicago in the summer of 1968 (see his mordant rememberings in Studs Terkel's *The Great Divide*), he collected a BA from Columbia College in Chicago in 1971 and taught in their writing program until the mid-1980s. His grueling war experiences became grist for *Close Quarters*, published in 1977.

His second novel, *Paco's Story*, follows a Vietnam veteran meandering in a ghastly ghostly haze through an utterly oblivious America. It earned the Carl Sandberg Literary Award and the National Book Award in 1986. In 1992, he brought out a very funny but, shall we say, regionally specific novel, *Cooler by the Lake*, which was a loving lashing out at Chicago's many foibles, fools, and scoundrels. His short works have appeared in *Penthouse*, *Atlantic Monthly*, *Harper's*, *Tri-Quarterly*, and the *Vietnam Writers Association Journal of Arts and Letters*. He has conducted writing workshops at many universities, including Northwestern University, the University of Southern California, and the University of California at Berkeley. Without burdening the text with innumerable annoying parenthetical breaks it is difficult to convey the wry humor he injected into the interview through intonations, squints, and actorly pacing in an unhurried storytelling style. A lot of laughter, rueful or raucous, erupted, even during grim recollections. The interview took place in his Chicago home in December 2002, a few days before he embarked for Vietnam on a Fulbright Scholarship. This would be his fifth trip back to Southeast Asia. He had just completed a book on travel by train and bicycle around Vietnam, as yet untitled.

I GATHER YOU DIDN'T QUITE HAVE A PRIVILEGED UPBRINGING LIKE OLIVER STONE, WHO LEFT YALE FOR VIETNAM.

My old man was a bus driver. My mother was a farm girl from Michigan. My mother's side of the family, oddly enough, is connected to Abraham Lincoln. I'm a sixth cousin. My grandfather resembled him. He had high sunken cheeks, a high squeaky voice, which Lincoln apparently had, and those melancholy eyes staring off into space like you see in a lot of photographs. My father was born in Chicago, and my mother came here in the 1930s and worked as a nanny for a doctor's family up in Winnetka. She met my dad, got married in 1939 or 1940. I was born in 1944. Went to work when I was 12, caddying summers.

WAS YOUR FATHER IN THE MILITARY?

No. He had flat feet. My uncles were. They never talked about it.

DID YOU GROW UP EXPECTING TO GO TO COLLEGE?

No. Like a lot of other families of ordinary working stiffs who came up in the Depression and World War II, the expectation was you finish high school and get a job. Guys like Bruce Weigl and Tim O'Brien and I laugh and say we became writers because of the war, not in spite of it. But my mother was a great storyteller and my grandfather was a wonderful bullshit artist. So I expect I got it from them. I worked for a while after high school. Then I went to Kendall, a two-year junior college across the street from Northwestern. I had a vague ambition to go to San Francisco State and get into theater. In 1966, I ran out of money, dropped out, and was drafted like that. Bingo. I was 22. I went overseas at 23 where everyone else was 18, and they called me the old man.

How about other family members?

I have three brothers and I am the only one who finished college. Three of us were in the service, two in Vietnam. I was in the army and my youngest brother was in the marines. He and I were there at the same time in 1967. He got wounded and sent home and then went back for a second tour. When he came back the second time, he and I didn't speak a word for ten years.

Because of different takes on the war?

Oh, yeah. Extremely different views of the war. Not to say, opposite.

Is that because he had a "kill 'em all let God sort 'em out" attitude?

Yeah. That's what the Marine Corps does. He dropped out of high school and my mother signed him in. The first day of boot camp he volunteers for Vietnam. But you are brutalized in a way that's unconscionable. The first night of boot camp everybody is scared shitless. They've got these monsters in Yogi Bear hats who scream at everybody like they've never been screamed at in their lives. Drill sergeants stand over each guy and scream at him until he volunteers. If he doesn't, they take him out back and beat the shit out of him until he does. But the marines do know how to dress. Give them that. James Jones called it a "pointless pride." All these guys have is a really flashy fucking uniform. On the other hand, some of my best friends are former marines, and they'd give you the shirt off their backs.

How does army training compare?

Compared with the Marine Corps, army basic training was a piece of cake. The one thing it was good for was the physical training. When I went in, I weighed about 140 pounds. Skinny, rundown, and nervous was the phrase in my family. After basic, I weighed about 160. Romping stomping dynamite [laughs]. I was in the best shape of my life. As an ordinary rifle soldier, if you're not in good shape, you are going to die. The work is just too hard.

STORIES CIRCULATED ABOUT THESE SUPERBLY CONDITIONED AND BAT-
TLE-HARDENED SOLDIERS BEING SPAT ON BY PROTESTERS, WHICH SEEMS
KIND OF UNLIKELY.

We all heard the stories of getting spit on, that mythology, when we
were overseas. I can tell you that when I arrived home I was not in the
mood. Some years ago I read from *Paco's Story* at the University of Wisconsin, and it was the only time I ever lost my temper at a reading. This
guy, a history professor and the faculty pill, I was later told, said that if
he had met me at the airport he would have spit on me. I came out from
behind the podium. I was shaking with anger and I said, "Shooting
someone with a rifle and spitting on them comes from the same place in
the heart. Second, I had just come from a place where I didn't take any
shit from anybody. You spit on me and you get your ass kicked within an
inch of your fucking life." I am not going to be ashamed that I came
through the war in one piece. I'm not proud of what happened in Vietnam, either. How can an honest person be proud of such a thing? But I
am not ashamed.

I HEARD THAT FROM OTHER VETERANS.

I've talked with a lot of veterans, and I never heard anybody say they
got spit on. Let me back up. I came back in March of 1968, about a
month and a half into the Tet offensive. Three weeks later, Martin
Luther King was murdered. On June 5, Bobby Kennedy was shot and
died on the greasy hot kitchen floor in Los Angeles. I got a job on a
Chicago city bus and drove through the Democratic Convention. Driving a bus—a horrible job for somebody in my frame of mind. It's one
thing about being a soldier that people here didn't get. We said it flat out
loud, "I don't fucking care." There were those days when you said, "Just
fucking kill me. I'm tired of this."

I can't think of another kind of work that is as soul-deadening, as
dispiriting. I remember coming back to the airport and just feeling ex-
hausted. You've been working on three or four hours of sleep a night for
a year. You feel as if you have been taken out of time. Saturday I was in
the 90th Reeple Deeple in Saigon. Sunday we stayed overnight at Oakland army terminal. I just want to go home. Please do not fuck with me.
It wasn't as if I had a chip on my shoulder or an attitude. I didn't have
any attitude at all. Or maybe it was more like, "Are you ready to fucking
die? Cause I don't care one way or the other." The next night I was home
in my own room. I slept on the floor.

THINK YOU NEEDED A PERIOD OF ADJUSTMENT?

Thinking back? God, yes. Back then? Get me the fuck out of here. I don't want a fucking parade. I have had it. They take your khakis and give you a brand-new uniform so you smell like the box of mothballs it came in. I put it on that afternoon about one o'clock, wore it home. I mustered out a sergeant, and it was the one and only time I wore my stripes. I looked like a toy. Got home that night, took it off, balled it up, hauled it to the garbage, and threw it away. I don't want anything to do with this anymore. I am a private citizen, thank you very much.

SO YOU START AT COLUMBIA COLLEGE IN 1968.

We're sitting around that first night in writing class, talking about what we want to write about. I say I just got back from overseas and I want to write about that. And there was this kind of suck of breath that went through the room. There was this look on everybody's face, like "You're one of them?" My attitude was, Yeah. I am one of them and if anyone wants to talk about it we can step out onto the fire escape six stories up from Ohio Street and talk about it out there.

SO HOW DID THEY WIND UP TREATING YOU?

Actually there was a great deal of empathy. A serious understanding by me of what they were trying to do against the war and a serious understanding by them for who I was and what the war was really about. After the news of the My Lai massacre hit the streets, it was, Whoa. They asked, "This happen a lot?" And I said that the spirit of atrocity was in the very air. We were all working-class kids. We were the first kids in our families to go to college. This was Columbia College in downtown Chicago. We found out we shared a great deal. They started out, "You should be against the war, Larry." And I was telling them, "Let me tell you why you should REALLY be against the war."

If there was an antiwar attitude among the troops I was with, it didn't get any more sophisticated than "Fuck this. This is bullshit." When I came back from overseas, I was just furious, and probably more radicalized than anyone I was in school with. I was extraordinarily bitter, and for a long time I thought I was the only one. I had this remarkable energy. This "thing" that just blew through me has got to make sense, has got to mean something. I got into writing because I had this story that will not go away. The thing that hooked me was the second week the teacher comes up to me—I didn't know then that he'd been a medic in Korea—and says, "Larry, if you want to write war stories read these." He hands me *The Iliad* and *War and Peace*. Everything that should be in a war story is in the *Iliad*. And *War and Peace* is just a great yarn and a beautiful piece of work. Plus we were reading *Moby Dick* and *The Painted Bird*.

IT APPEARS THAT *THE PAINTED BIRD* WAS A FIGMENT OF JERZY KOSIN-SKI'S IMAGINATION.

I don't care if it's phony, what a great fucking story. Turned out Kosinski was pretty strange. So I came into writing telling war stories. Never to my face did anyone say anything about being a soldier. The closest anyone came was to say, "How dare you tell those stories, how dare you use that language, and how dare you represent that point of view." That's when I knew I was on to something. I mean, I wanted to take the war and just shove it up your ass. I've run into people like that since, writers and writers who teach, and they act as if there is just one kind of story. They are doing the craft of writing and teaching, an extraordinary disservice. How dare you tell any young writer that they may not write about something because of subject matter or language or point of view just because you can't deal with it? That's your problem. Go find another line of work.

The worst kind of teachers think stories happen from the neck up, that there's a polite intellectual's armchair distance. But if a story doesn't make your skin crawl or make your bowels ache or your eyes fill with tears—well, what's the point? Goody goody talk never gets anybody anywhere. The way I learned anything was always the hard way. I opposed the war because I was up to here in it. I learned what love really means when I had kids.

WHAT DID YOU WANT TO SAY?

I always tried to talk about the war in terms of the work. It seemed like a good place to start. What struck me about *Moby Dick* was that Melville talked about what the work was so that you get an honest-to-God appreciation. There is a reason why the passing of that work is not mourned. Rowing after whales. You're engaged in slaughterhouse work and you're up to your eyeballs in blood. I started writing *Close Quarters* in 1968. I'll hang the story on the work, the same as Melville. It struck me that folks back here not only did not know what it was like to be in an army barracks but also knew nothing about the war as work. In every sort of work, there is a literal physical satisfaction that comes over you when a job's well done, a personal pride. But if you're an infantryman, your job is to kill people. "Close and engage," the lifers call it. I've heard historians refer to it as "state-sanctioned murder." But it's still murder. And how can you possibly have any good feeling about that? The aftermath of a firefight is all exhaustion, and downrange it's all meat. In half an afternoon, you are standing in a smell like no other in the world. The stink of body-count corpses. I was in mechanized infantry, a sort of junior armored cavalry. We had APCs, armored personnel carriers. Tracks.

What exactly was the work? Well, there's a .50-caliber machine gun that weighs about a hundred pounds and throws a slug about the size of your thumb and can blow your head off at a mile. Joseph Heller's Snowden in *Catch-22* was a fifty-gunner. That's what they used to shoot down Messerschmidts. A very serious weapon. I had never seen an APC before but learned quickly because I was the driver. I was in a recon platoon, so we had four guys on each track. If you fuck up, three guys hump. You hump, but they hump too. On the back were two M-60 machine guns. Basically, you're driving around in a thirteen-ton bunker.

We had Chevy 283 V-8s with a four-barrel carburetor and a blower about the size of a room fan and a 90-gallon gasoline tank. So you're always messing with machinery. So I told stories about night ambushes, search-and-destroy missions, and firefights large and small. What you do with body count. Smoking grass, drinking ourselves stupid. I never heard the word marijuana until I went to Vietnam, and we smoked it all the time. Stories about how the war worked, the same as you would go at any strange "process." It's the same in Robert Mason's book, *Chickenhawk*. He talks about what a helicopter is, for what, the first sixty or seventy pages? And if there's one symbol of Vietnam, it's the Huey chopper. Mason called it "hauling ass and trash." We just hauled ass.

I REMEMBER A MAGAZINE PHOTOGRAPH OF A TRACK PULLING VC BODIES BEHIND IT.

I don't need to see the picture. We did that a time or two. You get in a firefight and afterward go out and do what we referred to as a dismount, just like the cavalry. Searching the bodies and making the count. You tie the heels together with commo wire, which is like extension cord, and drag them out to the road and leave them. There were some outfits that left playing cards, but we never bothered with that. The strong inference was "Fuck with us and this will happen to you." Sometimes we had to drag the bodies a good long way. That's what got to me about reading *The Iliad*. Achilles ties Hector's corpse to a pair of horses. He gives them a whack on the ass and Hector's body gets dragged round and round the city until there was nothing left but what was tied at the ankles. How's that for "Fuck you"?

We had maybe 10,000 rounds of ammunition, which will last you all day. Crates of hand grenades. M-79 grenade launchers with both high-explosive rounds and canister rounds, which were 40-millimeter casings with double-ought buckshot. The barrel was eight or nine inches long, so you're walking around with a serious sawed-off shotgun. The M-16s back in those days were junk. I took an M-16 on my first ambush and fired three rounds and it jammed. Fuck this. So after that I took the M-60, the pig, we called it. You really did carry it like Sylvester Stallone [laughs]. You tied a long strap to the barrel and the butt plate and slung it over your shoulder, and you've got Pancho Villa–style bandoleers of ammunition. I had a 12-gauge shotgun for a while, and then an AK-47, which has to be the best in the world. You couldn't keep an M-16 clean enough. If I ever run into the motherfucker that sent that rifle overseas, I'm going to make short work of him. The other motherfucker I want to talk to is the asshole who sent gasoline-powered APCs. Just behind the driver is a 90-gallon gasoline tank. An engineer told me that one gallon of gasoline is equivalent to nineteen pounds of TNT, and nineteen pounds can blow the back of this house off.

WAS THE ARMOR EFFECTIVE?

It's inch-and-a-quarter aluminum alloy. Small-arms fire will ricochet. My track was all nicked up. By the way, it's the same armor that they use to make the Bradley Fighting Vehicle the army uses nowadays. And they're both death traps. A rocket-propelled grenade will go through inch-and-a-half aluminum alloy armor plate like spit through a screen. You hit the gas tank, the track goes up like the head of a match, mushroom cloud and all. Happened more than once. The drivers had their bodies separated from their heads. Many drivers got killed or burned to death. I ever run into the fucking genius who sent gas-powered to Vietnam, he and I are going to have a serious discussion. I would gladly do time in prison for the chance of showing Mister Genius what I think of his scheme.

DIESEL WOULDN'T DO THE SAME THING?

Diesel will burn, but it takes more to get it going. The only trick we had was to keep the tank full. That was the myth anyway. The RPG round has a magnesium core that burns of itself because it carries its own oxygen. So if you get whacked with an RPG, the shrapnel will burn right through you. Lots of casualties from that.

IT SOUNDS LIKE COMPLICATED MACHINERY DIDN'T WORK VERY WELL. WHAT DID WORK?

We used our bayonets to clean our nails and open our mail. Shotguns never failed. The M-79s were much coveted. The .45 pistols weren't much good beyond twenty-five or thirty feet but looked stylish. A lot of guys had personal weapons. A good friend of mine's father gave him a handmade Bowie knife. We drove our tracks hard, but they were beaters to start with. Take a thing so ordinary as C rations. We were once issued rations labeled October 1952 for Korea. And here's the one war souvenir I've got that I cherish: my P-38 C-ration can opener. It's the only thing the government ever gave me that worked as advertised. I keep it on my key ring for luck. C-ration food was terrible. But a couple years ago, I met a North Vietnamese army veteran and poet who said that they would have given anything to have C rations. What they did was boil up this really godawful rotgut wormy rice so it got real sticky and formed it into a log about a foot and a half long and carried it in their shirt. And that's what they ate.

OTHER ENEMIES IN YOUR BOOKS ARE "TICKET-PUNCHING LIFERS."

I have a strong memory of having it in for the lifers just as much as I had it in for the VC. One of the things almost nobody talks about is the fraggings. The boy scouts, the wannabe heroes, the John Waynes, the guys who buy the bullshit, the control freaks who really think they're in charge, the guys who want their Purple Hearts and their little medals, I mean they really want it—the clowns who simply will not leave you alone—these were the guys who got fragged: shithead lifers, the NCOs who were just assholes. Racist black sergeants, racist white officers. Look at it this way. When it was time to get rid of somebody, everybody was in on it, and there'd often be a pot. Everybody would kick in. And the easiest thing in the world was to fake a firefight at night, and somebody gets up behind the guy and simply shoots him. But the great appeal of hand grenades was you could booby-trap the guy's hooch and be, well, elsewhere. I read in [James William] Gibson's *The Perfect War* that the general who ordered the assault on Hamburger Hill wound up with a $10,000 bounty on his head but left for home before anyone could cash in. By the end of the war, there'd been thousands of fraggings. But their names are on The Wall too.

YOU PUBLISHED A STORY CALLED "THE FRAGGING" A FEW YEARS AGO. WAS THAT THE START OF A NEW NOVEL?

That's the only short story I've ever published that was never intended to be anything but a short story. For a while I had it in the back of my mind to follow the guys "who knew of the matter" after they got home. But no. No more war stories.

ANY EXCEPTIONAL LIFERS?

I've met a bunch since. Decent and intelligent men. When I was at Fort Knox, we had a first sergeant who got the entire gag. He was a full-blood Navajo Indian, First Sergeant Alva, and I will never forget him. Built like a fireplug. The day I left Knox, he took me aside and said, "Heinemann, remember, this is not a white man's war." What do you say to that? "Um, yes, First Sergeant." The best officer I knew was a University of Wisconsin ROTC graduate with a degree in history. He comes into the platoon, calls a meeting of the NCOs, and says, "Gentlemen, our job is to make sure everybody goes home in one piece." We look at him and say, "Lieutenant, this is a very good plan. How can we help you?" That's when we stopped doing a lot of the dumb things, like ambush every fucking night. Lieutenant Eric Opsahl was a prince. The lifers were there to punch their career tickets: get their medals and their promotions and their overseas pay. This is what gets me about listening to pilots, any pilot, who say they "were just doing my job." Well, they're doing their job and punching their tickets. Pilots never had to get down on the ground and wallow around in the mess they'd made.

SO YOU SAW THE AFTERMATH OF AIR STRIKES.

I remember sitting around a mess-hall kitchen table in the enlisted men's club at Dau Tieng, which was a dirt-floor tent with a sawhorse bar and couple of coolers full of semicold beer. We'd hear B-52 airstrikes in the distance and the cans on the table would start dancing around. And the airstrike is ten, fifteen miles away. Then they'd send us out to check on the damage. The bomb craters were just a swathe, maybe 100 meters wide and 500 meters long. It was just a hole, a nothing. The first time I flew into Hanoi was back in 1990, sailing in to the airport. Broad swathes of bomb craters all over everything. This was what Henry Kissinger saw when he flew into Hanoi, what year was that, 1973? I wonder what he thought?

PACO'S STORY IS A VERY PAINFUL BOOK THAT YOU GO ON READING ANYWAY. PACO, UNLIKE YOU, JUST DIDN'T FIND A VOICE.

Here's a guy who is probably a reflection of my younger brother. I hate to make it sound so pat. But you see it a lot. The war just choked some guys. Homeless veterans may well be the dictionary definition. My brother Philip came back and never said anything about the war. I could not shut up. Something happened to my brother in the two years he spent overseas that he simply could not get around. Lots of things are taken from you when you are soldier.

SUCH AS?

Ordinary human feeling. When you get R & R, you have your choice of cities. I chose Tokyo. Everybody on the plane was hornier than a five-peckered billy goat. I was twenty-three and I had $1,000 in my poke. In 1967, $1,000 was a great deal of money. Got to Tokyo and signed into, I swear to God, the Perfect Room Hotel. Could you think of a better name for a whorehouse? Any room you pick is going to be a delight. I wanted to sleep with a woman, not to say fuck my brains out, and find out if it was still possible for me to feel good in my body. Skip the date, skip the dinner, skip the movie. And yeah, I found out I could. I have a strong hunch my brother found out he could not. When you're nineteen, you don't even know what has been taken from you. And, sometimes, as I say, you don't get it back.

Bullshit counseling by some chaplain isn't going to do it. A parade isn't going to do it. All the Veterans Administration dope in the world isn't going to do it. Getting on your knees and praying twenty hours a day to Saint Expedite isn't going to do it. You are strictly on your own to rediscover all of these things about what it is be human and humane. There are a lot of guys like Paco. You get characters like him in Shakespeare. There are Paco characters in *The Iliad*. Psychologists have jargoned it to death, calling it post-traumatic stress disorder. The term I prefer came into use after the Civil War: soldier's heart. It amounts to a deep sense of grief that does not go away. Paco is transformed into a piece of meat. He feels as if he's been left behind. Because the guys who are narrating the story are the ninety-three dead guys of his platoon, and they aren't happy about being dead at all. So it's an odd irony. Wishing you were dead. But Paco is not innocent. You don't find that out until pretty far along in the story. Paco is a pretty creepy guy.

BUT THE STORY IS STILL SURPRISINGLY POIGNANT.

I worked on that book for eight years, and what I came to appreciate was that everything contains its own irony. There is a shadow side, an irony, an opposite to everything. Some people say the story is overwritten because the description gets to be too much. But there's a texture to the story, just like there's a texture to everything. Look around. There's always more than one thing going on. I don't know about poignant. At bottom what I tried to say was "Let's be honest about this."

Paco never says, "Why Me?" It would never occur to him. That's whining. What makes you think you are so fucking special? The big wheel turns, so why not you? Then, at the same time, you have the energy of the dynamic of the war. The central scene is the rape. Gallagher drags the captured VC woman into a hooch and forty guys rape her to death. They all understood that this was a moment of evil—but it couldn't have been any other way, because the whole energy of the dynamic points right to that. Let me put it another way. War is a special evil all by itself. The politest way to say it is that we were not pleasant people, and the war was not a pleasant business. We were not fun to be around. This is the thing about George W. Bush's determination to have a war in the Middle East that just breaks my heart, because these stupid motherfuckers haven't the faintest idea what they are getting us into. And they're not going to be able get us out. Maybe the kindest thing you can say about President Bush is that he's just not smart.

WHAT DO YOU ANTICIPATE?

The war is going to radicalize more Muslims, and then look out. President Bush is going to turn this country even more so into a country of serious racists. During the Vietnam War, it was "gooks." Now it'll be "raghead sandniggers," a slur I've heard they're using. There are already blacklists, and people being pulled over a million times. I saw a piece of film during those random sniper killings around Washington. They had pulled over a SUV with a woman and her kids, and the cop had the shotgun pointed right at her head through the windshield. Well, good morning to you, ma'am. Keep your hands on the wheel or I'll blow your fucking head off. The only thing I've seen since 9/11 is more nosy cops and snitches and trigger-happy air marshals. Try to get on a plane without being searched half to death and hassled if you ain't right on the bubble. I had a security guard give me lip for my P-38. What's this? Turns out the Vietnam War is so long ago she had never seen one, or the cops either. See what happens when you walk into City Hall, or the Cook County Building? Up against the wall, motherfucker. Cops just love it. They get to be in charge. Every epoch of war is a social catastrophe. Things accelerate. The changes are not just inventions and such. We're not talking penicillin. We're not talking Jeeps. We're not talking Tang. We're talking about a serious hit on ordinary civil rights. What was Goldwater's phrase, extremism in defense of liberty? Where're you going? What's your business here? It's only going to get worse, so the other side of the coin will be an explosion like the civil rights movement and the antiwar movement. When they start this war and the body bags start coming back by the planeload, maybe that's when folks are going to get religion.

IT LOOKS LIKE A PURE CHICKEN-HAWK PRODUCTION.

I'll go along with the war when I hear that the draft-age blood kin of the Bushes and Cheneys and McCains sign on. The day I hear that the graduating class of the Harvard Business School has dropped out three weeks shy of graduation and volunteered for Airborne Rangers, that's the day I'll go along with it. The U.S. government has had the last of me and mine. My son is draft age—and my daughter is draft age too—and I swear on the grave of my father that if Preston is drafted, he and I are leaving the country. I don't want anything to do with it.

HAVE YOU GONE PACIFIST?

I'm old enough to know that when evil comes into the world, you have to kill it. You're not going to buy them off; you're not going to negotiate with them because then you get Munich. The sticky part is, it depends on who is calling who evil. The Arabs, the Palestinians, clearly have a legitimate bitch with the United States and the Israelis. The one true thing that President Bush has said is "He tried to kill my daddy." On my block, that means that his argument with Saddam Hussein is strictly family business. As far as I am concerned, his moral authority to conduct this war does not extend farther than you can throw a chair off the porch of his ranch house in Texas. It's none of my business, and it's none of the business of any of the draft-age men that I know, kids on this block, my nephews, the kids I've been teaching down at DePaul. The war is about oil, and the Bush family business is oil. They're going to make a fortune while the rest of us take it in the neck, and the ground-pounders, not to mention working-stiff Arabs, are going to take it up the ass. It's amazing how this National Guard no-show has got everybody cranked up.

BACK TO NOVELS. A REVIEWER OF *COOLER BY THE LAKE* COUNTED FORTY WAR REFERENCES AMID ALL THE WISECRACKS.

It took two and a half years to write. My daughter Sarah said it was the first time she heard laughing come from my studio. It was great fun to write. I tried to get even with just about everything that irritated me in Chicago. Stupid cops, dumb baseball teams. Rum-dumb politicians. The references to war? Well, you can't get away from them. The stock market. Football. Politics. The evening news. Pick a topic and you get war jargon.

WHEN DID YOU FIRST RETURN TO VIETNAM, AND DID YOU HAVE THE HEEBIE-JEEBIES?

In 1988, I was invited to go on a genuine writers' junket to China for two weeks. That group was headed by Harrison Salisbury, and it was a great tickle to hang out with him.[1] The China trip was an ah-ha moment. I really do like hanging out in this part of the world. The Forbidden City. What a place. Then we went out to the Great Wall. You look out and there's nothing out there but scrubby mountains and you try to imagine guard duty. It must have been a stone-fucking bore. Sort of like the Kentucky hills, and you've got to know that on the other side of that is more hills, or a zillion Mongols on horseback. Then we went to see the terracotta warriors at Xian. That snapped my head back. They are modeled after real guys, so all the heads are unique. Folks on the trip said they saw soldiers that looked like me, that had my face, which was pretty spooky.

DID YOU CHECK IT OUT?

I don't need to know that I was a soldier in a previous life.

DO YOU PUT ANY STORE IN REINCARNATION?

I'm not going to say it doesn't happen. But if does—good God. Belt whippings. Again? High school. Again? Soldier. Again? Anyway, after the China trip I started thinking about going back to Vietnam. Then, in 1990, I got an invite to join a delegation of American veteran writers to travel to Hanoi and sit around and bullshit with the Vietnamese writers association. The group was, ahem, in no particular order [laughter] Phil Caputo, Larry Rottman, W. D. Ehrhart, Bruce Weigl, Yusef Komunyaka.[2] Yusef is a black poet who got the Pulitzer Prize for *Neon Vernacular* a couple years ago. This is going to look so dumb on paper, but there's a kind of aura about him. He is perhaps the most naturally elegant man I've ever met. By the time we landed in Hanoi, I couldn't wait. The city that had always been forbidden to me, even to my imagination. The long and short of it is, I love going back. By 1990, it was already a cliché that American veterans got a more warm welcome from the Vietnamese than we got when we came home. As a general thing, Americans wanted to shame us. Well, fuck that. And I don't go back to heal, God help us, or have one of those famous crying jags. It is a beautiful country, and there is an ease and a grace that I deeply appreciate. The food is great, and the women are beautiful, and riding the train is all kick.

WHICH VIETNAMESE WRITERS DID YOU MEET?

A fellow named Le Luu, who is basically the Ernest Hemingway of Vietnam. Another fellow named Pham Tien Duat wrote a poem called "White Circle," which is probably the most famous Vietnamese poem to come out of the war. And filmmaker Nguyen Quang Sang, who lived ten years in the Cu Chi tunnels. He still had the look of a guy you want on your side in a bar fight.

DID YOU MEET BAO NINH?

I met him in 1997 when a bunch of us went over. He came to Boston three years ago. I have great respect for Bao Ninh.[3]

DOES *SORROWS OF WAR* SEEM A COUNTERPART TO YOUR NOVELS?

I am not going to compare anything I've written to that. The one thing I know about the literature that came out of that war is that there is a subgenre of ghost stories. I don't know if there is anything comparable in other war literature, but in the Vietnamese and American writing that came out of the war there is a strong streak of that. I guess you'd say that the voice of the war is speaking.

DESCRIBE BAO NINH.

Bao Ninh is a pen name; it's the name of his village. No one calls him Ninh, his first name in Vietnamese fashion. It's Bao Ninh. I don't know if I've ever seen anybody drink as hard. He drinks with what Tennessee Williams would probably refer to as "some dedication." When people found out he liked Jack Daniels, everyone was laying fifths on the guy. I would be the last person in the world to tell Bao Ninh to stop drinking. But you could see it on his face. He's one of the few Vietnamese I've met who actually looks his age. Bao Ninh just looks like he never had an easy day in his life. Never.

He didn't write a lick until he was in his forties. The story I heard is that in classes and lectures he would sit in the back and drink. Never took a note. Basically, with *Sorrows of War*, he invented a form. I told him that the story just gave me chills. The beginning of the story where the guy strings his hammock above a truckload of North Vietnamese MIA corpses while they are driving through what they refer to as the valley of screaming souls. Whoa, what a way to start a book. Anybody who thinks that the Vietnamese don't have any ordinary human feelings or that they are somehow evil people should read this book.

ABSOLUTELY. DID YOU CLICK WHEN YOU MET?

I think he is the first Vietnamese writer I really connected with. He and I shared a great deal. He came to writing because he had a story, not the other way around. He's not university trained; he has no background in literature, particularly. He was an ordinary grunt, drafted in 1968, and was in a battalion of 500 guys who walked it down the Ho Chi Minh Trail which took, you know, six months. He was in the final battle for Tan Son Nhut Air Base in 1975. He told me that the morning of the last day of the war there were twelve guys left from the original battalion of 500. By the end of the day there were three. And he was as pissed off as any American veteran I've met, and pretty much said so in his novel. Give him credit for that. I once asked him as a soldier, as an ordinary, every-day garden-variety, ground-pounding grunt, what was the hardest thing he had to do. He said it was to bury all his friends. That's when I stopped complaining about how hard I had it.

WHAT DO YOU AIM TO DO IN VIETNAM?

I just put my Vietnam train travel book in the mail. Vietnam has this funky little narrow-gauge railroad. There is no better way to see the country. The original impulse for the book, my question, was: Who are these guys? How did they do this? What aspects of national character gave them the resources? I mean, on paper, we were unbeatable. Right? The lifers in Washington were saying that these were a bunch of fucking dirt farmers. Vietnam was going to be a walkover. Right? I'm going on a Fulbright to collect, transcribe, and translate Vietnamese folktales, about the cleanest expression of a people's imagination and self-image as you can find. But my real work is a "family novel" I've had in the back of my mind for ten years and more, and I want to write it in classic Grimm brothers folktale style. In the last ten or fifteen years, I've developed a serious interest in folklore and mythology. It seems all the elements of story have been there from the beginning. It's about as pure a story form as you can possibly get.

You've written about the mountain near your base camp.

The Nui Ba Den. What we called the Black Virgin Mountain. Everybody I know who has ever been around it remembers it with great warmth. It's like putting Mount McKinley out in the middle of Kansas. It was the one thing that we saw every day that didn't have anything to do with war. When I go back to Vietnam and folks ask me where I served, I say Cu Chi, Dau Tieng, and Tay Ninh. But when I mention Nui Ba Den, absolutely every Vietnamese I've ever met, North or South, man or woman, young or old, knows the mountain and knows the story. A young woman waits for her soldier-husband to return and he never does, and her faith and loyalty was so, what's the phrase, thorough and poignant, that when she died her spirit became the mountain. How's that for the origin of a place? And the fact that every Vietnamese knows the story says something very special about them. And even though we had no idea of the story, and probably wouldn't have cared, that image of the mountain touched us in a way that got tucked someplace until we needed it. Nui Ba Den is an astonishing place.

You've said you especially regret not having met James Jones.

I just loved his writing. And I've heard he was a real character. He wrote about war from the point of view of an ordinary soldier using ordinary language. If memory serves, he was the first American writer to use the word "fuck." *From Here to Eternity* and *Thin Red Line*, his World War II books, are his strongest. He really did call a spade a spade. He came back with an attitude not dissimilar to the soldiers coming back from Vietnam. Jones wrote about guys like Prewitt who would be PFCs for thirty years. Jones really nailed it. The moment Pearl Harbor was bombed, that all changed, of course, but what was preserved were the endless lifer stupidities. Jones died the week my first book was published. The same week, by the way, as my father.

Paul Fussell, a serious scholar, was a platoon leader in the army in Europe. I did get a chance to tell him what his writing meant to me. From *The Great War* and *Modern Memory* you got a sense of what being in a trench was about, living in a ditch for four years and going mad. He said he will always look at life through the eyes of a pissed-off infantryman, that there is something about being a soldier that does not go away. True enough. You read *The Thin Red Line* and you understand that a soldier's work is never going to change. You can only mechanize it so much. I'd love to be there the day all the computers go crunch. Now what, colonel? You can bomb a thing to kingdom come, but there is a point at which you must occupy the ground, and the pilots ain't gonna do it. The guys who go and stand on it are the guys with the hundred-pound packs and the serious guns. And by the time they get there, these are the guys who will slit your throat for your shoes. The guys who develop what psychologists refer to as combat psychosis, your basic take-no-prisoners, stone-fucking psychotic. There are those days when guys like that were worth their weight in gold.

How do you view the Bob Kerrey massacre scandal?

Bob Kerrey should be ashamed of himself. And he probably is, but only because somebody blabbed. He got a Bronze Star for murdering those people, and he wore it. A month later he gets in a scrape, loses a good bit of a leg, but they gave him the Congressional Medal of Honor. How dare he trade on that? If you want to be an officer, you had better have your shit together. You're the one who has to say no. Like the helicopter pilot, Thompson, at My Lai, who landed his chopper between Calley's troops and the Vietnamese civilians. Give that guy a medal.

The heat of the moment? I don't buy that. Of course, it happens, but you don't let it hang for thirty years. You're supposed to man up to it, Bob. It's something the same with John Kerry when he voted for the Iraq war resolution. What the fuck was that? He is definitely off my list. John, where is the moral outrage you had in 1971 at Dewey Canyon III when the VVAW showed up to throw their medals away? He ought to know better. And Hillary Clinton betrayed herself as an opportunist of the very first rank. Talk about punching your ticket.

WERE YOU INVOLVED IN THE VVAW?[4]

I often laugh and say that during the 1970s I hardly stepped off the porch. I hardly remember the music. I was, what would be the word, definitely inner-directed. I thought the one good thing I could do was write a good book. I'd been invited to antiwar rallies. But the VVAW? It was run by officers, and I had pretty much had it with them.

FINALLY, DID YOU EVER FEEL YOUR WORKING-CLASS BACKGROUND WAS A DISADVANTAGE?

No. Looking at the world from down where the rubber meets the road has a long and honorable history. Sam Clemens never finished grammar school, and he did just fine. I do know that I had to start from square one and read the books I was already supposed to have read. Well, you get to read with a very clean eye. And it goes straight back to the energy of ambition that I brought to school and the fact that my teacher gave me a leg up and a good shove. A great gift. Probably the only disadvantage I feel is that I don't have much of an organized background in American literature. I'm still working on Shakespeare, still working on Faulkner. I'm not a philosopher, and God knows I'm not a scholar. I'm a storyteller who got lucky. I can't think of doing any other work. If writing were taken away from me, I would wither. Anybody can be a barstool bullshit artist. I take great pride in my craft. And let's get this straight. There's nothing cathartic about writing as a craft. Just because you write it down, put it in a box, and send it out of the house does not mean it's gone. The people who write because they think it's therapeutic are, well, I don't know what they are, but they're not writers. You have to let the chips fall where they're going to fall. I do know this. I will always be able to reach back and touch the war and find a story. That's a mellow irony of the richest kind. And the stories have less and less to do with the war, and more and more are, well, just stories.

NOTES

1. Former *New York Times* correspondent in Asia in the 1960s and 1970s.
2. Philip Caputo, *A Rumor of War* (New York: Holt, Rinehart and Winston, 1977) and *Indian Country* (New York: Bantam Books, 1987); Larry Rottman, *Voices from the Ho Chi Minh Trail: Poetry of America and Vietnam, 1965–1993*

(Desert Hot Springs, Calif.: Event Horizon Press, 1993), Rottman et al., eds., *Winning Hearts and Minds: War Poems by Vietnam Veterans* (Brooklyn, N.Y.: 1st Casualty Press, 1972), and Rottman et al., eds., *Free Fire Zone: Short Stories by Vietnam Veterans* (New York: McGraw-Hill, 1973); William Daniel Ehrhart, *The Outer Banks and Other Poems* (Easthampton, Mass.: Adastra Press, 1984) and *In the Shadow of Vietnam: Essays 1977–1991* (Jefferson, N.C.: McFarland, 1991); and Bruce Weigl, *The Monkey Wars* (Athens: University of Georgia Press, 1985), *Song of Napalm: Poems* (New York: Atlantic Monthly Press, 1988), and *The Circle of Hanh: A Memoir* (New York: Grove Press, 2000).

3. North Vietnamese army veteran and author of the widely acclaimed half-memoir, half-novel *The Sorrows of War.*

4. The VVAW is Vietnam Veterans Against the War. Dewey Canyon III was a mocking label for a clever and courageous domestic-dissent campaign waged by these dissident veterans. For chroniclers, see Gerald Nicosia, *Home to War* (New York: Crown, 2001) and Andrew Hunt, *The Turning: A History of the Vietnam Veterans Against the War* (New York: New York University Press, 1999).

❸

JOHN NICHOLS

novelist and screenwriter

"All my life I've been torn between writing *War and Peace* and writing something small and delicate," says John Treadwell Nichols, who most recently has converted the former into the latter, an artfully abridged novel, *Voice of the Butterfly* (2002). Nichols is a slim New England émigré (to New Mexico) with an easygoing demeanor, loads of charm, and a steely underlying toughness. During our interview, for relief, he disconcertingly removed his false front teeth, a gaping souvenir from glory days as a hockey jock in college. Nichols leans toward novels of epic sweep that, when they work out, are rollicking blends of darkness and daffiness. *The Milagro Beanfield War* (1974) and *The Magic Journey* (1978) are portraits of a poor rural community in the Southwest that resist as resourcefully as they can the omnivorous juggernaut of capitalism. Together with the sardonic New Age farce *The Nirvana Blues* (1981), they constitute his splendid New Mexico trilogy.

At the time of the interview, Nichols lived on the edge of Taos in a small house with an outdoor convenience, which he has since departed in the wake of a divorce. Hockey injuries spared him from the draft, or spared the army from him. The polylingual Nichols moved from New York to New Mexico in 1969. For several years, he edited *The New Mexico Review*, an investigative journal, which provided a great deal of seamy grist for his trilogy. He also co-wrote *Missing* for film director Constantine Costa-Gavras (without credit) as well as the screenplay of *Milagro* for Robert Redford.

Returning to novels, Nichols penned *American Blood* (1988), which was a brutal imaginative reverie of a Vietnam veteran's wayward search for redemption. After a number of nonfiction expeditions, he brought out more novels: *Elegy for September* (1992), *Conjugal Bliss* (1994), *Ghost in the Music* (1996), and then *Voice of the Butterfly*, which is his "Keystone Kops comedy about the ecological crisis." A group of ecological "zanies get a rare no-account butterfly declared an endangered species" to foil developers running a highway bypass through an environmental haven. Nichols also has published a memoir, *An American Child Supreme: The Education of a Liberation Ecologist* (2001), and a book of essays, *Dancing on the Stars* (2000). I supplemented the interview with a phone call to Taos in the spring of 2001.

PLEASE TELL US ABOUT YOUR UPBRINGING.

I was born in Berkeley, California, July 23, 1940. I suppose you could say I grew up in a white Anglo-Saxon Protestant home, a very narrow-minded atmosphere. Sex wasn't talked about. I grew up pretty repressed. You did not show your emotions. You kept those kind of things to yourself. This was sort of the Calvinist puritanical ethic. I remember I used to shake my father's hand when we met. I think I called him "Sir."

My mother was French but was raised in Barcelona. She died when I was two. We moved almost every year of my life. From Florida to Long Island, where I spent three years living with cousins because my father went overseas in the marines during World War II. He got remarried when I was six. I lived in Montpelier, Vermont, about a year and a half, where my second novel is set. We moved back to Long Island. Then my father went back to school in 1949 to get his degree at Berkeley.

DEGREE IN WHAT?

He's a zoologist and ornithologist.

THERE CAN'T BE VERY MANY EX-MARINE ORNITHOLOGISTS RUNNING AROUND.

Well, my grandfather was curator at the Museum of Natural History in New York, and the whole family was involved in the natural sciences. My father thought that the Soviet Union was ahead of the United States in many areas of biology and zoology, and he wanted to read all the magazines and reports in Russian. So he majored in Slavic languages and minored in zoology. Later he went back to Berkeley during the time of the Free Speech Movement when Mario Savio and all those characters were around to get a Ph.D. in psycholinguistics and wound up teaching psychology at the University of Colorado.

DID ANY FAMILY MEMBERS HAVE LEFTIST LEANINGS?

Oh, no. My great-great-great grandfather William Floyd signed the Declaration of Independence. The Floyd House, built around 1720, stayed in the family until 1978. This house on the south shore of Long Island has a family graveyard where everyone's been buried for the last 250 years. So the family had this powerful rooted connection to both history and the place. Finally, when my grandmother died, the family got together and instead of splitting up the estate and selling it and becoming billionaires, everyone agreed that the house and 600 acres of virgin forest right on the ocean should be turned over to the government as a conservation area. Now it's part of Fire Island National Seashore. But when you come from that kind of background—well, I believe people voted Republican.

A LOVE OF NATURE CAN BE EXTREMELY SUBVERSIVE.

I really tuned into the natural world. By the time I was ten, I could identify seventy species of birds by their silhouettes when they were flying or when they were tweeting. I remember my stepmother, who was a teacher, would flip a new record on the Victrola and say, "This is Errol Gardiner. He's a wonderful pianist. You should listen to it." When Tolkien came out with the Hobbit trilogy, before it was popular she'd get a hold of it and read it to you. There was interest in everything. Nevertheless, it was no liberal or left family—no red-diaper babies or anything like that.

It caused real consternation when I sat around playing Chubby Checker, Elvis Presley, Chuck Berry, Screaming Jay Hawkins. It was all banned from the house until I brought home a Ray Charles record, a very slow bluesy thing. I remember that cutting through. But otherwise, it was the way I wound up feeling when my kids all shaved their heads and went punk and were grooving on New Wave music and Sid Vicious and the Sex Pistols and I'd say, "Oh my god what is the world coming to? Why can't they like good old-fashioned rock and roll," you know? My father had a vast knowledge of French folk music, Russian folk music, Elizabethan ballads, and cowboy tunes. I know all those wonderful old songs. I really loved blues music. I got into the whole scene—Leadbelly, John Lee Hooker, Brownie McGee, Sonny Terry, Memphis Slim, Willie Dixon. I venerated those people. I remember when I was a sophomore in Hampshire College, Josh White came and it was as if the pope had arrived. To see him playing tunes like "Hollywood Bed" or "Strange Fruit" was one of the most powerful experiences of my life.

DID YOU HAVE OTHER CONTACT WITH BLACKS THEN?

In 1951, I was going to an all-white high school when *Brown v. Board of Education* went down. All my friends came to school the next day with baseball bats, brass knuckles, knives, chains, switchblades, potatoes with razor blades in them, to beat the blacks out of the school if they tried to get in. Another scene made an impression. My stepmother lost her wedding ring and thought she threw it in the garbage. So we had to go to the black garbage man's house, which was near our home, going to this house with no windowpanes, just a shack with this guy and this woman and three or four children dressed in rags, surrounded by mountains of garbage. In other words, there was no landfill—the landfill was his land around the house. I remember me and my well-dressed mom rooting through the garbage looking for the wedding ring and these raggedy people standing around silently and staring at us. Things like that really stick in my head.

I SAW SIMILAR GRIM STUFF IN NORTH CAROLINA.

I was in Mississippi five years ago. It's all integrated, you know. Blacks and whites shop in the same stores. But the minute you get a couple of white people behind closed doors or at a restaurant table, it's just nigger this and nigger that. I was there five days, and it's lucky I didn't get into some brawl or get put into jail because white people would come up and make an automatic assumption that because I was white I was racist. People would say just as their goodbye greeting—"Well, okay, we'll see you, been nice talking to you, take care of yourself." The final thing they'd say is "Watch out for niggers." I don't know how many times I heard that. I know we live in a real racist society and you find it in Boston as well as in Taos, New Mexico. The divisions and the exploitation are there and very powerful. But Mississippi was really pushing it, you know? I wrote a novel in college about the exploitation of black people in the South. Yet I didn't get up on soapboxes. I was not a radical political person well ahead of my time. I was heavily involved in music and sports. I was enthralled by Spanish culture, language, music. Also, I was a sports fanatic from the age of seven. I spent a lot of time crossing those lines even though I was raised in the best private school money could buy in both prep school and college and was trained to be a member of the ruling class.

DID YOU GET ANY PARENTAL PRESSURE TO BE A PROFESSIONAL, MAKE A LOT OF MONEY?

Curiously, I never felt that kind of pressure. My parents got divorced when I was fourteen. My father got custody of me, and from that point I was going away to school and summer jobs away from home. I became independent pretty early. I remember the piece of advice my dad considered to be valuable in life. He said always pull your weight with the team—don't be a shirker. And you should be honest with people. That was it. He never said you gotta get good grades, you gotta make money and that's the way to success. I mean in prep school and college, you're trained to be a doctor or lawyer and make a lot of money. None of it took hold. The same way I went to church for God knows how many years and stopped the minute I didn't have to go. I never had a belief in God or Christianity. It was just all baloney to me.

WHO WERE YOUR LITERARY HEROES WHEN GROWING UP?

L. Frank Baum. The Oz stories. Probably the most influential literary hero I had was Damon Runyon. I just loved the gangster thing, loved the style, loved the slang. From a real early age, I loved language, joking with language, and puns and slang. All my life I picked up things by ear really quick because I grew up in an essentially tricultural family. I loved accents and ways of talking. It's hard for me not to mimic people. When I first learned to speak before my mother died, I spoke French. My father spoke fluent French, Russian, Chinese. Because my mother was raised in Barcelona, the Spanish side was real important too. I was always enthralled by Spanish culture, language, and music.

WHAT SORT OF ADOLESCENT WERE YOU? SULKY? BRASH?

The marriage between my father and stepmother was a real bad one. There was a lot of tension in the household. Tight-lipped. Tiptoe. Don't make waves. Which means the minute I got on the school bus, it was Jekyll-Hyde. I became a real wise guy, an arrogant, noisy, and popular person. I went to Loomis, one of the big prep schools in New England, and I flunked courses every year and was always being disciplined for long hair, arrogant attitude, that kind of stuff. Wound up with the rebels in the school, doing whatever was contrary to how you were supposed to do things. What saved me was I was an athlete, lettering in three varsity sports, captain of the hockey team. I got into Hamilton College because I was a good hockey player. It was 1958 to 1962—the tail end of the silent generation. I played sports, worked on the newspaper, acted in plays, played a lot of music.

I got crippled playing hockey, so I was 4-F in the draft. I was not a radical political person well ahead of my time. Hamilton was a conservative, isolated little place and yet it was also a place where I was allowed to be a jock and a bohemian. That kind of place makes you aware of class, race, and ethnic divisions and the need to overcome them. I spent a lot of time crossing those lines. There were a few blacks at Hamilton—not many, of course—that made you aware of the start of the civil rights movement. I wrote a novel there based on Emmet Till, a young black kid from Chicago who got lynched in 1957 or 1958. After that, it was almost as if I never met a book I didn't like. I was also a movie freak. The first film I saw was Roy Rogers in *Riders of the Purple Sage*. From then, any time I could see a movie I went. I read comics assiduously. I cut and pasted them in scrapbooks. I had every crime-stoppers textbook from Dick Tracy. I learned to draw.

When I got out of college, I figured I'd be either a cartoonist, a writer, or a musician. I spent a lot of time drawing. For much of the sixties and seventies I did political cartoons for Liberation News Service. Later, when I worked for *The New Mexico Review* from 1970 to 1972, I did a lot of cartoons for them. And *Seer's Catalogue*, an underground magazine in New Mexico. I published a couple in *The Nation*, *The Guardian*, things like that. The last artwork I did was a series of *calaveras*, which are black-and-white etchings of little skeletons in the Mexican tradition, which illustrated *The Magic Journey*. But the paperbacks each have a *calavera* done by José Guadelupe Posada, a Mexican graphics artist most well known during the revolution.

WHAT WAS YOUR FIRST MOVE AFTER COLLEGE?

I went to Spain for a year, where I taught English in Barcelona and worked on *The Sterile Cuckoo*. Then I came back to New York in 1963 and got a little apartment on the corner of West Broadway and Prince

Street for forty-two dollars a month. Now it's the chicest address in New York. I had three or four books going at once, writing my ass off. Played guitar in these little cafes every night. I did nude drawing on the streets at five bucks a pop. That was a wonderful time, sort of hustling and scuffling along. I took *Sterile Cuckoo* around and got real lucky. The eighth or ninth publisher gave me a five hundred dollar advance. So I put the money in my sock and I went down to Guatemala to visit my best friend, who was working on a Fulbright grant.

WHAT THEN?

Guatemala just blew the top of my head off. I went down as a lark. I'd never been in a place where people maimed themselves in order to beg, where people were so crippled and sick, where everybody seemed to have filarial worms in their eyeballs, where 80 percent of the population was barefoot. I'd never been in a country where you could walk down streets with little horse stalls with three women to a stall and you could get laid for fifty cents a pop. I'd never seen open sewers. There were hundreds and hundreds of vultures around. And it all could be laid directly on the shoulders of the United States. Because my friend was working with Guatemalans, I got to listen to people who told me about the CIA coup in 1954 that overthrew the Arbenz government.

I learned about people like Miguel Asturias, who won the Nobel Prize with novels like *El Señor Presidente*, about the United Fruit Company. It was an education in imperialism. It was like opening Pandora's box. The more I would read, the more I entered a kind of culture shock, which happened to a lot of my generation in the sixties, who'd say, "My God, what kind of country do I live in? I thought it was George Washington and the cherry tree, Abe Lincoln and free the slaves, this benevolent country that was out to spread democracy around the world." Instead, you read what really happened. So I wound up turning my value system upside-down. The American dream was over.

WAS *THE STERILE CUCKOO* OUT BY THEN?

I sold *Sterile Cuckoo* and *The Wizard of Loneliness* within a year of each other. *Cuckoo* was a Literary Guild alternate, went out on film option, and within two years was filmed by Alan Pakula. But *The Wizard* came out and sank like a stone. From that point on, I was trying to write different books, the books were very political, very angry, very polemical, very badly written.

I SAW *WIZARD OF LONELINESS* ON VIDEO. IT WORKS.

Jenny Bowen went back and extrapolated on the book and we wrote the script. She said that she never again would make a film about something she really cared about without having enough money because they were really strapped for bread. They had about a million—and they couldn't even do reaction shots. They'd do a master shot and the actors had one take and that was it. It's put together very simply. Her husband is a wonderful photographer. The look is just exquisite. That's where they put the money; everybody else did it for equity scale. But the ending is terrible. Also, they ran out of time. They had no budget. They couldn't go over. They wanted snow and it snowed in October and didn't in December when they needed it. And they didn't have money to correct that. They hired a few dump trucks to bring snow out of the mountains. It was a real shoestring operation. Yet it's a real lovely, very delicate, quite beautiful film.

THE THIRD BOOK WAS *MILAGRO*?

Milagro Beanfield War is the third published book. But between 1965 and 1972 I wrote seven novels, which dealt with Vietnam, U.S. history, that kind of thing. None of which ever got published.

DO YOU AGREE THEY SHOULDN'T HAVE BEEN PUBLISHED?

Yeah. They were all bad. One of them was about a guy who wins the Medal of Honor in Vietnam and comes back to the United States and is so blown away by the inequalities inside this country he was supposed to be defending that little by little he really loses it and goes bananas and slaughters his whole family and walks to the edge of the ocean and rips off his medal and throws it in the water.

I SEE WHAT YOU MEAN.

And that was probably the most coherent one. But it was nihilistic and so unartful.

DO YOU FEEL YOU GOT IT RIGHT IN *AMERICAN BLOOD*?

In *American Blood*, I finally came to write what I was starting to work on in the sixties. I figured out a way to either control the anger or to forge it into some coherent manner.

WHY MOVE TO NEW MEXICO?

I lived in New York from 1963 to 1969 and wanted to get out. We were really broke. Got married in 1965 and we had a kid and lived in a tiny apartment. The good times were over, right? I wasn't selling anything. A lot of people were burning out at that stage, moving to communes in Vermont or California, getting into peace, love, and grooving. Withdrawing from the struggle. I wanted to go where the atmosphere was such that you had to continue being politically active. There was a lot of social agitation going on. New Mexico is almost the poorest state in the union but is also a cultural bazaar. I can't live in a place that isn't multicultural, and multiclass too. New Mexico seemed like a colonial country. The majority of the people were minorities, Chicano or native American, and there was incredible exploitation.

WHAT'S THE ATTRACTION OF TAOS?

Well, Santa Fe is just a joke and Taos is a real tough little town, a very picturesque little ghetto. Sixty percent of the county lives below the poverty line. Yet it's set at 7,000 feet at the foot of 13,000-foot mountains. At the time, I didn't understand how wonderful the natural landscape really was. I was more interested in politics, the different cultures, the economics of it. So I went to work for *The New Mexico Review*, a high-class investigative journal, for three years, 1970 through 1972, doing articles every month on land and water struggles in northern New Mexico. Though it paid no money, it was a reason for being. It had power, was read widely in the state, a communal operation with contributing editors who decided what to cover. I edited it the final six months. Now it's sort of a classic.

But at the end of 1973, I couldn't keep going any longer. I was broke. I figured I had to find some way to resurrect my literary career or bag it. I sat down and thought how about entertainment again? Whatever happened to my sense of humor? So I bent over backward to be funny and wrote a book about class struggle and people trying to stop cultural genocide from occurring in their community. But tried to do it with humor and some kind of love and compassion and not be so fucking serious. Then one of those weird little situations happened where you are blessed by luck and have no idea why. I churned *Milagro* out in five weeks—a 500-page book. Spent three more weeks correcting it and sent it to my agent, who sold it to Holt. They gave me a $10,000 advance, and my literary career was saved. Ten years earlier, I got $38,000 for the rights to

Sterile Cuckoo, so we're not talking here about going upward. But it did go on film option for fourteen years and kept me alive in my limited lifestyle. That was a savior, because I had several novels rejected over the next four or five years. Then I managed to sell *The Magic Journey*, which became an underground cult book and started to be used in schools.

Then in 1979 I managed to publish two books. One was a little novel called *A Ghost in the Music*; another a nonfiction book called *If Mountains Die*. Knopf brought it out, and it actually was my first popular book. It stayed in print for twelve years, which is unusual for a photo-essay book. Bill Davis, the photographer, came to me and asked if I would write blurbs for his book of photographs. My agent and editor weren't interested. Knopf finally brought it out, and that got me started in nonfiction books. I thought this was kind of fun and a nice way to do something useful in between novels. Since then, I've published four photo-essay books. *The Last Beautiful Days of Autumn* is a 100,000-word book with 65 of my own photos. *On the Mesa* has a few of my photos and is 70,000 words. *A Fragile Beauty* is mostly photos and excerpts of my work with an introduction geared to the *Milagro Beanfield War* film. This last one is called *The Sky's the Limit*, which is a radical environmental essay with photos.

I TOLD A FRIEND WHO DIDN'T KNOW YOUR WORK THAT YOU WERE FROM TAOS. HE SAID "OH, ONE OF THOSE," MEANING THE KIND OF TRENDY YOU LAMPOON IN *THE NIRVANA BLUES*.

Outside the center of touristic bullshit, Taos is a real heavy, dark, scary place. It's a very picturesque ghetto, but still you're dealing with the socioeconomics of Bedford-Stuyvesant. Even Anglos who go there to live the trendy life wind up working at minimum-wage jobs because there is no real work to be found. One of the things that is undermining the community is that people with money are going in and building second homes that they go visit three weeks of the year. As more land gets bought up that way, it erodes the community, which is made of year-round residents. So Taos is one of those situations where you have a mansion surrounded by ghetto where everybody uses an outhouse. So it's a real schizophrenic situation.

WHAT'S YOUR LIVING SITUATION THERE?

I ended up buying the cheapest place I could find. It has indoor plumbing for a sink and bath, but you have to use an outhouse. It's a small place. But it has a half-acre field in front and a half-acre in back fed by two little irrigation ditches. It's like a microcosm of Taos. You see, the area is an agriculture-based economy. Almost everyone augments whatever cash income they get by raising a few cows or sheep, by having a garden, by putting in fruit trees—the whole subsistence scuffle. Land is real important. A lot of people who are desperately poor have a lot of land because it's been in the family for three or four hundred years. Someone with an income of $2,500 a year may own their own adobe house and thirty or fifty or a hundred acres. So long as they can hold on to the land, they can survive. The minute they become so involved in the cash economy to where they want fancy cars or VCRs or television sets and start selling off the land, they get involved in a journey of no return because there are no jobs. They are not going to be incorporated into the cash economy. They also get caught—as middle-class newcomers move in, demanding services—in a rising tax base that they can't pay for. Consequently, people will sell off an acre here and there simply to pay taxes. They wind up being displaced.

DID YOU NEED TO EXAGGERATE THE PLIGHT AT ALL?

The situation is exaggerated in *The Nirvana Blues*, where there's only one land-based Chicano left in the valley. Today, many people in the indigenous culture are in a huge struggle to sustain the irrigation system and keep water rights. You see, it's difficult to go in and develop because the resources are so limited. If Holiday Inn wants to build 500 rooms with flush toilets, it has to buy water rights for them. The town doesn't have any excess water rights to sell. So they have to go find some farmer willing to sell them water rights to flush the toilets. Then the farmers no longer can irrigate their lands because they transfer their rights. So there's a virulent struggle going on between the developers and the people who don't want the valley completely destroyed, who want to save that land and the Spanish-speaking culture that depends on it. I work for a group that goes into court almost every day to stop the state from transferring rights to developers.

IN *THE NIRVANA BLUES*, YOU SHIFTED YOUR AIM TO SILLY AND SELF-DESTRUCTIVE NEW AGE PIETIES.

The Nirvana Blues is a book I wanted to write attacking the "me" generation, EST, Eckankar, the selfishness of yuppie self-absorption. I thought of it as the third panel of the *Garden of Earthly Delights*. In fact, I wanted *The Magic Journey* to be sort of a *War and Peace*, a huge novel that incorporated everything that also is in *The Nirvana Blues*. I couldn't work the juxtaposition, the tragedy versus the farce. I had this huge novel that just wasn't functioning. I finally dropped the tack on the futuristic look at where this is all going, and then sat down on *The Nirvana Blues* to complete the picture.

DID YOU EVER KNOW SUCH A WOMAN AS APRIL DELANEY, YOUR LEAD CHARACTER IN *THE MAGIC JOURNEY*?

April Delaney was based on two people I had known very closely. They were very powerful to me. So she was there from the start.

THE MAGIC JOURNEY READS LIKE A MAGICAL-REALIST VERSION OF *DAS KAPITAL*.

I wanted to trace the development of the town over a forty-year period. How capitalist development functions. I did more planning for that book than anything I've ever written. For *The Milagro Beanfield War*, I sat down on a one-sentence premise, you know, you got a thirty-five-year-old unemployed Chicano handyman who cuts water illegally into a half-acre bean field and all hell breaks loose. I just sat down—"Once upon a time. . . ."

But for *The Magic Journey*, I had maybe 200 manila folders following skullduggery in a small town, corruption in the police, corruption in the mayor's office in the application of federal programs. I had files on everything from the Ladies' Garden Club to scandals within the highway department. I typed out synopses of every file and how these might relate to a novel. Then I typed the first draft—about five or six hundred pages—and there wasn't a line of dialogue in it. All it was was this convoluted, contorted macroscopic overview of a society with very little emphasis on character development. Most of it was putting together this complicated Chinese puzzle describing the workings of this system. Then little by little, after rewrite and rewrite, I began to developing characters more and more and fit the story to what I wanted to say politically.

HOW LONG DID IT TAKE?

I started writing *The Magic Journey* in 1973. A good four or five years. I was collecting information for a long time. It was a case of the more you read the more you learn the more you become politicized by understanding the whole picture, trying to develop a macroscopic overview of life.

WHAT EXAMPLES SPURRED YOU ON?

I really loved books like William Shirer's *The Rise and Fall of the Third Reich*. Robert Caro's book on Robert Moses was a real inspirational thing. The Beards. Ida Tarbell's history of Standard Oil. That kind of thing where somebody tries to encompass the overall picture. I suppose Tolstoy in *War and Peace*. Emile Zola's *Germinal* was real powerful. I used to love Dickens novels. George Eliot's *Middlemarch*. Another major influence was muralists: Bosch, Breughel, Jan van Eyck or Diego Rivera, Orozco, and Siqueiros. These fantastic murals depicting history, armies, war, revolution, huge factories, the poor, the rich. All that stuff.

I'M SURPRISED NO ONE SLAPPED THE LABEL "MURALIST WRITER" ON YOU.

That would be a good label. One of the great benefits of having a privileged education is that people made me read Faulkner and Dickens and Katherine Anne Porter and Carson McCullers. I don't know if I ever read Zola in college, but they made me read *Middlemarch* and things I never would have known about if I was just on the streets, you know? All my life I always loved the great macroscope; at the same time I loved Camus. I'd really like to write something like *The Stranger* or *The Great Gatsby* or Truman Capote's *Breakfast at Tiffany's*. Or Jim Harrison's *Legends of the Fall*. It's one of the most beautifully written precise things. God, if only I could put together a 90-page perfectly sculpted novel.

I'm always vacillating about what's the next project gonna be. Am I gonna shoot for 10,000 pages or some perfect little gem? I've been working on a book that started as a 1,400-page manuscript. That didn't work out. I rewrote it as a 900-page manuscript and that didn't work. Then I got really pissed off and chopped it down to a real tight 300-page manuscript and that didn't work. Then I just threw away everything except for maybe 100 pages. A little gem, you know, and started in another direction.

IS THIS YOUR JUDGMENT OR YOUR AGENT'S JUDGMENT?

I sent the 900-page draft to my editor because I was desperate for money. Hoping she would give me an advance. She's a wonderful editor, but she's harsh. Her letter said this book is like a great oil spill, going in every direction, meaning nothing, and she was right. I sit down and I have some vague idea or notion, and it takes me forever to realize it. I'm not a person who seems to have the discipline to actually forge the thing

I'm after the first or second or third time around. Most of my writing is trial and error, badgering and badgering it, writing in pieces until it falls together. *The Magic Journey* was a hellacious process of molding. I never felt I actually got it the way I wanted it to be. I wanted to put everything I got into this. You know, you start out and it's gonna be this wonderful, incredible novel, and in the end you wind up just trying to stay sane long enough to salvage something.

YOU MEAN YOU ARE DISAPPOINTED IN *THE MAGIC JOURNEY*?

I think I'm proud of it now. I get so burned out on writing books that once I go through the galleys I never ever want to read them again. I have this little fantasy that when I'm eighty years old and dying of cancer or something, I can sit down and read whatever books I've published and be curious to see what I did. It makes me nauseous to read anything—you go through one page and you say, "Oh fuck, there's six dangling participles, three split infinitives, blah blah blah blah."

DID YOU FEEL BETTER ABOUT *NIRVANA BLUES*?

In *Nirvana Blues*, I really wanted to savage that part of the culture crush—what did Ayn Rand call it?—the virtue of selfishness. So I figured I'd write a book paralleling the building of the house because yuppies come in and they've just been married and they have little children and put them in Montessori schools. They get some land and then they start to build their house and then everything goes wrong. By the end of the whole thing, the husband and wife are off fucking sixteen different lovers and the kids don't know which end is up, and as soon as the house is finished they get a divorce. One of them turns into a drug addict, the other goes off selling real estate as a slum lord in Brooklyn or whatever. They're all into ecology and yogurt and natural foods. At the end of it, they've turned into the worst beasts that anyone can imagine.

I wrote 600 pages and had only gone from Saturday night to Tuesday morning. Furthermore, the thing didn't have a plot. So two or three drafts into it, I decided this guy is gonna make a coke deal to get money to buy land. I imposed a running thread to make people turn the pages and read my railings against this and that. I threw in the Hanuman monkey unveiling. And that's the way the books get written. It's real hard in the beginning to know where they're going. I guess that's what makes it fun. Fascinating. It's like entering a relationship where you don't know whether it's gonna work out.

YOUR NEXT NOVEL WAS *AMERICAN BLOOD*?

Yeah. After *Nirvana Blues*, I worked five years with Costa-Gavras on three different films, including *Missing*. A year with Karel Reisz. Six or seven months with Louis Malle working on a *Magic Journey* script and two and a half years with Redford working on *Milagro Beanfield War*. Also a couple of years with CBS working on a film on the life of Pancho Villa and the Mexican Revolution. Somewhere around 1985, I said I gotta do another piece of fiction before I forget how. I'd been planning to do a huge historical novel on the rise of industrial capitalism from 1870 up to the Vietnam War. God, it was a wonderful project. I went about it the same way I did *The Magic Journey*. Starting files and taking voluminous notes and clipping articles. You get to read about Rockefeller, Harriman, Stanford, Gould, Fisk, Morgan. You get to read about Chinese immigration, the building of the railroads, the destruction of the buffalo, the rubbing out of the Native American people.

You should see the library I put together just for this book. I wanted to start with the Sand Creek massacre and the killing of the buffalo, which seemed to me the central metaphor for the climax of the industrial revolution in the United States. I would have a little town be founded where this massacre took place and build it to a city of two million people. I wanted to give America a history lesson from a different perspective than we usually get. But I was working on one or two scripts all the time, and life was complicated. I realized I needed ten uninterrupted years to get it together. So I took this metaphor of violence and wrote *American Blood*, a quite emotional book around the violence in American culture.

THEN YOU BROUGHT OUT A MUCH GENTLER NOVEL, *ELEGY FOR SEPTEMBER*.

I wanted to write an impressionistic prose painting about a season I dearly love, the month of September, and in the course of it a story about a three-week affair between an older guy and young woman. The book begins with one of my favorite quotations: "Not to know the pain and tragedy of your own life is not to know the joy of being here at all." It's a little novel about not playing things safe as you grow older and more fragile. People have a real tendency at that age that all they think about is get the house, get the insurance, get the retirement. The book deals with avoiding that. It takes place while the guy is getting a divorce and leaving his wife and a house he's had for twenty years. It's about accepting loss, about the beauty and richness of life even as it wanes. It's a little novel of one hundred twenty or thirty pages.

SO IT'S A CRACK AT ONE OF THOSE SMALL GEMS.

Yeah. The most difficult part of writing the book was to keep it very simple and not add things or explain. I kept having to take out and take out and take out. That was the hardest part. Just letting it be very quiet. It takes much more discipline for me to write something small and controlled like this.

YOU VISITED A VERY UNQUIET NICARAGUA IN THE MID-1980S. HOW DID THAT AFFECT YOU?

I don't think people here understand how psychologically and emotionally close Nicaragua is to the United States simply by being a satrapy for so long. At the time I visited, toward the end of 1983, they expected the U.S. to invade. There was the mining of the harbors and things were blowing up. So you read a newspaper like *Barricada* and the first page would be cursing at Reagan and you'd turn two pages over and the real important news would be that Dennis Martinez was traded from the Baltimore Orioles to the Cincinnati Reds. Nicaragua is a nation of athletes, and baseball is the national sport. There was so little hostility toward North American culture and North Americans. I remember when I took a bus to Guatemala in 1964, a guy got on in Mexico carrying his shoes, which were all in tatters. His feet were swollen to twice their size. The guy had hitchhiked from Managua to Mexico City to see a professional baseball game, like between the Dodgers and the Cubs. Afterward, he begged money to get a bus ticket back.

It seems so symbolic to me that this person almost out of *Don Quixote* would make a pilgrimage just to see a stupid baseball game. Kind of touching too. How we're all connected. I went on a tour that had access to a lot of Nicaraguan bureaucrats and politicians. You'd sit down with them and instead of trying to proselytize you about the revolution, they'd tell you about the mistakes they made and poke fun at themselves. At the same time, they were very, very serious about the revolution. You could get into some heavy-duty arguments, but then they'd always make these self-deprecating jokes, right? Because they saw themselves as an ant being stomped by an elephant. They had no illusions about resisting Uncle Sam. At the same time, they made it clear that if the United States wanted to take over, it would have to kill everyone in Nicaragua. They also made it clear that the United States probably could do it. There was a lot of humor in that country. Then you look at the U.S. reaction to Grenada and Panama. Why is a country that is so powerful so paranoid and humorless?

WITH A GOOD DEAL OF HELP FROM THE UNITED STATES, THE SANDINISTAS LOST POWER.

The U.S. concept of free elections is to blockade a country for, what, eight years, finance a counterrevolutionary army to destabilize it, and force the government to put all its energy into fighting the mercenaries. Then, on top of it, the United States demands elections in which the opposition leader is financed by U.S. dollars. Have you ever seen anything more cynical? I feel terribly sorry for Nicaragua, and I hate my country for what it does.

CAN YOU NARROW THAT DOWN TO, SAY, REPUBLICANS AND RIGHT-WING DEMOCRATS?

I dunno. You know, you think of Franklin Delano Roosevelt as kind of a liberal American president, right? But down in Nicaragua he was just another motherfucker. He was famous for that quote about Somoza: "He's a son of a bitch, but he's our son of a bitch." So whether it's Democrat or Republican, it doesn't change much for people outside of the country. "A capitalist is a capitalist is a capitalist" is a famous quote by Gertrude Stein.

THE VOICE OF THE BUTTERFLY IS A SERIOCOMIC LOOK AT ENVIRONMENTALISM. CRITICS OFTEN SAY IT IS A SAFE ISSUE BECAUSE IT DOES NOT NECESSARILY ENTAIL A POLITICAL PERSPECTIVE.

Yeah. Well, to me environmentalism includes everything. The environment is air, earth, trees, topsoil, Bedford-Stuyvesant, South Chicago, Indiana steel mills, civil community. If you are concerned about the spotted owl, then you have to be concerned about the people of Bangladesh, the street people of Calcutta, the U.S. blockade of Cuba. You can't separate the squawfish or the snail darter from the homeless in New York and Chicago. It's all environment. Pretending that the South Side of Chicago is less an environmental problem than the wilderness of Wyoming is absurd. So that's where I'm always running into problems with the Sierra Club and Audubon Society. To solve any part of the problem, you have to understand the whole. If people are worried about the slash-and-burn techniques in the Amazon destroying a rain forest upon which we depend for a certain part of our oxygen, well then they ought to start investigating the whole structure of Third World debt and how First World demands for everything from ceramics to coffee to wood creates devastation of the environment in the Third World. If they try to isolate the struggle from the struggles around the globe against finance capital, then they have missed the point.

My favorite quote from John Muir is that whenever we try to pick out anything by itself, we find it connected to everything else. If people could understand that in its entirety, we would at least be on our way toward creating some kind of consciousness to deal with the problem. If each individual understood the amount of influences creating every liter of air that they breathe, which has 10,000 compounds, then they might be more concerned about all aspects of society that create the poisons that go into their lungs and create the cancer that's going to terminate their lives twenty years early. But people don't think that way. They don't make those connections at all.

GEORGE W. BUSH IS THE MOST OBLIVIOUS, IF NOT THE MOST MALICIOUS, AMERICAN POLITICAL LEADER IN MEMORY WITH REGARD TO THE ENVIRONMENT.

Bush is oblivious but he is not a unique creation. He is [the kind of leader] this economic system supplies; the educational system is oblivious. This is not a man who arises out of nowhere. You can shit on his stupidity but you are shitting on the stupidity of a culture that cultivates this kind of character.

DO YOU SEE ANY DIFFERENCE IF AL GORE OR EVEN RALPH NADER HAD BEEN ELECTED?

If Gore had been elected there could have been some improvements, but it would be very difficult. I don't think Nader offered a serious political alternative.

YOU SEEM TO FLOURISH ON BOOK TOURS. DO YOU ENJOY THEM?

I prefer not to go out or make speeches. I'd like to live simply in a room and concentrate on writing eighteen hours a day for however many years I have to live.

4

STUDS TERKEL

writer and broadcaster

Studs Terkel, born in New York City in 1912, moved at the age of eleven to Chicago, where his family, among other things, ran a boarding house. He earned a law degree at the University of Chicago in the inauspicious year of 1934. Law did not appeal to him anyway; show business, beginning with the Chicago Repertory Theater, did. The Depression-era Works Progress Administration's Writers' Project provided him with his opportunity to get into radio. For more than four decades, he worked at WFMT radio in Chicago as a disc jockey and an interviewer. A lifelong champion of social reforms, he was blacklisted in the 1950s for refusing to name names.

His international reputation is based on his memorable "memory books," as he calls them. These mesmerizing oral histories include *Division Street* (1967), *Working* (1970), *Hard Times* (1974), *American Dreams: Lost and Found* (1980), the Pulitzer Prize–winning *"The Good War"* (1984), *The Great Divide: Second Thoughts on the American Dream* (1988), *Race: How Whites and Blacks Feel about the American Obsession* (1992), *Coming of Age* (1995), *The Spectator* (1999), *Will the Circle Be Unbroken?: Reflections on Death, Rebirth and Hunger for a Faith* (2001), and *Hope Dies Last* (2003). He also scribbled a memoir, *Talking To Myself* (1995), and a tribute volume, *Greats of Jazz* (1975).

Show-biz credits include his pioneering but short-lived TV program *Studs' Place* over 1950–1953; stage appearances in plays such as Arthur

Miller's *A View from the Bridge*; a creditable cameo performance in John Sayles's 1989 film *Eight Men Out* as Hugh Fullerton, the Chicago reporter who broke the story of the 1919 Black Sox scandal; the narration of *The Good Fight*; a documentary on the Abraham Lincoln Brigade in the Spanish Civil War; and an appearance in a PBS television production of a musical based on his book *Working*. We first met at his WFMT office in 1992, several weeks after four police officers were acquitted of beating Rodney King and race riots erupted in Los Angeles. I interviewed him again more than a decade later in November 2003, during his book tour for *Hope Dies Last*. Everyone says that Terkel, with his phenomenal memory, remembers everyone he meets. It's true.

Terkel is now at the Chicago Historical Society, where he is Distinguished Scholar in Residence. What surprised and dismayed me is that many of our exchanges in 1992 fit the present all too well, if one only changes "Reagan" to "George W. Bush" and "Clinton" to whoever— "Howard Dean" or "John Kerry"—emerges as the Democratic presidential candidate in 2004. So I have run together these two interviews conducted eleven years apart. One hardly notices the jump.

1992 INTERVIEW

A THEME RUNNING THROUGH *RACE*, AND EARLIER BOOKS, IS THAT THE REAGAN ERA GAVE AMERICANS PERMISSION TO BE THEIR WORST SELVES.

There is a black woman named Leona Brady, a school principal, who says American white people are not really a racist people. They're a docile people. In other words, they're not the independent people we like to think of Americans as. They are very obedient and obeisant to power, and if they actually were made to obey a law—a civil rights law— they would eventually adjust to it and be all right. It's like a traffic light. If you cross a red light, you're gonna get a ticket. So people abide by it. I'm oversimplifying. But if the guy up there winks at the law, he's telling you to wink at it too. It's not that there wasn't racism before. But there was leadership. Not the greatest, God knows: Lyndon Johnson. A civil rights act was passed while he was there. And with it there was a hope.

I don't want to glorify the South, but there is quite a difference when it comes to social behavior. Of course, there are still horrendous things going on. But if you go to Jackson, Mississippi, you see people at the counter, blacks and whites together. You think of the stuff that was dropped on the kids who sat in in the 1960s, all the humiliations. If there is, from the top, a sort of civil obedience, people will go along. But it gave you the word not to obey. . . .

IS IT ALL REAGAN'S FAULT?

The average guy who voted for Reagan will never confuse him with Einstein. He knows the guy's not bright, and he likes that. Because if the president's not bright, I don't have to deal with heavy issues and these goddam things. I can talk about Joan Collins and *Dynasty*. It's easy. I got the okay. Reagan's got style and he's got charm. Of course we know he's a mean-spirited prick. There are his comments about people on welfare. We also know he was an informer for the FBI when he was president of the Screen Actors Guild. He appeals to all the worst instincts. So the trickle-down theory has worked, perversely. The trickle down helped the big boys. That it would help the small guys was, of course, a joke. But the mean-spiritedness trickled down. That worked.

IN CONTRAST TO THE CYNICISM OF THE REAGAN-BUSH ERA, THE 1960s, MUCH ABUSED TODAY, WERE ACTUALLY A TIME OF SOCIAL PROGRESS AND REAL HOPE.

When Abbie Hoffman died, this clown Raymond Coffey [an editor at the *Chicago Sun-Times*] had a column about what a bum this guy was, a no-good bum who perverted America's youth. Well, Abbie was a delight and a joy and a reverence. At the same time this guy is putting down Abbie, he's putting down the 1960s, and so were Evans and Novak and dozens of others. They put down the 1960s because it was a moment of true challenge not only here but all over the world. It was a moment of nondocility. Were there extravagances? Of course there were! There was also a certain exhilaration. I think Abbie represented it with his humor and his put-ons. The French kids had a slogan, "All power to the imagination." Think of Lennon's song "Imagine" too. Precisely the opposite of imagination is what you had in Reagan and, for that matter, in Bush, who is a preppie version of Reagan.

It's always agitators who change things. Take the American Revolution. Half the American population, maybe more than half, would just as soon have gone along with the Tories. It was agitators who did it. Certainly Samuel Adams was one. He destroyed the property, the tea. Our whole history has been that way. The abolitionists got the crap beat out of them. Then in the times of the robber barons came the labor agitators, Gene Debs and the rest. They're the guys who changed things.

ANOTHER THEME IN ALL YOUR WORK IS THAT PEOPLE ARE CONFINED BY THEIR OWN IGNORANCE OF HISTORY.

I hate to use the word "yuppie" because yuppie is not what most of the young are. Most are bewildered and lost and worried stiff that they are not going to do as well as the old man. But I bumped into this couple on the street who really are yuppies. So I'm waiting for a bus where I live. I'm on a street of haves in an area of have-nots. This couple are the ones you see in the suds-sex-beer commercials. They have plenty of bucks in their pockets. So I just talk out—because I talk everywhere— while we're waiting for the bus. It's a few days before Labor Day, so I say Labor Day is coming up, a celebration of American trade unions. I'm talking to these kids, I don't know them.

"Unions?" they say, "God, we despise unions."
"Oh, you do?" I say. "How many hours a day do you work?"
"Eight hours."
"Why don't you work eighteen hours like your grandparents or maybe great-grandparents did? You know why? Because four guys got hanged so you could work eight hours a day. The Haymarket martyrs [in 1886]. Don't you know that people got their heads busted fighting for the 40-hour week?"

They just don't know. The point is that we have no sense of history. There is no past. There's just the ten-second sound bite. Aside from that, the cards are stacked. They've been stacked a long time. Long before Reagan. How did Reagan get in? You pick up any newspaper. There are sections, right? There's the feature section, style, arts, a financial section, or business. Is there a labor section? Is there a labor page? Is there a labor columnist? This is what we're talking about. The cards are stacked, you see. Reagan was a little peddler for General Electric for years before he became governor of California. [pauses] You know [former California governor] Jerry Brown is crazy.

YOU MEAN THE FLAT TAX PROPOSAL?

Oh, the tax is ridiculous. But a great moment in the campaign was in the first debate on NBC with Tom Brokaw as the moderator. All six of the Democratic candidates are there. Brokaw knows Brown is gonna put up that 800 number asking for $10 bills up to $100. Sure enough, Brokaw says there will be no pleading for funds on the program. Brown defies him, and they have a real encounter. Brown says, "You're telling me I can't ask for ten dollars? NBC is owned by General Electric." Talk about dollars being put up for candidates. That for me was the high moment of the campaign. The rest was anticlimax. We're talking about a stacked deck. You do the best you can with a stacked deck.

THOSE YUPPIES SEEMED TO BE HOSTILE TOWARD ANYONE THAT LOOKED TO THEM LIKE LOSERS, WHO ARE ANYONE AGAINST WHOM THE DECK IS STACKED.

You use the word "loser." A loser is not just someone who is a victim, someone who has lost. A loser is someone who deserves to lose. "I'm not going to be with that guy. He's no good. He's a loser." In the 1930s—not to say that those who had dough were any nicer then, because they weren't—but there was more sympathy. The word "loser" has taken on new connotations so that instead of pity or compassion, or even just a sense of "it could be me," now it's contempt. You got to win no matter what. What are the commercials stressing? The "competitive edge"? The point is to win. What's been ruined is the sense of community. Einstein said long ago that Americans look upon community as a threat to their personal freedom when it's just the opposite. It gives the person greater power, contributing to something outside himself.

There's a very good book by Robert Stone, *Outerbridge Reach*. It's about this handsome Annapolis guy. Something's wrong with his life. And another guy is a filmmaker and a phony who speaks of heroism, and his hero is Vince Lombardi—remember he made the famous comment "Winning isn't everything, it's the only thing"? It doesn't matter how you win, see? Lombardi, this guy people look up to, was a brutish bastard. He won, so what? Losing is unpardonable today.

Brecht wrote a play, *Mahoganny*. In this town of Mahoganny there was one crime, being poor. You can do anything you want, but the crime was being poor. We're living in Mahoganny right now. At the same time, here's the Pollyanna in me. There are more grassroots movements than ever today. Crazily enough, the environment is a blanket issue. Out of that come a lot of other things.

Any sign of it in the [1992] presidential race?

I'm going to vote for Bill Clinton. I'm saying I'm voting for tuberculosis against cancer. It looks like he may change a few things for the better. You know, Arkansas is a scab state, a right-to-work state. But he's come out against scabs permanently taking strikers' jobs. The very phrase is almost comical and absurd. Even in the worst days, that never was the case. That's why I call the 1980s the "unashamed decade." Until Reagan fired the air traffic controllers and got the country's applause, scabs—even in areas where companies ran towns—came through the back door. They'd sneak through. But today they don't go in through the back door. I remember a scab football game during the professional football players' strike. They were horrible games, you know. But these two teams were playing on TV. The camera shows kids in the stands. You know those Rambo kids, these idiots with bare chests in the wintertime. They're holding up a sign—"We Love Our Scabs." It's on TV. We love our scabs? At another time, the kids would have been beheaded, certainly deballed.

Can you really support Clinton?

Apparently, he's amenable. But amenable to all sorts of change. So far as we know from his whole record, he has no principles at all. But he's wooing black votes, and that's a good sign. So, in a sense, he's an improvement on Bush. Here's the interesting question. How come [Tom] Harkin didn't stand a chance? The pro-labor guys. Maybe there's something wrong with their campaigns. But more than that, the Democrats don't want to win. If they win, they win begrudgingly. Not since 1972, when they were terrified by what happened at the McGovern convention. That's a key moment. The McGovern campaign brought in new people, new constituents: the feminist movement, the blacks, other colored movements, gay/lesbian, labor—and they're called "special interests." This is interesting. Special interests? In political science or civics, special interests were big corporations. That's why we had antitrust laws, to protect us from them. Now the people who are up against the wall are called special-interest groups.

The Democrats don't want to win. They'd rather it be the way it is. So, after McGovern's campaign, they're wooing the same constituency the Republicans are. But they're called "the middle class." Now what does that mean? Don't people work? Isn't it called the working class?

Remember Michael Dukakis? That, that fool. Dukakis and Bush are in a debate and up comes the "L-word." Liberal. Card-carrying member of the American Civil Liberties Union. All the guy had to do was pick up a dictionary. He could have carried a pocket dictionary. "What did you call me?" "A liberal." "You're anti-liberal?" "You bet." So he looks up the word "liberal." There are two definitions. Every dictionary has them. First definition: "generous of heart, helping others." We Americans are so proud of that. "You mean you want us to be mean-spirited, miserly, selfish so-and-sos, Mr. Bush? Is that what you want?" Second definition: "tolerant of the opinions of others." In America, we always say you can say what you're gonna say. "Of course, I'm liberal. What are you if you are anti-liberal? You want us to be totalitarian?" He'd have won. Instead, he says, "I'm not liberal, not really." Gore Vidal said it some time ago: we need a second party. A second party, you know?

CAN A DEMOCRAT WIN?

I think Clinton can win. If people can't rub two quarters together and they are worried, they'll forget the Persian Gulf and the battles. Which leads to a big question: Must you personally feel it, the depression? A recession, they call it. It's a joke. We love euphemisms. You can't call it a recession for the steelworkers who aren't working and for the family farmer. You go to Iowa or Minnesota. You see ghost towns. It's *Grapes of Wrath* all over again. I talked to a fourth-generation farmer. He's so desperate. His little girl, eight years old, is watching for the deputies. Thinks they're going to repossess her tricycle. It's no recession to him.

YOU STAYED PUT IN CHICAGO TO WORK ON YOUR BOOK *RACE.*

Chicago has everything. Chicago is the country. It's a metaphor for everything. Here they came, the blacks and the Appalachians, in two waves. I stayed here except for a trip to Durham.

THE PEOPLE WHO GET PAST THEIR RACISM ARE UNABLE TO RUN AWAY OR SIMPLY SEEM TO BE EXCEPTIONAL FOLKS—WHICH IS NOT ENCOURAGING. DO YOU FEEL HOPEFUL OR NOT?

Well, both. At the very end of the book is the young guy—Lloyd King, who is half white and half black. I ask, "How do you feel?" He says it's like kids coming home from the prom. They've had a few drinks and are high. Will they make it home? So the word is guardedly optimistic. We are at a crazy moment; it could go either way. You know, we get David Duke getting 55 percent of the white vote in Louisiana. What is it that made this occur? Then there's Diane Romano [a white woman interviewed in 1965 for *Division Street* and in 1990 for *Race*], who knew blacks and was friends with them and now is less friendly. She lets the racist words be used, laughs when they make those horrible jokes. Never did before. She says, "I go to church. I feel it's wrong. I am not a low-class person. A low-class person uses the N-word." See, there's that ambivalence, that ambiguity. Blacks have their own. The playing up of Louis Farrakhan. They don't give a damn about him. What they get a kick out of is the white reaction to Farrakhan. The guy is telling whitey off. Who builds him up but the white press?

DO YOU HAVE YOUR NEXT BOOK IN MIND?

I was debating a book about old people who are scrappers. I got that from an old Maine radical. He pinned me against the wall. A strong, wiry guy. My arms were bruised. And he says, "What about people over seventy? Maybe the hope is in us." You remember Maggie Kuhn of the Gray Panthers? She tells the story of how they were formed. She said to friends who were forcibly retired, who were crying: "What are you talking about? We're free. What have we got to lose? We've got a mimeograph machine." The Vietnam War was going on. "Let's put our warm bodies out to save these kids. We've got nothing to lose." So the image of the little old lady peering through a room window in a nursing home or retirement home, that's only one image. The other is older people who are in there scrapping, challenging the establishment.

You know, John Sayles did a wonderful short story, 'The Anarchists' Convention.' A pretty funny one, about these old-time battered radicals having a reunion. They're sick and some are dying. They come to the hotel and the manager tells them he made a mistake. They can't have this huge room they're in. The Rotarians are out there. It's their room. Of course, the old guys weren't giving in to this authority, to management. Hell, no. They think it's discriminatory to begin with. They think it's a plot. So here they are, cripple and old and holding hands singing "We Shall Not Be Moved." And the cops come in and the cops don't know what the hell it's all about. Marvelous. Well, it's that kind of book.

WHEN LOS ANGELES ERUPTED IN 1992, GEORGE BUSH PREDICTABLY BLAMED IT ALL ON THE 1960s.

People call upon authorities of the past to comment on things going on now. I think in this case, as so often is the case, George Bush called on W. C. Fields. It wasn't de Tocqueville he called upon, or Jefferson, but W. C. Fields. To blame those who tried to ameliorate the situation. This was Fields's great comic technique. The outrageousness. He'd beat up old women or kick Baby Leroy in the fanny. Fields appealed to the mean-spiritedness in us, though he did it with a certain humor. So you have the president of the United States using the same technique. The outrageousness of it. Here they were, Bush and the people Bush represents, in every way trying to stymie any chance people of color have. In desperation, finally something happened. The Rodney King verdict was simply the spark that set off the tinderbox.

BUSH BACKED OFF IN A REAL HURRY.

Oh sure, he backed off, as any politician would. The cynicism of the guy is incredible. Also the banality. I think if I were to find the key word for this, it's banality. When Hannah Arendt described Nazism, she called it the "banality of evil." For these people I reverse that: I call it the evil of banality. That's what I find so horrible in Bush and Reagan.

DO YOU SEE ANY PROSPECT FOR CLOSING THE GAP BETWEEN THE SIMI VALLEY JURORS AND THE RIOTERS?

There are two separate classes living on different planets. The people in L.A.—the rioters—know a lot more about the Simi Valley people than the Simi Valley people know about them—which is a long tradition of servants and masters. You know, *Invisible Man* by Ralph Ellison. People talked in front of blacks as if they weren't there, like servants. Jimmy Baldwin wrote a book called *Nobody Knows My Name*. The subtitle easily could have been *But I Know You*. That's not to say there isn't prejudice in black society. Of course there is. There has to be prejudice on both parts to have the situation it led to.

In a crazy way, the huge gap has narrowed and it hasn't. People for the American Way did a survey, and it indicated that many more whites today have a black friend than in the 1960s. Far more. But what they say is, the person they know is different, is the exception to the others.

Those I know, I like.

The person I know, I like. But the person I don't know, the great many whom I hear about from the six o'clock news or from my parents or whatever—they're no good. So you see, we're in a crazy situation where your own experience, your own eyesight, means nothing compared to what you hear about. For example, we had the riots. On the six o'clock news, we see black kids being led away in handcuffs. But some weeks ago, we also saw 9,000 people, mostly black, standing in line in the cold [in Chicago] for a few hundred jobs at the Sheraton Hotel. But that's a reason they've eliminated. A key thing: jobs, of course. But that's blocked out by a picture of black kids attacking white persons during the riots. The reason for that happening is never discussed. And the reason is that 8,000 people who didn't get jobs are out there somewhere. They're young. They're full of energy. We don't figure that those rioters are the same people who didn't get jobs. Two plus two equals four. You know? Eight hours a day. A few bucks in the pocket. And life is okay.

What can be done?

There has to be more open talk. I mean real talk, no matter how outrageous, between blacks and whites about real honest-to-God issues. You blast each other and you dissect what it's all about. But the big thing is government. "Big government" is the term used by Ronnie and by George. They got away with it all these years. Well, big government saved the asses of their fathers and mothers in the 1930s. They don't mind big government when it comes to bailing out the S&L crowd. They don't mind big government when it comes to pouring all that dough into the Pentagon. They like that. This is John Kenneth Galbraith's theme in his new book, *The Culture of Contentment*. These guys don't mind big government helping the haves. But when it comes to helping the have-nots, wait a minute! So we have to expose this double standard.

But the fact is that government has to play a role. Here the infrastructure, we're told, is falling apart. Roads and highways. We could use railroads and mass transit. Low-cost housing. Nurseries and child care. Obviously we have the hands to do it. Eight thousand people waiting with no jobs. You could multiply that so many times. The hands are available. The need is there. The dough is there. The raison d'être for the crazy bloated military budget was the Evil Empire. But if it's no more, you get not just billions but multibillions. So what we need is the vision and the will. We needed leaders to do it, and obviously we ain't got 'em. So that's got to come up from the grassroots, a bottom-up protest. And there you have it.

2003 INTERVIEW

WHEN WE LAST SPOKE, THE L.A. RIOTS OF 1992 HAD JUST HAPPENED. DO YOU SEE ANY PROGRESS IN RACE RELATIONS SINCE YOUR BOOK *RACE* APPEARED?

Yes and no. The answer is ambiguous. Are we in some little ways better off? There is a black middle class that wasn't there before. But you pick up the magazines [catering to them] and it's just bullshit, the same as the others. Harold Washington's election played a role in changing Chicago, but at the same time the [minorities] may be worse off now in that people are saying "You had your chance," you know? There are all the attacks on affirmative action. You go to Jackson, Mississippi, today and you got black and white people in the restaurant. But the great many haven't got the buck—or the ten bucks or fifteen bucks—to go in. So the right is there to the toilet. The right is there to go into the hotel. But is the wherewithal there for the great many? No.

CIVIL RIGHTS NEVER MEANT THAT YOU MUST BE BETTER OFF ECONOM-ICALLY.

We think that we made progress but are little better off so far as amenities are concerned. In terms of the economics, we're probably worse off. Now, we're not starting again from scratch. No. You know the hymn, "We are Climbing Jacob's Ladder"? Every rung is higher and higher—but there's two steps forward and one step back. Sometimes it's two steps forward and three steps back. It's a long haul. It's not an overnight thing. The racial situation is a rough one. When it comes to economics, we've fallen down on the job.

HOW DO YOU COMPARE MAYOR DALEY JR. TO DALEY SR.?

Daley [Sr.] loved power. He bent toward powerful people and he had disdain for those who did not have power. That's why he was unique as a city boss. It wasn't the dough, it was power. Richard M. Daley—no more silver-tongued than his father—was elected mayor in 1989. The manner of speech is similar but never would the son do what his father did. He uses power in his own way, but not in the outwardly brutish way Daley Sr. did in 1968. It's different now, although there still is police brutality, as we well know.

He's not the same as his father because the situation is different. When the old man was mayor it was the post–World War II boom period and any mayor pretty much had it made at the time economically, you see. Now we come to Chicago. It changed overwhelmingly when Harold Washington won in 1983. Until then it was plantation politics. [Daley Sr.] owned the black vote. He had an overseer named Bill Dawson, the [black] congressman of the First Ward. So there was Daley, head of the plantation. But then came Harold Washington. Harold died too soon. He would have been fantastic. If he were alive today, the country itself would have been affected for the better by him. There's no question in my mind. Harold was brilliant, funny, and heads above the others.

Daley Jr. is not brutal like his father. I'm not saying he's nicer than the old man. The brutality is in the situation. Things have altered to some extent. So it's not the same and it's just the same. The trouble is there is no organized opposition. When the older Daley was mayor, there was a core of dissenters: Leon Depres and Dick Simpson and others. Now there's no dissent; there's co-optation. There's a few who say no. [Chicago Alderwoman] Helen Schiller, who is in the book, has to make compromises to survive. Gentrification plays a role in her neighborhood and she has to allay the fears [of her incoming middle-class residents] while maintaining her principles, and she is doing a pretty good job.

JUST SIX MONTHS AGO, IT SEEMED THAT WE WERE DESCENDING INTO AN ORWELLIAN PIT WHERE BUSH HAD EVERYTHING HIS OWN WAY. NOW IT LOOKS LIKE ALL THE DECEITS ARE UNRAVELING. WHEN WE LAST MET, I ASKED IF A DEMOCRAT COULD BEAT THE SENIOR BUSH; HOW ABOUT BEATING JUNIOR BUSH?

Ever since Reagan, the Democratic Party—thanks to that Democratic Leadership Council that has to be kicked out on its ass—has been moved to the right. [Senator] Joe Lieberman is a case in point. If I were Karl Rove, the Rasputin of Bush, I would immediately draft Lieberman as my VP candidate to run with Bush. [Lieberman and Bush] agree on all the major issues. The Democratic Party is the story of the betrayal of the best of the Roosevelt administration, the best of the New Deal. It's been under attack ever since Reagan. Then, after those [Reagan–Bush] years, you thought, well, [progressive policies are] going to come back. But even before 9/11, there was nothing much. The welfare reform program that Clinton put forth in 1995 was a complete cave-in.

I remember a gathering for an anniversary celebration of the 1960s. It was about a month after the welfare reform bill went through, and Clinton was running for reelection against Bob Dole. Bella Abzug, Tom Hayden, Norman Mailer, and Vic Navasky were there. *The Nation* was sponsoring it. Bella Abzug said, "Clinton's got to be reelected." It was my turn to talk. I said, "Clinton has to be criticized." But I didn't say all that I should have said then. Since Reagan and the counterrevolution, there has been a complete perversion of our language. Where going toward the right is described as going toward the center, where Lieberman is described as a moderate. A moderate! In fact, George W. Bush is described in some quarters as a moderate conservative. I wrote a little piece way back for FAIR (Fairness and Accuracy in Reporting), Jeff Cohen's organization. I called it "No Brass Check Journalists." You know the Upton Sinclair book of that title [*The Brass Check*] in 1916?

Don't know that one.

In the old days when a guy went to the brothel, he paid two dollars, and the madam or the pimp gave him a brass check and then he handed the brass check to the girl. At the end of the day the girl cashes in her brass checks and she gets half a buck apiece. And so Upton Sinclair was talking about the brass-check artists where [he identified] the reporters and publishers. They were whores. Take Teddy Roosevelt, an overrated president. The trust-buster. Here we go again. Teddy Roosevelt loathed the muckrakers. It was a derogatory term used by him against Lincoln Steffens and Ida Tarbell. Later on, George Seldes came along, and Izzy Stone. With the exception of the muckrakers, there were these brass-check artists who played a tremendous role in the language becoming perverted bit by bit by bit. As a result, the American public reads what, sees what, hears what?—[media] run by fewer and fewer people. We know the most powerful media mogul today is that Australian Neanderthal Murdoch, who's become a citizen.

Where is the hope?

Here's the optimistic part. I like to read letters to the editor. I said to *Chicago Tribune* editor Bruce Dole, who edits the editorial pages: "I see letters there about Israel and about the Middle East and about Bush, and a surprising amount are anti-Bush letters." And he says, "It's fifty-fifty, and in fact it's a little more anti than pro." And this is the *Tribune* [a conservative paper]! The *Tribune* does not publish anti-Bush letters. They go the other way. There's a turn taking place. Of course, the *Tribune* is not the same paper it was under Colonel McCormick. They have these columnists who appear once a week. Molly Ivins gets the most mail. Con as well as pro, more pro than con. So something is popping.

There's something underneath that's happening, but there's no umbrella organization. Dennis Kucinich of Ohio, the leftist candidate who is in the book, is the one who gets the least ink, is always the last one mentioned of the nine candidates. He has no money and the organization is all in a mess. We know he's not going to win the nomination, but name recognition [matters]. Now only one in a hundred knows his name. But if he runs third in Iowa, for example, name recognition would force the Democratic Leadership Committee to give him time at the national convention, which would be seen by multimillions. That could be pretty exciting. So the big thing is name recognition.

KUCINICH, AS YOU SAY, IS NOT EXACTLY A SHOE-IN. WHAT ABOUT THE REST OF THE CANDIDATES?

As far as the rest of the candidates, I suppose [Howard] Dean is the best of the lot, I imagine, if that says anything.

WHAT ABOUT JOHN KERRY?

Here's Kerry. Long ago when he came back from the Vietnam War, I interviewed him. I had a whole series on Vietnam, including officers who returned, and he was one of them. I have a tape with him but I can't find it now. He was one of the officers opposed to the Vietnam, and he was good. He was very good. But then he comes out for [Bush's resolution after] 9/11. It's a matter of guts. That's the big thing, whether you have the guts. He didn't. Wesley Clark? Clark, I understand, has a group of advisors who are the worst you could possibly think of. Kerry and Dean are the best of the lot. But what does it say? We have more and more dissenting groups, whether it be environmental issues or peace issues or whatever, but there is no umbrella group. Dennis is not given much press, but when he gets up to talk to the audience—not just one of these brief two- and three-minute rebuttals back and forth—he gets standing ovations wherever he talks.

HOW DO YOU FIGURE SCHWARZENEGGER IN CALIFORNIA?

The victory of Schwarzenegger was not a Bush triumph at all. It was a vote out of frustration, out of anger, out of fury. They would have voted for W. C. Fields—who would have been wonderful, by the way. If the Democratic Party loses to George W. Bush, it must dissolve. The DLC [Democratic Leadership Council] has been urging it more and more toward the so-called center. Now the opposite has to be the case. I do run into all sorts of people, as you know, whether it be waitresses or cab drivers or CEOs. And everyone says, "This guy has gotta go." So it's a question of the Democratic Party choosing someone who is militant, who is against Bush. People know what's happening with the tax cuts, Enron and the corporate accounting.

THERE'S NO END OF RUBBISH SPILLING OUT.

You know I'm a hambone, a ham actor, and I ramble pretty good up on a platform. I go to a town in DuPage County, which is the only county in all of Illinois to vote for Goldwater in 1964. There is an audience of Republican women there from the opera house, and I'm talking about Bush. I start off, laughing, of course, "I'm ninety-one and I have my two martinis a day and I ask my cardiologist about it. He says, 'At your age your cholesterol count is as relevant to you as truth is to George W. Bush.'" They erupt in laughter.

I go on in the same vein. I say I'm an alumnus of the University of Chicago. My fellow alumnus was John Ashcroft, and although I preceded him by thirty years, he is considerably older than I am. I figure he is about 320 years old. You saw him in Arthur Miller's play *The Crucible*. He was the reverend way up there, the Reverend Parris. I'm telling this to the women. Remember Salem, Massachusetts? The witch-hunt? Those old women living in the town considered witches by the hysterical girls: they were the terrorist of their day. And here is this prosecutorial officer, the Reverend Parris: "If you're not with us you're against us. If you challenge me, you're consorting with the devil." That's John Ashcroft.

I also have great difficulty with my hearing. The volume [of my hearing aid] goes up, but the clarity does not. So I say, "During our triumph in Iraq when we finally democratized the country"—the women are chuckling—"I heard the phrase 'embedded journalists' continuously. But with my bad hearing it comes out 'in bed with journalists.'" Of course I'm in the opera house and you know Puccini's *Tosca*, the story?

And so I say my hearing is so bad that when I hear "Justice Scalia," it comes out "Scarpia."

SCARPIA BEING THE WICKED VILLAIN OF THE OPERA.

At the end of that I get a standing ovation. And this is a Republican community! Next day I pick up the DuPage County paper, "Studs wows them." And they quote the stuff in that Republican paper. Something is going on. Of course Bush can be beaten. Who ever had a president who had a war and a depression at the same time? See, it was the Second World War that ended the Depression, even though the New Deal—the WPA and everything—saved millions of lives. There were eleven million unemployed up until the [war started]. So then women get jobs in defense plants and guys go in the army. It was the Depression that knocked off Hoover. Now we have a president with a depression and war, or I should say wars, since he speaks of an axis of evil. Who's next, after Iraq? So if this guy would win, it's a one-party country. All I want Dennis Kucinich to do is keep on going. In any event, we come back to reality, Dean or Kerry. I would guess either, I suppose. I say this with a sigh. I'm pretty certain the Democratic Party will win. If they don't, then they must dissolve.

HAVE WE SHAKEN OFF THE "ME" GENERATION, THE YUPPIE HYPE?

Young kids now are so taken with trivia and with self. But they're bright; they're not dumb, many of these kids. That guy named Eminem, there's a remarkable article about him in the *New York Review of Books*. The kids are up on a lot of this stuff but there's no one organization— meaning a political party—that can really hit it. The Democratic Party is not really doing a damn thing, but despite that there's more recognition that things are unraveling. It's clear even to people who can't spell "cat."

So despite everything I have said, I feel hopeful. My old friend Pete Seeger says he sees crazy movements all around the world. You know, with all the violence and the horrors, things are happening. Just picking up a fascinating article on Bolivia this morning, and look at what happened at Cancun with that WTO conference. So it's a question of finding the spearhead—what I call the umbrella that could cover these groups. I think the Democrats will win, but I want them to win in a way that the country itself will know has a meaning. The key thing should be the United Nations, which, of course, was the hope of the world. We are part of it. We are the strongest part, but only part of it. We have to blast this whole idea of unilateral action.

OUR LEADERS' PARANOIA, OR ULTERIOR MOTIVES, DECIDES WHAT WE AS A NATION DO ABROAD.

In the book, one of the most revelatory things is one of the most modest interviews, one with former Olympic winner Adolf Keefer. Keefer's a Bush man. I have these people in to mix it up. But it's his wife who says, "Why are we in so many countries today?" She represents, I think, the great, great many. What the hell are we doing in these places? And then there's Enron and those revelations. Who do you most mistrust? In the old days it was always car dealers and lawyers. Now it's corporations. In the polls, big business is up there at the top. So these are the hopeful signs. My own feeling is one of what I call guarded hope. The key word is guarded. This sounds crazy to say, it sounds goofy and romantic, but underneath there is a stirring.

A SUBURBAN LAWYER ONCE SAID TO ME, "ISN'T STUDS AN OLD-FASHIONED NEW DEALER PEDDLING OBSOLETE IDEAS?" SHE HERSELF WAS A REPUBLICAN SPOUTING MARKET RHETORIC STRAIGHT OUT OF THE EIGHTEENTH CENTURY. LIKE MANY PEOPLE, SHE DOESN'T KNOW A NEW IDEA FROM AN OLD IDEA FROM A GOOD IDEA. PEOPLE ARE VERY CONFUSED. I THINK ARLO GUTHRIE TALKS ABOUT THAT KIND OF CONFUSION IN YOUR BOOK.

We're suffering from a national Alzheimer's disease. There's no yesterday. Those who are against "big gummint" in health, education, welfare—not the military—are the ones whose very asses were saved by "big gummint" in the 1929 crash, and how they pleaded—please save us. So this woman suffers from national Alzheimer's disease. We live by the clichés of the day.

THERE ARE NEW CLICHÉS COMING AROUND EVERY MINUTE.

The other big obstacle is the trivia itself, the overwhelming trivia. It leads to Schwarzenegger again. Here's Oprah Winfrey with the largest women's audience ever probably in the history of TV, the most powerful sales force. She has a kiss-kiss hour-long program with Schwarzenegger and his wife, Shriver's kid, during the campaign. And [Oprah] says, "We never talked about politics, it was only a good family show." An hour! No one of the opposition was on at all, so no one can contest Schwarzeneg-ger. It was just assumed [that it was okay]. He's on an hour, and hun-dreds of thousands of women are watching. I see that most white women voted for Schwarzenegger.

ISN'T THIS CONFUSION—MAYBE A CAREFULLY CULTIVATED CONFU-SION—AGAIN?

But the big thing is how it is so one-sided—even in the case of Oprah, who undoubtedly would vote against Bush. Of course she will, but it doesn't matter. And talk about perversion of language. Talk about liberal media? Liberal media! A term that is an obscene assault on our intelli-gence.

THAT'S A STRONG THEME THROUGH MANY OF YOUR BOOKS.

September 11th was an obscene, horrendous event. But the far big-ger assault is on our native intelligence, the assault on our innate decency. This I know about the intelligence of the so-called ordinary person—a term I dislike because it is patronizing—the anonymous many are capable of extraordinary things. We know there is an intelli-gence there. It's a question of the information coming through to them. There's a great quote Tom Paine comes up with that fear causes you not to think. He didn't write those books just for freedom-loving Americans but for thinking people. It's always good when you make the audience aware that it is thinking. You know, "It is thinking Americans such as yourselves, such as yourselves. . . ."

BUT AREN'T MANY PEOPLE IN YOUR BOOK TALKING ABOUT JUST HOLDING STEADY? NOT LOSING MORE GROUND?

It's more than holding steady. I think, despite ourselves, that the changes are there and ready for action. The voices are there, but, again, there's no umbrella. Take the word "activist"—to act, to do, to take part, to partici-pate. Like this one writer in the book, she's a good writer. She says, "I'm not moved. I don't take part in those demonstrations. They don't hit me." And then she says "I don't know why I have these headaches all the time."

Well, something I forgot to include in the book is a news item from England. A psychiatrist there says taking part in an action is therapeu-tic. When you take part in something, whether it is a peace march or a rally somewhere, it actually is medicinally good. It's good in that it lifts your spirits but it also makes you physically feel better. He had proof of it. So I'm saying to her, "The reason you have the headache is because you don't take part in these things" [laughter]. But it's true. I wish I had that item now. I'm a slovenly guy, you know. I tear these things out of the papers and save them but I lose them. I don't know where it appeared now. It was wonderful. It was a health piece.

It's there. It's just waiting for more voices to be more articulate and more outspoken. And those who are in the book should be reaching more and more people. There has been such an unraveling of the deceit. How do you feel when you are being lied to regularly every day? I think there is hope provided that there is this opposition that has a kind of umbrella and at the same time principle, backbone, and some guts and has nothing to lose. And humor. Try to put humor in there if you possibly can.

YOU TALK TO A LOT OF YOUNG PEOPLE IN YOUR NEW BOOK. DO YOU THINK THEY ARE REPRESENTATIVE?

I'm not saying they are representative. I think they represent what could be, not what is. When Ralph Nader ran for president in 2000, who do you think went to Nader rallies? They weren't old lefties; they were young people. So Willie Nelson and Eddy Vedder from Pearl Jam were there, but would the kids have paid ten cents a head to hear Bush or Gore? The Illinois Coliseum was jammed. But they didn't vote. They didn't vote. It's a question of getting them to turn out.

I WONDER WHAT THEY WOULD THEY MAKE OF AN ABBIE HOFFMAN TODAY? A FEW YEARS AGO, A WELL-INTENTIONED BUT VERY BADLY WRITTEN FILM ABOUT HIM, CALLED *STEAL THIS MOVIE*, FLOPPED.

I think Abbie killed himself because he was a romantic, but a romantic in a good sense. He wanted to build a New Jerusalem. All his dreams, his romance with the future, were being shattered. Along come the MBA kids, you know? He didn't live long enough to see the streets of Seattle and things of that sort. The sixties are always being put down because it was a moment when kids had causes outside themselves. A woman I know says the sixties are put down by those who delight in the failure of dreams. That's a wonderful quote.

DID YOU HAVE TO LEAVE OUT ANYONE YOU REALLY WANTED IN THE NEW BOOK?

Recently, four guys were pardoned by Governor George Ryan from death row. All were so obviously innocent it wasn't funny. Only one of them is in this new book. I wanted a couple more in there. Like Merle Haggard. This rough, gruff guy is changing. He has got this new song: "That's the News." I got a hunch he would have been very interesting. But it was too late to get him for this one. I love to get people in transitions, like that Klansman [in *Race*] who changed. They're the ones who attract me the most.

RUMOR HAS IT YOU HAVE ANOTHER BOOK UNDER WAY.

It's about musical artists I've had on my show. Opera and jazz and folk. It'll be the other aspect of my life. The musical aspect. I'll call it *They All Sang* and it's subtitled *Guests of an Eclectic Disk Jockey*.

WHEN DO YOU EXPECT TO BRING IT OUT? NEXT YEAR?

Oh, who knows? I'm ninety-one, you know. I'm working on a great presumption [laughing]. A great presumption.

5

J. P. DONLEAVY

novelist

James Patrick Donleavy, known as Mike to friends, was born in New York City, saw combat in the U.S. Navy during World War II, and attended Trinity College in Dublin on the GI Bill afterward. There he met the indelibly wild cast of Irish characters and fellow émigrés who stampede through his comic marvel of a first novel, *The Ginger Man*, published in 1955 by Maurice Girodias's Olympia Press. (Donleavy later purchased the press.) He followed *The Ginger Man*'s international success with *A Singular Man* (1963), *The Saddest Summer of Samuel S* (1966), *The Beastly Beatitudes of Balthazar B* (1968), *The Onion Eaters* (1971), *A Fairy Tale of New York* (1973), *The Destinies of Darcy Dancer* (1977), a short story collection *Meet My Maker the Mad Molecule* (1964), and play versions of several of the novels.

At the time of the interview in his home, a refurbished Anglo-Irish mansion in Westmeath in Ireland, guarded by two friendly wolfhounds tall enough to play in the NBA, he was working on *Schultz*, published in 1979. Since then he has spun out several highly diverting nonfiction books: *J. P. Donleavy's Ireland: In All Her Sins and Some of Her Graces* (1986), *A Singular Country* (1989), *The History of the Ginger Man* (1994), and *An Author and His Image: The Collected Short Pieces* (1996). Further literary forays include the Darcy Dancer sequels *Leila* (1983) and *That Darcy, That Dancer, That Gentleman* (1991), the *Schultz* sequel *Are You Listening, Rabbi Löw* (1987), *The Lady Who*

Liked Clean Rest Rooms (1997), and *Wrong Information Is Being Given Out at Princeton* (1998). The interview below "caught a moment" of revealing reverie about the origins of *The Ginger Man* that I thought worth preserving. Here it is as it appeared twenty-five years ago.

YOU WERE BROUGHT UP IN NEW YORK, ENTERED THE NAVY, THEN ATTENDED TRINITY COLLEGE ON THE GI BILL. WHY DUBLIN?

Well, I heard stories about Europe and about Dublin from the odd person returning from the European Theater of Operations, so I decided to apply to Trinity. In those days, one's whole object was to spend time happily doing nothing. I studied natural science and basically enjoyed but wasted my time.

YOU OBVIOUSLY DID NOT WASTE ALL YOUR TIME. HOW DID YOU MAKE THE TRANSITION FROM NATURAL SCIENCES TO LITERARY AMBITIONS?

I recall John Ryan as among the very first people I came across in Dublin. I remember one night at some roaring-drunk party being absolutely astonished overhearing this man who actually liked listening to music, who was interested in painting and, indeed, in literature. He was also, compared to the rest of us, well-heeled. I spent a lot of time with him. He was acquainted with people like Desmond MacNamara, the sculptor, who had a studio somewhere where people used to meet.[1] And they seemed to know all the people interested in the arts in Dublin.

READING ACCOUNTS OF PARTIES IN THE INFAMOUS BASEMENT FLAT KNOWN AS THE CATACOMBS, IT'S EASY TO BELIEVE THAT PUBS AND POETS MIXED VERY EASILY.

There was no literary clique as such that I knew of at the time. I mean about 1946. One established itself later around Ryan's magazine *Envoy*, about 1949. The life I knew that was written about in *The Ginger Man* had nothing to do with it. The few poets and journalists were very much physically parasitic on the actual life—and richer protagonists who were committing literal suicide. The Catacombs became a place where people gathered when pubs closed to continue things.

SO DID YOU MANAGE TO BALANCE YOUR PARTYING WITH YOUR WRITING?

Well, I don't think I wrote much then. It was only later that I began to write, to become conscious of myself as a writer. However, first I was a painter, as was John Ryan. And somehow in writing my forewords to my exhibitions, I gravitated toward and finally took up writing exclusively. People like Ryan, MacNamara, and then Ernie Gébler came into one's life and possibly gave me encouragement in that direction. Gébler had the most astonishing literary background of any man that I'd known at that time. He left Dublin for London early on, where he became a successful author.[2]

THERE IS A STORY THAT BRENDAN BEHAN HAD BEEN PRETTY INSTRU-MENTAL IN GETTING *THE GINGER MAN* INTO PRINT.

That's true. Brendan was writing for newspapers at the time, I think. Well, I had this place in Wicklow by the sea, and when I was gone, Behan arrived and broke in and discovered this manuscript that I had been writing in secret. When I returned, I found two manuscripts. One was mine, which he had written his comments upon, and next to that was a sheaf of papers that turned out to be *Borstal Boy*. I also had about forty pairs of shoes at that time. This discovery must have amused Behan, because he threw all of them into a suitcase or something and on his way to the local pub, when he had walked far enough to wet a pair, he just flung them into a field and put on a dry pair. At that time it wasn't so funny. Anyway, that's how Behan came across *The Ginger Man*.

YOU SAY YOU WERE WRITING IN SECRET. WAS ANYONE ELSE IN ON THE SECRET ACTIVITY BEFORE YOUR FIRST PUBLICATION?

Yes, another man who was, perhaps as much as anyone ever could be, an influence in Dublin at that time—though he was there very briefly, only nine months or so—was A. K. O'Donoghue.

HE WAS THE MODEL FOR *THE SADDEST SUMMER OF SAMUEL S*?

Yes. And the model for O'Keefe in *The Ginger Man*. I remember he would come up to my room at Trinity to look for food or whatever and while there he would look at what was in the typewriter and stop and ponder and then say that it was just shit. Each day he would do this. He was a Greek and Latin scholar. So one day I wrote instead passages from

Virgil or Horace and planted them in the typewriter and he came in and I invited him to look at it and he pronounced it just shit too. It demonstrated something that I learned very early—that where art was concerned there was only one critic, just you. Nobody else.

WHAT WAS HE CRITICIZING? WAS *THE GINGER MAN* UNDER WAY?

There were various attempts at novels, short stories, other things. I also was compiling notebooks, which I used later on. Descriptions of people, buildings, streets, and so on. I can recall sitting down and consciously attempting to write *The Ginger Man*. I can't tell you the exact origins and circumstances, but I recall attacking it and deliberately sweating and struggling with it. It might have taken a week to get the first page or two out. It subsequently took about two or three months to write the first forty or fifty pages. And I simply stayed with it.

WERE YOU STILL A STUDENT AT TRINITY THEN?

I had deliberately decided to stop attending University. I sold the place I had and I stayed briefly in England. Then I went to the United States, where much of *The Ginger Man* was written—near Bridgewater, Connecticut; Boston; and also in my family's home in the Bronx. John Hall Wheelock of Scribner's was one of the first to give the manuscript serious attention.

He said, "There are four people who have read this manuscript here. Three of them think it is one of the best that's ever arrived at this publishing house. The fourth thinks that it is the best manuscript she's ever read." But then he said, "I must tell you that because of the book's obscenity we are unable to publish it." So at that point I realized that I might never find a publisher in America and decided to go back to Europe.

BUT DUBLIN WAS NO OBVIOUS IMPROVEMENT ON NEW YORK.

I certainly had thought of that. Ireland clearly was a dead end. Some stuck it out there, people like John Ryan and Brendan Behan. But for many reasons I realized I couldn't take America. I wrote something about this, "An Expatriate's View of America," for *The Atlantic Monthly*.

IS THAT WHEN BEHAN TOOK YOUR SHOES FOR A STROLL? HOW DID YOU REACT TO HIS LITERARY COMMENTS?

No. Behan had read the manuscript before I went away. He had made little additions and marginal notes. For example, certain phrases that struck me as slightly flowery and that I crossed out he said to put back in. At any rate, when I returned to Europe, we met one night in Fleet Street in London. He knew a lot of journalists and would drink with them. That was also the night I had kind of a famous fight with Behan. Anyway, in the early course of the evening, he said, "What about the manuscript?" He said, "If you want to publish it, there's a publisher in Paris." He gave me the name, and I wrote off to Olympia Press and that was how *The Ginger Man* first was published. That was in 1954 just before Christmas. It was published in the spring of 1955.

RIGHT. SO HOW DID THE FIGHT START AND END?

The fight happened because I ended up paying for drinks that evening with about ten dollars or so that I had. American currency was rarer in those days and I had needed it for something. Anyway, I brought this money out and Behan became incensed that I hadn't brought this money out sooner. I then became incensed with Behan. Now, poor Behan, he was a big man all right, but he never really knew how to fight well. Without a weapon, that is. But one thing I did do well was fight. We dodged around on the street until I recall hitting Behan once and the fight was over. We were soon arrested by the police. They released us quite quickly, though. We were of course in five minutes close friends again. It was only some months later that I had found out that Behan had visited Paris himself and written for the Olympia Press.

WERE YOU ABLE TO CONTINUE WRITING DURING ALL THE DISAPPOINTMENTS?

Well, yes. I did have the advantage of having slightly established myself as a painter, and that gave me self-confidence and a basis for staying with it. Partly, I also had the scientist's point of view. I developed patience. I was aware that observation was such an important thing, precise descriptions and various ways of looking at things.

WHAT ABOUT THE DEVELOPMENT OF YOUR STYLE? WHO INFLUENCED IT? JOYCE SEEMS OBVIOUS.

I suppose one has been influenced by people like Joyce. But also possibly—and this is not too apparent in my work—by Henry Miller, who was then literally a private god, arrived in Dublin through his books. He was someone who influenced people in a much wider sense in their daily lives. You might say that through Joyce I became aware of the use of words, the use of sounds, the impression made upon one by a page. As a serious author, you know, it is very difficult to get a publisher to bring out a book with everything exactly as you want it.

THE MODEL FOR *THE GINGER MAN* WAS ANOTHER TRINITY STUDENT, GAINOR CRIST. WHERE DOES CRIST LEAVE OFF AND THE FICTITIOUS MAN BEGIN?

Well, Dangerfield, perhaps, was the most fictionalized character in *The Ginger Man* of the many Dublin people in it. I recall Behan, after reading the book, saying that he thought the character was not really Crist. That was his opinion, anyway. But I certainly did draw upon certain events in Crist's life. Places he had lived in.

DESPITE THE VITALITY, DANGERFIELD ULTIMATELY WAS A SELFISH BAS-TARD. WHAT WAS CRIST LIKE?

He looked like the Duke of Windsor. Perhaps taller and better looking, but that's who he looked like. He was extremely elegant with marvelous manners, enormous charm, and an English accent. He could walk into any pub and impress upon people that he was a gentleman and eminently worthy of extended credit from any bartender.

WHERE WAS HE FROM?

Dayton, Ohio. I can remember someone once suggesting that perhaps Crist might have stolen jewelry from someone's house. I recall being actually quite angry about what I thought was a malicious slander, and I totally disbelieved it. Which I still do. But then I thought once or twice over the years that perhaps, through eyes that would find no fault, I did not want to have my image of him tarnished. Although I did see him do all kinds of other outrageous things.

ONE CAN DO CERTAIN SORTS OF OUTRAGEOUS THINGS AND STILL NOT BE CRUEL. WHAT ARE SOME EXAMPLES OF OUTRAGEOUSNESS?

Yes, say, there was an incident in which Dangerfield in *The Ginger Man* was getting a lift to the Brazen Head, a pub, in a horse carriage.

The driver tries to cheat him and Dangerfield drags him off and lectures him about his lack of love. That was a bit of Crist. And of his behavior that sometimes was tantamount to sainthood, like Christ driving the moneychangers out of the temple. Many, many years later, George Roy Hill, the film director, who knew Crist also, and myself, spent a couple of days talking about what Crist was all about. What he meant in our lives. We had both liked Crist. Well, finally, I concluded that he was a saint, literally a saint. And I was fascinated to find that Hill absolutely agreed with me. And that is how I would describe him, as a saint.

PLEASE GO ON.

I remember traveling with him to the west of Ireland for four or five days on foot out on the country roads. He had come to my room one afternoon at Trinity and said, "Let's go, Mike. Get your toothbrush." He always carried a toothbrush and little else. We headed off. We ended up in a pub on a night I'll never forget. We were heading toward Kerry and now were in the town of Kells in County Meath, which was more than slightly north of our destination. Anyway, while we were there, the only other patron in the pub began to talk. He recounted his life to Crist. Staring at the ceiling, he'd say, "I went down to the hedge and I looked down the road," he'd begin the refrain. "And then I came back to this." Then he'd reach for his pint and drink it down. This already had gone on for two hours or three, and I felt we were too indulgent. I said we should go, but Crist stopped me and said, "Stay. This man knows something." And that was his refrain to me. And we were there the rest of the night till dawn.

AND DID YOU FIND HE "KNEW SOMETHING"?

Well, he knew the marvelous romantic vision he could create in his mind with a pint of Guinness. And Crist could spend hours like that in total contentment. In a kind of spell he could create. The world outside simply wasn't there. It had gone away. All was here. And that's all. Just this strange sense of now. Which seemed sort of forever.

DID YOU CONTINUE ON TO KERRY ON THIS ODDBALL ODYSSEY?

Yes. On another night heading by fields across country we came to a fair. At this fair, Crist found a girl who was crying because her father would hit her for being out too late. He asked me to wait and he took her home so her father wouldn't beat her. What happened along the

way, I don't know, of course, but he was gone half the night. At dawn
we were picked up by a wedding party from the side of the road, where
we had slept. It was like that with Crist. Everything seemed to happen
wherever he was. This must have been the only such party in the
county.

Again, the next morning I woke up by the side of the road and found
that Crist was already sitting awake and had taken off his jacket and cov-
ered me with it. Very rarely had I ever seen him asleep. I always remember him just sitting there alert. Thinking. Now this was another
side of him. His thoughtfulness and kindness and his utter selflessness
shown anyone he regarded as being in need of help or aid. Especially inside a pub. And I do think of him as a saint.

VERY UNLIKE DANGERFIELD. WHAT BECAME OF CRIST?

He died some years ago. His death was just as bizarre as his life
was. The peculiar connection dates back to his earliest decades, when
he had met some army major on the streets of London during the
Second World War. Crist, incidentally, was in the navy. They somehow ended up three days later in a lorry on the Rhine River four or
five hundred miles inland in Germany. Well, Crist met this same man
all those years later in the streets of Barcelona and this man was in
Crist's company when he died aboard a ship and was buried in the Ca-
nary Islands.

HOW DID CRIST REACT TO THE BOOK?

Well, in reading some of his letters, he very much liked the book, and
during some of my more discouraging moments encouraged me.

THE GINGER MAN WAS USUALLY FOUND EITHER ENORMOUSLY ATTRAC-
TIVE OR ENORMOUSLY REPULSIVE DURING ITS EARLY GOING. WHAT EFFECT
DID THE CRITICAL CROSSFIRE HAVE ON YOU?

I don't know. I was simply too busy trying to get my second novel published and attempting to protect my interests in the enormous litigation
that was growing over *The Ginger Man*. But I suppose despite the criticism *The Ginger Man* clearly went on working for me in the sense that
it established my reputation as an author and it became a safe thing to
say that it was a good book eventually. Although there are many of my

readers now—who came along after that book—who don't even know it exists.

DID YOU WRITE *BALTHAZAR B* OR *THE ONION EATERS* AND SAY TO YOUR-SELF AND THE CRITICS, "THERE, THAT TOPS *THE GINGER MAN*"?

No. Measuring one of my books against another totally disinterests me. Nor do I encourage academic interest in my works. In any event, critics are such a cozy lot. And their influence makes no impression on me. But it does amuse me over the years that everyone is saying *The Ginger Man* is such a fine book. All forgetting how it had been so criticized, so abused. Although praised too by a handful who had the guts. Dorothy Parker being one. Now I suppose the conforming many identify themselves with Dangerfield, but it's fascinating that no one ever identifies with Samuel S of *The Saddest Summer of Samuel S*. Certainly it's a key book to understanding the world of Dangerfield, being as it follows the character of O'Keefe. What I'm pointing to is this: that it's usually not the quality of a book that matters to a critic but how his opinion of it can be safely reinforced.

THAT'S AWFULLY CLEAR REGARDING NOVELS. NOW WHERE DOES *THE UNEXPURGATED CODE* FIT IN?

Well, *The Unexpurgated Code* [1975] has a long history. I guess people like A. K. O'Donoghue, who first made me conscious of classes and his preoccupations with the basics of social and sexual survival, had a lot to do with its background. I can't think why I wrote it except that one is very much concerned with social manners and how in their implementation they keep people's hands from each others' throats.

MY WILD GUESS IS THAT IT SERVED AS A WAY OF PURGING FEELINGS, DEALING WITH PET PEEVES THAT MIGHT HAVE SLIPPED INTO YOUR FIC-TION. DARCY DANCER LOOKS SUBDUED, IN COMPARISON.

Perhaps. And there are still hundreds of things that I'd like to add that I hadn't dealt with in that edition—expanding it, I suppose.

WOULD YOU DESCRIBE YOUR WORKDAY?

I wake up and work as long as I comfortably can work. That's generally until two or three o'clock. I work seven days a week and I take a day or two off occasionally.

NOTES

1. MacNamara is interviewed elsewhere in this volume.
2. Ernie Gébler (1915–1998) was the Irish-born son of Czech immigrants. He launched his writing career with best-seller *The Plymouth Adventure* (Garden City, N.Y.: Doubleday, 1950), which was made into a Hollywood film with Spencer Tracy. Another novel was made into the film *Hoffman* (1970), directed by Alvin Rakoff and with Peter Sellers in the starring role. Gébler was the model for "Gentleman" in his ex-wife Edna O'Brien's first novel *The Country Girls* (New York: Knopf, 1960). They divorced after twelve years. Recently, his son Carlo Gébler published a deeply unflattering account of his domestic life: *Father and I: A Memoir* (New York: Marion Boyars, 2001).

6

DESMOND MACNAMARA

sculptor and author

Desmond MacNamara (b. 1918), who resembles an affable cross between Methuselah and Ho Chi Minh, is an Irish artist, sculptor, and
novelist who has resided in London with his decidedly English wife
Skylla, a film-studio script reader, since 1951. Their West Hampstead
flat is packed to the groaning Pompeian-red ceiling with artworks,
masks, books, and other memorabilia. In Dublin, he worked as an in-
genious set designer for the Abbey and the Gate Theatres and, before
the term was properly noted in credit rolls, as a prop designer on films,
including Laurence Olivier's 1944 film of Henry V.

MacNamara is the inimitable model for the kangaroo-suited character MacDoon in J. P. Donleavy's *The Ginger Man*, and his sculpture
today is exhibited in the Irish National Gallery and the Dublin National Writer's Museum. He also has published books on puppetry,
uses of papier-mâché in sculpture, the art of picture framing, and a
short biography of Eamon de Valera. In 1994, his Celtic comic novel
The Book of Intrusions won plaudits in the *Washington Post*, the
Chicago Tribune, and the *LA Times*. A second novel, *Confessions of
an Irish Werewolf*, had just been completed at the time of the interview.

ACCORDING TO MEMOIRS WRITTEN ABOUT THE 1940S AND 1950S IN DUBLIN, YOU ARE PORTRAYED AS THE IRISH ANSWER TO GERTRUDE STEIN IN THAT YOU RAN A NONSTOP SALON IN YOUR SCULPTOR'S STUDIO ON GRAFTON STREET WHERE MOST IRISH NOTABLES—AND SOME NON-IRISH, LIKE PHYSICIST ERWIN SCHROEDINGER—WOULD SHOW. HOW DID THEY ALL COME TO GATHER THERE?

It's simply that by accident I had a studio in a tall house in the middle of the city in the narrow ravine of a street, and I started using a pub around the corner, McDaid's—and people would drop in casually. My wife at the time, Beverlie Hooberman, kept an open house. When pubs shut, people dropped in. People dropped in before pubs opened, people dropped by when the pubs were open, and people dropped in for a free cup of coffee instead having to pay for it because there was usually coffee bubbling away.

People sunbathed on the roof. There were three studios on the floor. One used by John Ryan, one by me, and one by a sculptor called John Bourke. There was no furniture whatsoever. No living accommodation. So I furnished it with everything that I had. Theatrical props. Cows' heads. Anything to reduce the room from the empty barn it was when I first saw it.

HOW DID YOU COME BY IT?

Through John Ryan.[1] It was over the Monument Creameries, which is now gone. So there it was. Up on the Gothic heights opposite Woolworth's, where I could watch pigeons fornicating on ledges that no one else could see from below. That's really all there was to it. This period of my life lasted only three to four years, but it was a formative three or four years for me. The end of my life as a student and my first evasions of the obligation of living elsewhere or in some other way.

WERE YOU BORN IN DUBLIN?

I'd been born in Dublin. Born in a Georgian crescent near Merrion Square. My mother was Dublin-born, although my paternal family comes from Killaloo. My grandfather was a bespoke shoemaker. He had a small shoe factory that made riding boots, livery boots, and things like that. He was a Fenian.[2] He was out at the rising at Tallaght in 1867.

HE WASN'T NABBED BY THE BRITISH?

He came home in a cab. Buried his gun and came home in a cab. When the redcoats appeared.

YOUR SCULPTURAL MEDIUM SEEMS TO BE PAPIER-MÂCHÉ. YOU'VE PUBLISHED A BOOK ON ITS USES IN ART. YOU BEGAN BY APPLYING IT TO STAGE-PROP DESIGN, DIDN'T YOU?

Yes. A lot of my work was theatrical. Papier-mâché was simply an accident. I had trained in sculpture and done my diploma at the National College of Art, as it then was called. I had always been interested in the theater and I had belonged to rather a progressive theater group.

CONSISTING OF WHOM?

Oh, various people. I can't recall many names. Many are quite well known in the theater now. An ambassador in Luxembourg, Stockholm, and Delhi, Val Iremonger, was our last producer. The founder of the Lyric Theatre in Belfast was our secretary. Many others passed into acting. So I took to making theatrical props as one of my means of making—hardly a living—an existence, a subsistence, really. It so happened that at the time, Hilton Edwards discovered that I was able to do things that previously hadn't been obtainable in Ireland or, for that matter, in London. Certainly not at a cheap price. I started to reduce the amount of scenery, the amount of painted backdrops. That was a fashionable thing then. And I concentrated on huge props like statues of Apollo or Venus or whatever. And so, simply because people knew I was there, they tended to come to me from the Abbey and the Gate and other separate productions. And from the odd film when they were in Ireland.

DONLEAVY INDICATED THERE WAS A SEPARATION BETWEEN THOSE WHO LIVED UPROARIOUS LIVES AND THOSE WHO DID THE ARTISTIC WORK.

I don't remember any particular distinction of any kind. There were no separate zones of living that I can think of. I went many, many times to the Catacombs. On one occasion, I lived there for about ten days, in a most superior room.

IS THIS AFTER YOU VACATED GRAFTON STREET—ABOUT 1948?

I think that it was probably 1949. I've forgotten exactly when I left Grafton Street. I left quite early on because the huge place had been taken over. It was an entire floor of the most expensive property in the middle of the city. Grafton Street district was the equivalent of Bond Street in London or Avenue Louise in Brussels or anywhere like that. I was squeezed out and ended up in a Georgian mews off Baggott Street. It was a mews off a mews. It was full of hens. You had to pick your way through them to get to it. And so I moved everything up there and expanded to fill up the space. You could hardly move around in it. It was about that time that I met people like Gainor Crist, the "ginger man."

HOW DID YOU COME ACROSS THAT NEST OF AMERICAN STUDENTS AT TRINITY? HOW DID DONLEAVY, CRIST, AND O'DONOGHUE STRIKE YOU AT THE TIME OF YOUR FIRST ENCOUNTERS?

I can't remember any first meeting. But I do remember the first time I talked to Donleavy at any length. It was at Crist's house at 1 Newtown Avenue, Blackrock.[3] He had a little house there with two rooms downstairs and basically one room upstairs. I was there several times. There were problems with Gainor, who was rather given to the bottle. I remember one occasion when Petra tracked him down in Blackrock village waving a dirty nappy.

SO WAS CRIST GINGERY?

He had ginger hair. Not violently ginger, I've known more gingery people. He was about six feet tall, slender, very well spoken, a slightly T. S. Eliot way of speaking. I don't think this was an affectation. He actually used rather Dickensian phrases like "My good man," "God's teeth," and even "zounds." He would affect, very mildly, a satiric kind of pedantry, but he said these things in a comic spirit that you were meant to know, and you were meant to laugh. Many had reservations about it of a violent kind.

Somewhere in this flat, I still have his law notes in an old ledger with half an acre of foolscap. He left many pages untouched.

DID YOU EVER SEE HIM STUDY?

Law, no. But he read a lot. He read everything.

WAS HE RECOGNIZABLE IN THE STAGE PRODUCTION OF THE GINGER MAN YOU SAW IN DUBLIN IN 1999?

He is strangely recognizable. All the characters in *The Ginger Man* are recognizable—with exception of, I think, of Mary. There were moments in his life when he became very testy and rather outrageous. These were usually followed the next day by remorse and apologies. It was a feature of his character that Donleavy tends to forget or didn't find convenient to use. He came from Dayton, Ohio, and his next-door neighbors were the Wright brothers, Orville and Wilbur. Gainor's father had been a respected physician who had been to the South Pole with Admiral Byrd. He married a second time; Gainor's mother died when he was quite young. Some people attribute his slightly necrophiliac tastes to the death of his mother.

SKYLLA MACNAMARA INTERJECTS:

Gainor had this wily charm and would get anything out of you, your background, and whatever you were thinking about, your whole life history perhaps. This was truth night. And then when he had you really flung out, then he'd borrow money [laughter].

IT SAYS A LOT ABOUT CRIST THAT IT IS A FOND MEMORY. WHAT'S THIS ABOUT NECROPHILIA?

He was hitchhiking to County Down and got as far as Drogheda. It was a hot day and he entered the large cool cathedral, and, slipping off his shoes, sat in the back pew with his swollen feet on the cold marble. He fell asleep and was awakened by childish laughter and saw little girls putting pennies into a slot that turned on a light that lit up the mummified head of the blessed Oliver Plunket, now St. Oliver Plunket. Gainor was most taken by this and sent me a photographic postcard of it. Two or three years later, Brendan rediscovered it and dubbed it the B.O.P. in the box—B dot, O dot, P dot. Brendan sent me a beautiful postcard to pass onto Gainor and scribbled on it—I think it was Brendan's last piece of verse—"The blessings of Ollie, so jovial and jolly / be on you dear Crist till next we get pissed."

At Gainor's request, I made him a small copy of the B.O.P. fitted into a matchbox. He carried it around in his pocket and would show it. It looked very like the B.O.P., like someone very dead with teeth showing. a papier-mâché head. Years later, he showed me a brothel in Barcelona. They had a small morgue: a mortuary chapel and bier awaiting the next customer. I don't know if the brothel had any specialties—probably had to arrange that the day before. Another occasion in Madrid with Peter

Walsh, an ex-IRA man, he took me to see Spanish funeral hearses with jet-black horses with nodding plumes six feet high, lined with cut-glass windows and velvet linings. Then I was taken upstairs to a hearse garage, where there were very impressive ones with ebony life-sized angels—six more small hearses, pearly white, with weeping angels carved in them. About half life size. This was for kids. He thought it was one of the tenderest things he had ever seen. Very impressed by it.

WHAT WAS CRIST UP TO IN DUBLIN?

Trying to screw money out of the American government. His wife had access to his grant before he laid a hand on it. That's his first wife, an English woman, whom he met while in the navy during the war. They were just around, and I got to know them better. Mike Donleavy struck me as an appallingly bad painter, which he was and which apparently his then-wife M. W. still believed, since she'd barred his paintings from their stately home in Mullingar.

HOW WAS DONLEAVY FARING?

He had a house in Kilcoole, a cottage surrounded by concrete blocks that he built for pleasure, I think. Maybe they were abstract pieces of sculpture. They looked just like tank traps in the meadow by the sea. He painted pieces on plywood and Swedish hardboard. He raided the daisy market and bought off the frames. If the paintings didn't fit the frames, he'd saw them down until they did. The borders of the paintings, which were on scrap pieces of hardboard, were very large. I remember an exhibition Mike held on St. Stephen's Green.

WHAT WAS THE SUBJECT MATTER AND STYLE?

Many of them were fruit. They had titles like "Three Large Happy Apples" or "Rich Delicious Tomatoes"—and there were three circles. They were rather minimal; they were still lifes. Very often the tomatoes or cucumbers or whatever they were would just float into space. They were quite naive. Any resemblance to any school of painting that happened before or since is quite coincidental. One very avant-garde woman painter went to the exhibition with me. She said, "We'd better go along and see what Michael Donleavy is doing." She had previously slapped him down because of his tendency to ask people sexual questions about themselves. He never revealed anything about himself, but he'd ask people how many times they'd had it last week and that sort of thing. So on our way over, we met him standing on the corner of a side street off Grafton Street and she greeted him with "Michael Donleavy! Are you still in your celluloid penis stage?" He said, "What's that, Phyllis?"

"Sculpting your apples," she said. "Your celluloid penises."

Well, I went with her to Mike's exhibition and we walked around this beautiful Dublin painter's gallery with all the other people. Though tending to frankness, Phyllis did not want to offend Mike by saying anything openly. So when Mike asked her what she thought, she said, "Well, some of the color is quite interesting and indeed quite good." And Mike said, "So it should be. That chrome yellow cost me fifteen shillings."

HOW COULD SOMEONE OF THAT TEMPERAMENT STAY CLOSE ENOUGH TO RECORD THE ANTICS OF A MAN LIKE GAINOR CRIST?

I don't know. How did Boswell stay close to Johnson? Mike carried a notebook. I noticed him using it on occasion, and I thought he was writing down an address. I discovered that he had written down little bits and pieces and, indeed, comments of mine and John Ryan and other people that he changed in some way into aphorisms—directed at nothing in particular. They were rather like the pieces of verse that he used at the ends of chapters. Gnomic little utterances.

DID YOU SUSPECT HE WAS WRITING NOVELS?

No. I had no idea until Brendan told me about it. Brendan and I and two or three others had been at a weekend party in a very hospitable house up in the mountains near Glendalough. Brendan had a row with a journalist when they went out for a walk. The journalist was a very tedious man, but Brendan also overreacted. So Brendan decided he wasn't going back to the house if so-and-so was going with him. And he set off across the mountains and walked twenty miles down to Greystones, where he found Donleavy was out. And he broke in and found the manuscript for *The Ginger Man*. Donleavy was supposed to have appeared with a shotgun because Brendan, who had effected an entry, as they say, left a window open through which he came in. Donleavy crept up and crept up and looked in to see Brendan reading the thing. Brendan looked up and said, "Put that away. This book is fucking funny." That's all I know. That's what Brendan told me.

YOU MET BRENDAN BEHAN WHEN HE WAS IN THE FIANNA [REPUBLI-
CAN SCOUTS], THE JUNIOR IRA?

The first time I ever spoke to him, he was maybe sixteen and I was eighteen or nineteen. It was at the end of the Spanish Civil War. There was an attempt in the crumbling days of the Republic of Catalonia to get a food ship out to beleaguered Barcelona. A meeting was held and we were all issued with banners to carry—"Skim Milk for Spain" and things like that. I'm not sure what the Spaniards thought of skim milk, but that's what they got if they got it. The person carrying the other pole of the banner, marching past the General Post Office where Nelson's pillar stood, was Brendan. He was a very good-looking boy with a very bad stammer. A young Stewart Granger in appearance. His personality overpoured.

So I became quite friendly with him, although a youth of nineteen looks upon a boy of sixteen as very much younger than himself. Nonetheless, Brendan became part of my circle for a while, mostly connected with the theater group. The he disappeared, and I heard that he had been imprisoned in England. The Second World War had started by then. A year had passed. Then one day, coming into my Grafton Street studio on a tram—I had a flat in Rathgar—someone appeared behind me and tapped me on the shoulder and it was Brendan, who, wherever he was going, jumped off the tram with me and came down to the studio. It was then I discovered he had been released. The previous evening he had enacted the closing scene in his book with the customs officer greeting him in Irish off the boat in Dun Laoghaire. Had *Borstal Boy* been extended another paragraph, he would have said, "Next day on the 15 tram I met. . . ." He went home, but he wasn't too well received there. There were always rows going on in that family.

IDEOLOGICAL ROWS? PURE FAMILY ROWS?

I should imagine both. All mixed together. He spent the night there. I suppose that's where he was coming from. He didn't go back for about a fortnight. He stayed with me. No one drank a good deal at that time, although we went into McDaid's often. But we seemed to spend hours over a pint or a couple of half-pints. There wasn't a great deal of money then. And that was my meeting with Brendan. Later, he shot at the policeman and went into prison again.

WHAT WERE HIS AMBITIONS AT THE TIME?

His ambitions were not to do house-painting. So far as I know, they were purely negative.

BUT HE HAD BEEN WRITING POETRY.

Well, he made some infantile effort while in school. Many children do that. I think his interest was nurtured in prison, particularly in the Curragh, which was kind of a university with lectures going on all day by people like Roger McHugh and many others. People who subsequently took over the Folklore Commission were interned there. He started writing there and also in Arbour Hill, the military prison. His reason for writing poetry, as I wrote in a review of Colm Kearney's book on Brendan, is that the Irish Gaelic magazine paid very quickly and they always paid properly in guineas, never in pounds. Because guineas are for artists and gentlemen and pounds are for the commonality, you see. So it was two guineas a poem, which at the time was quite a lot. Many's the time that I and others waited while Brendan rushed off with a grubby piece of paper in his hand to come back with the money. If those two guineas hadn't existed, the poems would not have been written.

YOU HAVE A HEAD OF BRENDAN DISPLAYED ON YOUR MANTLE, BESIDE MANY OTHER BUSTS. DID HE ACTUALLY POSE FOR IT?

Well, Brendan, who was a monstrous egotist or egoist or both, conceived the idea of having a statue of himself erected in St. Stephen's Green. There were a number of grass bays around the perimeter of the north side of the Green, some of which contained statues, some of which didn't. In some cases, statues had been there originally that were blown up during the Troubles. It occurred to Brendan that if you erected a statue like that, how long would it be there before people noticed it hadn't always been there? The idea came to him, I think, because I had just done a life-sized replica of a statue of Queen Victoria that originally sat in front of Leinster House.[4] It was for the Annual Horse Show Review at the Gaiety Theatre. It was very uncomely.

SO WAS SHE.

She was. The statue was even more so. The monument was quite handsome, baroque. But she, sitting in the middle of it, was rather uncomely. It was known as "Ireland's Revenge." Anyway, I'd done this copy complete with dried pigeon and seagull shit. Very effective. And indeed, when taken to the Gaiety Theatre in the back of a lorry, it was mistaken for the real thing. Brendan didn't want his own name on the statue. He wanted a statue erected to Rabelais with Brendan's head on it. This was to be set up on a plywood base treated to look like stone, with which I had some skill. He had even gone to the extent of persuading an engineer to design a retractable trolley so we could wheel the thing over and press a lever, so it would settle in the grass as if forever. I had to come, for various reasons, to London then and later he followed me over and we started to do it. The important thing was to get a portrait head of him from which the rest could be fabricated.

SO HE ACTUALLY SAT STILL FOR YOU?

He slept still. He fell asleep half way through, no, a quarter way through. I had to prop up his head with half a dozen books.

WAS THE SCHEME THWARTED?

Well, I didn't go back to Dublin for sufficiently long to do it, but the hoax could have been done. Our mutual theory was that it would take about three weeks before some gardener mowing the grass would bump into the base and discover it wasn't granite.

WHAT CHANGES DID YOU SEE IN BRENDAN OVER THE YEARS?

The only change that happened to Brendan is that he was drinking heavily toward the end. He always drank a lot socially, but toward the end it was very bad, particularly since his visits to the States and Canada, it began. The chemistry of his body changed and his soul with it. Well, the two are inseparable.[5]

PATRICK KAVANAGH'S HEAD IS ON THE MANTLE TOO. WHEN DID HE ARRIVE AT GRAFTON STREET?

Kavanagh started coming into McDaid's when Bev and myself and John Ryan established ourselves there.[6] We hadn't much opportunity or domestic capacity for entertaining. Damp turf fires and all that. So we would just take visiting people over to McDaid's for a ham sandwich and half a pint of Guinness or porter, very often, at the time. And Kavanagh was one of the people there. I remember the first lengthy conversation I had with him, a rather irascible one. There was an exhibition of paintings by Irish painters. One was John Ffrench. Michael Morrow was another—he was Gothic even in those days—and I think Beatrice, Brendan's later wife, was one of the exhibitors in the Grafton Gallery, which was owned by Tom Nisbet and next door to McDaid's. There was a crowd of people at the opening. I was invited, but there was no room to get in at the door. Even the porch was filled. I'd thought I would go and have a drink next door and come back in twenty minutes, since I knew most people had come fairly early and would leave the gallery reasonably soon.

But Kavanagh sort of craned over my shoulder, looked in, and bawled over my head past my ear: "FRAUDS! IMPOSTERS! DECEIVERS!" Then he went into McDaid's, ordered himself a small whiskey, and he sat curled up in himself on a stool, not looking at anyone. I said, "That was rather cruel." He went on at great length to explain to me why it was true that every phony in the city was there. To some extent this was true. Every phony in the city was there. So were several dozen quite reasonable people. So was Oisin Kelly, who is now a celebrated sculptor. So, you know.

YOU KNEW BRIAN O'NOLAN TOO.[7]

I got to know him when a man called George Jeffares, who was doing a Ph.D. on Yeats, was having continuous rows with Nolan. I attended some of these argumentative sessions, and I got to know him. He wasn't a person one talked to. He talked to you. He held court. There was little to contribute. Oddly enough, although Brendan spoke louder and externalized more, he was a listener and he was a question-asker. He'd ask endless questions, and he'd pick you up on them. In between his mimicries and fantasies.

ERWIN SCHROEDINGER WAS LODGED AT THE DUBLIN INSTITUTE FOR ADVANCED STUDIES DURING THE WAR.[8] HOW DID ONE OF THE PIONEERS OF WAVE MECHANICS ENTER YOUR LIFE?

I met his wife. I found her a very charming Austrian woman. She then invited myself and others to visit over afternoon tea. I met Schroedinger and liked him very much. He invited me to Dunsink Observatory with him. His ideas were like toys to him, and he liked explaining them to people. I don't suppose I met him more than two dozen times, though most were lengthy occasions. I remember he had a loom, a shuttle loom that produced tapestries about eighteen inches in width. He changed the pattern the whole time. He'd try out mathematical curves and then arbitrarily stop them and change to another curve from a different equation. The effect was very beautiful. I wish I had one of them. He once offered to cut me off a couple of pieces. They went on and on in very long strips. He had them running down the walls. Random curves and slopes and colors.

HE HAD WOVEN FORMULAE ALL AROUND HIS ROOMS?

That's right. He dropped into Grafton Street a few times, mostly to hear a singer named Aine Woods, who was a superb Gaelic singer. My wife was compiling notebooks of traditional songs, and people used to come over to sing. Schroedinger left Dublin when the war ended.

SOME PEOPLE, LOOKING BACK ON THE YEARS AFTER THE WAR, OR "EMERGENCY," PORTRAY THE PERIOD TO BE AS NEAR TO A "GOLDEN AGE" IN THE ARTS AS DUBLIN HAS SEEN SINCE LADY GREGORY.

It wasn't a golden age. Each age is an age that is dying or one that is coming to birth. I never thought it was golden. Gilt potato bread, perhaps. It was a clearing of the lungs after the stagnation of those years of neutrality during the war. Ireland was spared the horrors of Europe, but it did pay a price. It was pushed back on itself. Became insulated and cut off from news. Dublin was a city of rumors. Actual news of events in the wide, wide world was very hard to come by because there was censorship on both sides. So you couldn't find out what was happening. I think most people I knew at the time favored the Allies. Most of the IRA then were more violently anti-Nazi and anti-fascist than the British government. Very much so. Many had fought in Spain. At the time the left was very Republican, and a large part of the Labour Party was Republican Socialist. It's the rump of this that you find in the Official IRA.[9]

YOU LIVE IN LONDON. WHAT'S YOUR RECEPTION BEEN LIKE OVER THE DECADES? AN IRISHMAN, GIVEN THE "TROUBLES" GOING INTO THE MID-1990s, MUST HAVE FELT QUEASY ON OCCASIONS.

Well, during rather critical times I've found myself rather embarrassed when going into pubs with plastic bags in my hand. I've been conscious of the fact. My attention has been drawn to them in pubs, but mostly where I'm known. The limeys, God bless them, are a very tolerant people. Harmless and tolerant. Not very imaginative or talkative. Or rather, they do talk but not about things that interest me very much. They're not disputative enough. If I were to make an ethnic choice before going into a previously unvisited London pub, I'd choose a fellow Celt of some sort. A Glasgow man. An Edinburgh man. A Welshman. You don't meet many Cornish, so I can't judge them. But the Welsh and the Scots are much closer to us than the English, I now realize. Anyway, in watching international sporting matches, for example, I am pleased when Scotland beats England.

WOULD YOU SAY DISPUTATIVENESS IS A CELTIC TRAIT?

It does appear to be. Years ago I would deny this, but I am aware of it now. Certainly the Welsh are as disputative as the Irish. I know that if I bump into a Welsh man anywhere, he'd talk the hind legs off me. About nothing very much. About life, death, and resurrection. From such talk anything can split off.

THERE IS THE CONTENTION THAT CELTS TALK THEIR BOOKS AWAY.

I've heard that. I don't know if there were any books there. I really don't believe that about writing. Because writing is an obsessive thing. Important writing is obsessive.

YOUR FIRST NOVEL, *THE BOOK OF INTRUSIONS*, WAS WELL REVIEWED. IT WENT THROUGH A LONG PERIOD OF GESTATION.

I like writing. It's a very pleasant thing to do. It's a bit awkward if you're arthritic, leaning over a hard table sitting in a hard chair. But otherwise it's a very pleasant occupation. It occurred to me that not only in Europe but over half the New World as well—Meso-America and South America—people built walls. I started to put down an essay, as it were, about walls.

WALLS AS METAPHORS, WALLS AS REAL WALLS?

Walls as everything. There were vast areas of western Ireland along the Atlantic seaboard up to Donegal and the offshore islands where people built walls in crazy abundance—small walls, tiny walls, all made of gray stone and well maintained. Since they were very old walls, it occurred to me that many of these walls had been repaired down through the endless centuries. As small peasant farmers marry and acquire a bit more land, they may take out a bit of the wall but usually leave the rest. Considering these things, I introduced a couple of characters—a suggestion of Flann O'Brien on some occasion that it was quite unnecessary to invent new characters. There were lots of characters already invented. You could take a lot of characters from Dickens and put them into a spy story, and you could have a detective named Nickleby. Out of these frivolous cogitations you could take entire stories borrowing characters of a previous generation of writers who are already written about quite satisfactorily and far better than you ever could. So I went on from there. It occurred to me that it would be necessary to write a story to link it to someone who had gone before. Then there was limbo. I read something about limbo having been abolished by the Catholic Church of Pope John. If limbo was abolished, I thought what did they do with the inmates? Did they just turn them loose? All these unbaptized babies and "meritorious pagans" like Virgil or Juvenal or Marcus Aurelius. So I got the idea very quickly of the emptied limbo and of squatters. There was a lot of squatting going on at that time in London. And I started to fill it with characters.

FROM KNOWN WORKS, ABORTED WORKS?

Exhumed aborted works. It was great fun.

THEY ROUND BACK VERY ROUGHLY UPON THE AUTHOR.

Yes. They become visible. The tougher ones escape through a fissure. I pictured limbo as a very old building made of ectoplasm. The ectoplasmic tiles were coming off and odd characters manage to escape. And two of them manage to escape through an early nineteenth-century novel. They invade the writer's psyche and get into his narrative. It's a roomy warm place into which they camp quite happily. He discovers to his horror some time later that they have completely taken him over and use him as a place to become encorpified. They use the literary notes to extricate and to free other people. One is an actual creation by Brendan Behan, a translation of the late eighteenth-century poem "The Midnight Court" by Brian Merriman. It's about a revolt of the women in Ireland, who convene a court on the shortcomings of Irish manhood. Brendan did a translation when he was in prison. The governor of the Borstal put in a request for Brendan of the Irish version of the poem. The manuscript was handwritten, sometimes in pen and ink, and sometimes in pencil. It was left on a scaffold. He lost the manuscript.

Your book was in danger of not getting encorpified itself. You had a galling experience with a British publisher.

Someone connected with them, an agent, someone I met in Bloomsbury in a pub near the British Museum took it. He was quite happy to take it to the publisher. Various people at Faber and Faber decided it was worth having a shot at. They had a final meeting on a Tuesday evening. An extremely important supereditor came in rather late. He'd been delayed on the tube or the train. They went through the business of the day very quickly, and someone said, "What about this Irish book?" He said, "Don't mention that bloody country to me. No more Irish!" At that time Belfast was ablaze. Newspapers were full of Celtic tedium and blood in the street. So the book was rejected on the assumption it was about the Provisional IRA.

If there is such a thing as a nice irony, one is that *The Book of Intrusions* was published by Dalkey Archive Press. You had designed the dust jacket for Brian O'Nolan's *The Dalkey Archive*.

Yes.

Did he request you specifically?

Yes. The editor contacted me. At about that time, I had modeled and cast a head of Joyce. One of the few photographs I had was from a death mask. All Brian said was that it had to be "under water." No one knew what he meant. When asked, he would say "I told you: Under water." He said, "You didn't put a miter on its head." I said, "Well, I meant to. Wasn't it obvious?"

A critic praised your book for making fun of artificial boundaries and unnecessary barriers, mental and physical.

All nations are composed of lesser aggregations and they tend under stress to protect themselves and to some extent to isolate themselves. That's how it is, and that's how it has been throughout history.

So you pit subversive cosmopolitanism against knee-jerk nationalism.

Well, that is so.

I GATHER FOR THE WEREWOLF NOVEL THAT IT WASN'T LON CHANEY
YOU HAD IN MIND.

I was taken by the title. There were a few stories I know from the
early Irish from around Kilkenny, which was a Norman town. It was famous for witchcraft. There was a story of three werewolf sisters who
slept in a cave who lured passersby and ate them. They were particularly
fond of pilgrims. I returned to Bram Stoker. I knew the Stoker house
very well. Then he was a well-known surgeon. I remember seeing a collection of risqué slides. Not very dirty.

IT IS A MURDER MYSTERY WITH THE WEREWOLF PLAYING DETECTIVE.

Well, I didn't plot anything out. At one time, he was a surgeon in the
early nineteenth century. He sets out to find out what he suspects—that
an artist's model wasn't drowned but murdered. But in the course of this
he discovers this Sapphic ring, which published this highly naughty
magazine [in order to support themselves and their cause].

THE SOFT PORN OF ITS TIME.

I've seen some of them. They are artful and rather beguiling indeed.
He goes to Paris at the time of the siege of the Commune. He hopes to
pursue the matter further. He goes to their Sapphic headquarters and
finds them completely guileless and cooperative. He also discovers, after
starting out as a fairly orthodox werewolf who couldn't pass a day without
a chubby child or a meaty piece of male or female venison, as it were,
that, like society, as the centuries pass, his moral attitude toward eating
has been affected. A degree of enlightenment begins. Just as in the time
of the Crusades, barbaric things were happening to entire cities, entire
populations were starved, slaughtered, burnt alive. As we came to an age
of more enlightenment, this became less acceptable. Similarly, he prides
himself on the fact that his taste for blood over the centuries is decreas-
ing and is less intrusive. He does not have to kill. He still does occasionally, because that's his nature. He follows the urges of his palate but never
very seriously. Very often he happily subsists on ordinary fare.

SO HE BECOMES A SYMBOL OF A MORE CIVILIZED SOCIETY.

Yes. In many ways, Western society is becoming more civilized. It's
unacceptable to eat each other. It still happens, you know, but only on
extreme occasions.

Do you mean this novel to be a kind of comedy?

Patrick Kavanagh corrected me and said, "The real truth lies in comedy. You wouldn't find much of it in tragedy." I believe it to be profoundly true—using comedy in Dante's sense of a happy or a hopeful ending.

Life, death, or resurrection: any parting remarks on any of these topics?

I seem to recall that when old Jack Yeats the painter was nigh unto death, about three weeks before he died, an American critic wanted to meet him. This was rather difficult because he was bedridden at that time. But finally he consented: yes, come along for sherry or whatever. And this rather eager young man—I've forgotten his name if I ever knew it—sat down respectfully by his bedside with the sherry and said, "Tell me, Mr. Yeats, what advice have you got for rising young artists?" Yeats looked around the room and then out the window at the mountains and he said, "Ah, well."

Well?

That's all. Just, "Ah, well." As soft as the end of Ulysses: "Yes. Yes. Yes."

NOTES

1. John Ryan, born to a well-off Dublin family, was an Irish renaissance man: literary editor, theatrical producer, and painter. He edited *A Bash in the Tunnel: James Joyce, an Irish View* (Brighton: Clifton Books, 1970) and is author of several books, most notably *Remembering How We Stood: Bohemian Dublin in the Fifties* (Dublin: Gill and Macmillan, 1975). See my interview in the January 1988 issue of *The Journal of Irish Literature*. I regret there was no room for it in these pages.

2. A Fenian is a nineteenth-century Irish nationalist of a particularly vigorous kind.

3. The Curragh was the County Kildare site of an internment camp.

4. The site of the today's Irish Parliament.

5. Behan died in 1964.

6. Patrick Kavanagh, born in rural Monaghan, is author of *Tarry Flynn* (New York: Devin-Adair, 1949), *The Great Hunger: A Poem* (Brighton: Clifton Books, 1970), *The Green Fool* (London: Martin Brian and O'Keeffe, 1971), and many other works.

7. Brian O'Nolan (1911–1966), a.k.a. Myles na Gopaleen, a.k.a. Flann O'Brien was a legendary Dublin satirist and wit. He was an *Irish Times* columnist and author of *At-Swim-Two-Birds* (London: Longmans, Green, 1939), *The Dalkey Archive* (London: MacGibbon & Kee, 1964), *The Third Policeman* (London: MacGibbon & Kee, 1967), and *The Poor Mouth* (London: Hart-Davis, MacGibbon, 1973).

8. Erwin Schroedinger, Austrian physicist, supplied the mathematical basis for Einstein's theory of relativity. He was the author of *What Is Life and Other Scientific Essays* (Garden City, N.Y.: Doubleday, 1956).

9. The IRA split in 1969 between the Provisional IRA, which waged the nationalist war until the mid-1990s, and the Marxist-oriented Official IRA, which called a cease-fire in 1972.

7

NOEL BROWNE

activist and author

Noel Browne (1913–1997) was the Irish equivalent of the United Kingdom's Tony Benn, South Africa's Nelson Mandela, and the United States's Michael Moore all rolled into one irrepressible package. As minister of health in the 1948–1951 Irish coalition government, the young Dr. Browne won renown when he instigated risky but successful measures to end the TB scourge. With a keen eye on the Labour government's social achievements in Britain, his ultimate goal was to install an Irish National Health Service and, to that end, he promoted a preliminary scheme for delivering free health care to mothers and children up to age sixteen. However, the timid Irish government caved in to combined pressure from haughty bishops and fretful doctors. Browne exposed their clandestine dealings and resigned. Here was a grimmer aspect of the Ireland of *The Ginger Man* era.

Afterward, he endured blacklisting, evictions, knee-jerk ridicule, and furious official opprobrium while fighting for sorely needed political reform and social policy improvements. Browne retrained as a psychiatrist and worked in state hospitals while continuing to be returned to the Irish Parliament to give voice to the otherwise voiceless. There was no imaginable progressive cause that he did not play a key role in promoting. Only with the publication in 1986 of his memoir *Against the Tide* did Browne reach the wider public in a manner unfiltered and unmarred by adversaries. It quickly became the best-selling autobiography of all time in Ireland. I first interviewed Dr. Browne in Dublin in 1978. In December of 2000 I freely but, I believe, aptly adapted that lengthier original interview for an "as if" Browne riposte from the grave in response to a dismayingly derisive biography that appeared that year. I retain the frivolous but purposeful introduction below.

> Out of the vasty deep arose the unrepentant shade of Dr. Noel Browne, presumably dry-roasted in the lakes of fire that so many Irish church metaphysicians (and even more physicians) judged the richly deserved fate for all his earthly impertinences. Our tremulous medium, a defrocked priest wielding his granny's heirloom ouija board, gasped "Jaysus, it worked!" and tremulously greeted the tenacious Irish trouble-maker, bane of all that is petty and smug on that small damp green island. Contrary to pious expectations, the spectral Browne looked wonderfully fit, and his wide grin filled the séance room with soothing warmth. No whiff of suffocating brimstone and sulfur; instead, a summery Connemara breeze accompanied the genial apparition. Whatever astral plane he inhabited evidently agreed with him.
>
> Through sheer Mephistophelean blind luck we had conjured up the notorious radical to respond to a severely crabbed and disparaging portrait rendered in John Horgan's biography, *Noel Browne: Passionate Outsider* (Dublin: Gill and Macmillan, 2000). The bemused phantom first remarked that he was as aghast as we were at his impressive ghostly manifestation, and assured us that he remained a thoroughly lapsed Catholic. Indeed, at Browne's insistence, and before we proceeded with queries, we ransacked the shabby quarters searching for concealed tape players, hidden ventriloquists, hovering holograms and whatnot. We came up utterly empty-handed, and so we commenced.

YOUR BIOGRAPHER CANNOT GRASP YOUR MOTIVES EXCEPT BY REDUCING THEM TO MENTAL QUIRKS, IF NOT ILLNESS. HE AGREES THAT YOU FOUGHT AGAINST "DREADFUL AND REMEDIABLE SOCIAL CONDITIONS," YET ON THE SAME PAGE HE INVOKES THE TERM "NARCISSISTIC RAGE" TO DISCREDIT YOUR ACTIONS. HE WANTS TO LOCATE YOUR DRIVE FOR SOCIAL CHANGE IN TIDY PERSONALITY FORMULAE, SUCH AS A LEFT-HANDED BOY FORCED TO WRITE RIGHT-HANDED, YOUR PLACE IN THE FAMILY BIRTH ORDER, OR, MORE LIKELY, YOUR MOTHER'S DEATH. WHICH, IF ANY, DO YOU REGARD AS FORMATIVE EXPERIENCES?

I saw an enormous amount of suffering. I don't say that I personally suffered, but I saw tremendous suffering in the lives of the people around me. My parents both died of tuberculosis quite early on. My father died first. Then my mother was left with [very little money] and seven of us. A lovely, gentle person. She was one of those people who had endless children and took all the crosses that kept coming as they came. We went down to Ballinrobe, where she had grown up, but we had a tough time.

Then a sister emigrated to the States. Eventually, three more went there. One wonderful sister, Eileen, gave up school at fourteen, went over to England, got work, did well, and managed to bring us over. I also had a hunchbacked brother [who] went into a workhouse, where he died in complete isolation and loneliness. I understand that before he died a plastic surgeon experimented on him. Then this lovely sister who carried us all caught TB and she died. Another sister went into a mental hospital. [I remember] my mother frequently was in terrible pain, crying and all that. Kidney disease, I suppose it was. We weren't able to help her. We couldn't afford a doctor. She died shortly after we arrived in England. She was kind of relieved, poor lady. She couldn't take it anymore.

That left its mark on one. I think it does. As for myself, astonishingly I was taken into an exclusive Jesuit school in Windsor. Quite up the line. Quite a crazy school for me, really. That's why I say I saw more suffering than I experienced myself.

YOU BECAME A DOCTOR AND WORKED IN TB SANATORIUMS IN BRITAIN AND IN IRELAND. WHAT BROUGHT YOU INTO POLITICS? DID YOU HAVE A NOTION OF PRESERVING THE IDEOLOGICAL PURITY OF YOUR POLITICAL PARTY EVEN AT THE COST OF YOUR HEALTH PLAN, AS YOUR BIOGRAPHER ACCUSES?

When I came into politics, all I wanted to do was stop tuberculosis. I met Harry Kennedy, a journalist, and Noel Hartnett, a politician who had [just helped form] the Clann na Poblachta Party.[1] They said the only hope [to eliminate the TB scourge] is to go into politics and you'll get something done that way. I was a complete infant in politics. Funnily enough, my sister Eileen was once asked to take me away from the [Jesuit] school because the rector complained that I was causing trouble as an anarchist—and I really didn't know what an anarchist was! After I entered politics, there were endless talks and talks with Kennedy and Hartnett. And Mae Keating, too, who was a serious Marxist.

WHAT ABOUT REPUBLICANISM? YOUR BIOGRAPHER SAYS YOU "SUPPRESSED" YOUR VIEWS IN YOUR AUTOBIOGRAPHY. WERE YOU A CLOSET REPUBLICAN AT ANY TIME? OR WAS THE RELEVANT INFLUENCE UPON YOU, LIKE MANY OTHERS, THE SOCIALIST THRUST OF THE 1930S REPUBLICAN CONGRESS, LED BY PEADER O'DONNELL AND GEORGE GILMORE?

The Republican Congress is the only thing I see in the last [century] with which I have any sympathy.[2] That was the only time when Republicanism was republicanism. At any other time it was a dreadful philosophy, the complete antithesis of serious republicanism. I [was] very close to George Gilmore and I [got] great help from him. He was able to explain the thread of republicanism that ran through the national movement. I am an internationalist.

YOUR BIOGRAPHER ARGUES THAT YOUR "SATISFACTION IN IDENTIFYING AND DENOUNCING ENEMIES OBSTRUCTED [YOUR] JOURNEY TOWARDS DESIRED OBJECTIVES." WHILE HORGAN HIMSELF SHOWS THERE WAS NO ROOM FOR COMPROMISE WITH THE BISHOPS AND THE DOCTORS, HE WINDS UP INSINUATING THAT THE FAULT WAS ALL YOURS FOR NOT ACCEPTING A DILUTED VERSION. DID YOU SEE SPACE FOR COMPROMISE?

No. And this is a very important point. Once [Clann na Poblachta leader Sean] MacBride [caved in to the bishops] and said that Browne was on his own, the Bishops no longer had any need to compromise with me.[3] The Cabinet was happy because they were on the side of the doctors and, of course, the bishops. The ministers were all deeply involved with the doctors, and the only way the doctors could be placated was by passing a poor law–type scheme, which they later got.

JOHN HORGAN ACCUSES YOU OF BEING NAIVE AND UNPREPARED FOR THE STRUGGLES WITH THE CHURCH AND THE IRISH MEDICAL ASSOCIATION. HOW DO YOU PLEAD?

I've no objection to any group making representations or lobbying, but the decision had been taken in the 1947 Health Act, and all I was doing as minister was implementing it on their behalf. We had to establish the right of the government to govern without interference by the bishops and the doctors. I knew Mother and Child was going to be rejected about eighteen months before I submitted.

I knew that the doctors would fight it and that gradually the bishops would be brought in. My plan was to use the scheme as a powerful educative incident and force in society. I set on a very systematic campaign detailing this marvelous scheme for mothers in motherhood and children up to the age of 16. No doctors' bills. No dentists' bills. Taking out half-page ads, distributing illustrated booklets, creating tremendous expectations. Perfectly legitimate.

IT FAILED, SO FAR AS THE INSTALLATION OF AN IRISH NATIONAL HEALTH SYSTEM, COMPARABLE TO BRITAIN, IS CONCERNED. YOUR BIOGRAPHER CRITICIZES YOU FOR OSCILLATING BETWEEN SUPINE COMPLIANCE AND MINDLESS HOSTILITY TOWARD THE CATHOLIC CHURCH. IS THIS FAIR?

I said to [my theological advisor], "What if I tell the bishops to go to hell?" Which is what I wanted to do. He said that that is a political decision that you must make yourself, but you will then effectively be a Protestant. And the bishops would say, "We are deeply sorry that Dr. Browne has taken this position which he has a perfect right to do, but he has rejected the teaching of the Church and he is no longer in communion with it." And you are totally cut off from your electorate. A 98 percent Catholic electorate! So the political decision I had to make was to accept the ruling and resign.

YOUR BIOGRAPHER SAYS THAT YOU DISPLAYED AN AMBIVALENT ATTITUDE TOWARD THE CATHOLIC CHURCH. DO YOU SEE, EXCUSE THE EXPRESSION, ANY REDEEMING FEATURES IN CATHOLICISM OR IN RELIGION IN GENERAL?

I was very impressed by [a folk mass I attended some years ago]. Because the general line of the bishop in his speech was sharing, that it was concern for other people that mattered most. One of the songs that little girl sang was lovely. God loved little children. Black, red, white, yellow, and so on. There's so little between my own socialism and what they were talking about. But the practice, you know, is different. Seven percent of the people here own 75 percent of the wealth. Still, it is an infinitely better sort of Christianity than the dreadful stuff one listened to about the blood sacrifice and the macabre interpretation of the crucifixion. But, on balance, I think that religion has done more harm than good. I don't care what religion you are talking about.

ARE YOU A CELTIC DON QUIXOTE? WAS YOUR LIFE ONE LONG TRAIL OF WINDMILLS AND BROKEN LANCES?

I've always tried to take up a position slightly in advance of the public without ever losing contact with them and always draw them a little bit farther. As soon as they took up that [issue], I'd move on to the next position. Take contraception. I didn't really bother with that [after a while]. I moved on to homosexuality, abortion, and so on. Way back, it was a fierce thing to talk about wanting a welfare state, to be a liberal or a socialist. You

couldn't be a Marxist. By having the welfare state accepted, I go on to revolutionary changes, [working for] a completely different distribution of
the wealth. That was the only function I thought I could serve.

WHAT DO YOU MAKE OF IRISH SOCIETY, THE BALLYHOOED "CELTIC
TIGER," TODAY?

One thing I noticed when I worked in Ballymun is that they have left the
very repressive but at the same time sheltering cocoon of religion that told
them what they should and shouldn't do and aided and consoled them in
its own particular way.[4] Many of them have lost contact with this religion,
with the extended family, and are facing the appalling demands of young
married life in these high-rise flats under pressures to which no one in my
opinion should be subjected. We haven't replaced the guidelines of the
Church, of the old parents. That's gone. There is no active alternative culture being provided in the form, say, of a socialist community concern.

WE SEE FORMER IRISH PRIME MINISTER CHARLES HAUGHEY'S HIJINKS EX-
POSED TODAY, AND COUNTLESS OTHER MONEY SCANDALS SURFACING TOO.[5]

Politics in Ireland is at a very primitive level of development. The
politician is a figure of fun, really. He's meant to be a self-seeking, self-
centered person who certainly does not want to change society in any
radical way. So there's no alternative.

WHAT OF YOUR BIOGRAPHER ALLEGING THAT YOUR SELF-ASSESSMENT
WAS AS A TRAGIC HERO? DO YOU FEEL REJECTED, OR LET DOWN, BY THE
IRISH PEOPLE?

They've been wonderfully loyal to me all through my political life.
Obviously, it was the job of my political opponents to do what they could
to damage me. I'm not complaining about that. But I was misrepre-
sented. Think of the unfortunate person who was listening to these
things about me. I was defeated a couple of times in elections. At the
same time, despite the confused picture they must have of me, they've
been wonderful. They've always given me support, even though they
know that I'm very antiestablishment. Conflict with the Church. Conflict with the doctors. Conflict with everybody in accepted society.
   I had a very quick education in that first coalition. The education was
that unless you have money, you are wasting your time in the Cabinet in
this kind of society. So thereafter I never had the slightest wish to be

cabinet member in any subsequent government. My job I considered to be one of an educator, a propagandist, and, to a certain extent, an agitator. I have tried to use Parliament for that purpose, to try and put forward a socialist idea on every issue. Now, looking back on my life, I don't think I could have done anything else, do you? I don't think you could say at any time that you could have turned your back on it.

Suddenly this pensive specter, who for so long had haunted a Celtic chunk of Europe and afflicted the comatosely comfortable groups within it, winked and withdrew—returning to the yellowing May 1978 issue of the *Journal of Irish Literature*, where this interview first saw light of day. Since Browne's death, the situation in Ireland between the Catholic hierarchy, public opinion, and the state has undergone a profound change, caused by the misbehavior of certain men of the cloth with regard to children (and, in one case, a divorcee) and the attempted suppression of these scandals. It's just not the same country anymore, except for the usual widening disparity between rich and poor, despite all the celebrated economic growth.

NOTES

1. In the late 1940s, Clann na Poblachta was a rapidly growing insurgent party whose inner circle was made up mostly of left-wing Republicans who were discontented with Fianna Fail Party rule under Eamon de Valera. In 1948, the clan leader Sean MacBride opted to ally with the conservative Fine Gael Party to form a coalition government to end sixteen consecutive years of Fianna Fail power. MacBride became foreign minister and Browne became minister of health.

2. The Irish Republican Congress was an attempt in 1934 by politically radical members of the Irish Republican Army to redirect its organizational sights to a democratic socialist agenda of reform, North and South, running parallel to James Connolly's aim to establish a workers' republic. Connolly was one of the leaders of the 1916 Easter Rebellion and was executed by the British.

3. Sean MacBride, son of Yeats's utterly elusive object of desire, Maud Gonne, was a former chief-of-staff of the IRA who later would be awarded both the Lenin Prize and the Nobel Peace Prize.

4. A congested working-class housing district in North Dublin.

5. Charles J. Haughey of the Fianna Fail Party was twice prime minister of the Irish Republic. In the 1990s, he became deeply embroiled in court cases with regard his alleged corruption, especially the whopping mismatch between his legitimate traceable income and his wealth.

8

BIANCA JAGGER

human rights activist

Bianca Jagger is a prominent advocate for human rights, social justice, and environmental protection in a wide variety of threatened locales. Born in Nicaragua, she studied political science in Paris, married and divorced Mick Jagger, and became deeply involved in upheavals across Latin America. From the late 1970s onward, she worked unstintingly with humanitarian organizations such as Amnesty International, Human Rights Watch, and the Washington Office for Latin America. Among other honors, Ms. Jagger received the 1994 United Nations Earth Day Award, the 1997 Green Globe Award from the Rainforest Alliance for her efforts on behalf of saving tropical rain forests and securing the rights of indigenous peoples, and the Abolitionist of the Year Award from the National Coalition to Abolish the Death Penalty.

Ms. Jagger has also spent a great deal of time and energy in the embattled Balkans and in AIDS-afflicted Africa. She visited Baghdad in January 2003 together with a peace delegation of American academics and was a strong antiwar voice in the run-up to the Anglo-American invasion. She is a member of the Executive Director's Leadership Council for Amnesty International, the Advisory Committee of Human Rights Watch/America, the Advisory Board of the Coalition for International Justice, and the Twentieth Century Task Force to Apprehend War Criminals. She is also a member of the board for People for the American Way and the Creative Coalition and a special advisor to Indigenous

Development International at Cambridge University. The interview was
conducted in September 2003.

YOU WERE BORN IN NICARAGUA, WHICH HISTORICALLY HAS BEEN A VERY
TENSE AND TROUBLED PLACE. DOES POLITICS RUN IN YOUR FAMILY?

My father was a businessman and he was not political. My mother was
a housewife and she was very political. There is no question that her
views influenced my vision of the world when I was an adolescent—she
was a staunch opponent of the Somoza regime. After I left Nicaragua to
study in France, she actively opposed the regime during the insurrection. Later on she became disillusioned with the Sandinistas and left
Nicaragua to live with us.

WOULD YOU CALL WHAT YOU HAD A PRIVILEGED UPBRINGING?

During the first ten years of my life, while my parents were married,
I enjoyed a privileged upbringing. After their divorce, my mother found
herself single, without a profession, and with three small children to
care for. In the Nicaragua of the 1960s, life was difficult for a working
divorced woman. It was then that I learned the meaning of discrimina-
tion. It was a traumatizing experience. She had to work in order to keep
us in the same Catholic school we were attending, because the child
support she was receiving was insufficient.

WERE YOU POLITICALLY AWARE IN YOUR YOUTH?

Yes, very much so. In the 1960s, before I left Nicaragua, I participated
in student demonstrations against the Somoza regime to protest against
the student massacres perpetrated by Somoza's National Guard. We were
tear-gassed and took refuge in a church. My father had to rescue me.

YOU WON A UNIVERSITY SCHOLARSHIP IN PARIS. WHY POLITICAL SCI-
ENCE?

I wanted to have a political career and I thought studying political science would be the best way to achieve it. I didn't want to face my
mother's fate—to be discriminated against because of my gender and
status. I promised myself I was never going to be treated as a second-
class citizen.

WHAT IMPACT DID PARIS HAVE ON YOUR VIEW OF THE WORLD?

I was avid to learn, to discover a new world, a new culture and wanted to escape the narrow perceptions of the women of the Nicaragua of the 1960s. I cherished French literature, and the first book I read in French was *L'étranger* by Albert Camus, which had a profound influence on my adolescent life. In Nicaragua, liberty, equality, and the rule of law were the stuff of dreams. But in Paris I discovered the value of those words, their precious meaning. I arrived in Paris on Bastille Day, July 14th, in the mid-1960s, a very significant time. I will say that I am closer to a European viewpoint of the world than an American one. I mean, my ethics and ideals are based on European concepts. At the same time, my links to Latin America and the developing world are very strong. My umbilical cord was never cut. I feel great identification with the developing world.

WHO WERE THE MAIN INFLUENCES ON YOU THERE?

Philosophers from the eighteenth century like Voltaire and Rousseau. Later on, Gandhi became my role model. I have always been interested in Eastern philosophy. Since early in my life, I've been fascinated by India, and I have spent a great deal of time traveling in that country. The more I know about Gandhi, the more I [value] his success through his power of persuasion by nonviolent action. There was so much he was able to achieve. But today when we think about terrorism—we talk a lot about terrorism but rarely talk about state terrorism—we sometimes see how state terror can drive people to terrorism, but it still would be important to highlight the achievements of Gandhian nonviolence.

THE USUAL OBJECTION IS THAT GANDHI WOULDN'T HAVE DONE SO WELL AGAINST THE SS AS HE DID AGAINST THE BRITISH.

I ask myself the question, "Would it be possible to achieve success if you adopt a Gandhi attitude to state terror? Would that really be successful when confronting the imperialistic and ruthless tactics of the Bush administration, who have absolutely no regard for the international rule of law and human rights? Are they capable of being persuaded?" I don't know.

YOU MET MICK JAGGER AND MARRIED HIM IN 1971. WERE YOU POLITICALLY ACTIVE DURING THAT PERIOD?

Was I as politically active as I was before and after my marriage? Perhaps not. What I can say is that it was a much-politicized period of my
life. I don't think there was really a time when I was not politically
aware. I inevitably became concerned with women's rights.

SO YOU RETURNED TO NICARAGUA IN 1972 AFTER THE EARTHQUAKE?

In 1972, on Christmas Eve, we were having dinner in our house in
London. The television was on in the next room. Suddenly I heard the
announcement that there had been a devastating earthquake in
Nicaragua. I rushed to see the news. I tried to contact my parents and
couldn't reach them. All flights were suspended. So we decided to fly to
Jamaica the following day, and from there we took a shipment of medicine in a small charter plane into Managua Airport. When we landed,
the airport was partially destroyed and was shut down. There were no
immigration authorities in view and there were hundreds of boxes scattered in the airport. The airport and surrounding area was teeming with
National Guard. They were making sure the supplies went to the government warehouses. Not far from the airport there were hundreds of
people pleading with the guards in front of the warehouses to let them
have access to food and water. It became apparent to me from the moment we landed that the aid that was pouring in from the United States
and other nations was not going to the intended victims. Only Somoza
and his cronies had access to it. People had to put red flags on their
doors to proclaim that they were supporters of Somoza in order to get
access to food and water. I was anxious to find my parents. Fortunately,
I found a British journalist to help us go through the city of Managua. I
still remember the stench of burned flesh. There were many fires still
burning, and I couldn't find my parents. It was a very upsetting experience. During that period, I witnessed the outrageous mismanagement
of the aid. Three days later I finally found my parents in León. I came
back to the United States and I urged Mick and the Stones to do a relief concert to raise funds for the victims. They raised $280,000. So I
went back to Nicaragua with the intention of building a small clinic with
the relief. The Somoza regime did everything not to allow that to happen. In fact, we had a meeting with Hope Somoza. Mick was present at
that meeting. There, Mrs. Somoza said, "I am in the process of building
a children's hospital and we would be delighted if you would donate the
money to help with the construction." I said, "Unfortunately, the money
raised is American tax-exempt money and we are obligated to the Amer-

ican people to make sure the earthquake relief will get to the intended recipients. I don't think they will be satisfied if we gave the donation to your government." Mrs. Somoza wasn't very pleased, and after that meeting I became persona non grata in Nicaragua. She was head of social security and consequently had some measure of control over doctors. Most of the doctors I tried to secure to help with the clinic were apprehensive because she had taken my rebuff personally. In the end, that clinic turned out to be an impossible task. So we donated the funds to a Nicaraguan foundation to build homes for earthquake victims. For many years I was afraid to go back to Nicaragua.

THE SANDINISTAS WERE TAKING POWER, OR ABOUT TO TAKE POWER, IN 1979. IS THAT WHY YOU WENT?

The victory of the Sandinista revolution coincided with the end of my marriage. Sometime in the spring of 1979, the British Red Cross asked me to help them spearhead a fund-raising campaign for the victims of the war in Nicaragua, After I was done helping them, I went to Nicaragua with an International Red Cross delegation to visit victims of the war and political prisoners. It was toward the end of the Somoza regime. I saw first-hand evidence of the brutality and oppression carried out by the Somoza regime against my countrypeople. It was a turning point in my life. It began my commitment to justice and human rights issues.

WHAT DID YOU MAKE OF THE SANDINISTAS?

The Sandinista revolution was without any question a popular insurrection. I think the difference between El Salvador and Nicaragua is that in Nicaragua you had a popular insurrection and in El Salvador you had a revolution. The revolution in Nicaragua began to take place only after the Sandinistas overthrew Somoza. There is a question for which we will never know the answer: Had the United States not launched the Contra War to overthrow the Sandinista government, would [the Sandinistas] have succeeded in bringing socioeconomic justice to the people of Nicaragua? Would they have succeeded in generating prosperity? Or would they have failed even without a U.S. intervention? We will never know. I think that for the U.S. government, the Sandinistas represented a threat to their dominance of Latin America. First you had the Cuban revolution. The Sandinista revolution represented a further threat to their economic monopoly in the region. U.S. government officials always invoked the domino theory. They feared that if the Sandinistas succeeded, that what happened in Nicaragua would [spread to] other countries and shake the economic dominance that America enjoyed.

You also were critical of some Sandinista policies.

At first I supported the revolution, like millions of people throughout the world. However, I became disillusioned after a while. In the end, some of the leaders betrayed the very principles for which they fought the revolution. It was a great missed opportunity.

Chomsky observes that a counterrevolution always forces the revolutionary regime to become authoritarian—works like a charm.

Not only did they force them to become authoritarian, but they were forced to invest a disproportionate amount of their budget on military spending instead of focusing on what they initially tried to do, which was invest in education, eradicate illiteracy, reform health care, and improve the economy. The Sandinista government became consumed with fighting a war of survival. They were up against the biggest superpower in the world. I think it is important to point out that the U.S. embargo imposed on Nicaragua, rather than weakening the Sandinistas, actually maintained them in power. It was only when the embargo was lifted that the Sandinistas were voted out of power. When the U.S. government imposes these immoral and counterproductive embargos and sanctions, the people rally to support their government even when they otherwise oppose it, because they consider their sovereignty to be under threat. Those who suffer are not those at the top but the less-privileged members of society. I saw the same mistakes in Iraq, where the sanctions were even more inhumane and cruel. I saw the appalling effects of two wars, twelve years of UN Security Council sanctions and the food-for-oil program. Today, people in the United States fail to understand the Iraqis' resentment and hostility toward them. It is very much based on the sanctions, which affected millions of innocent Iraqis. As a consequence, hundreds of thousands of children died. The Iraqis never forgot Madeleine Albright's statement that it was worth the lives of half a million children. When I left Iraq [in January 2003], I was convinced that Americans would not be regarded as liberators but as occupiers and that the Iraqis would profoundly resent the occupation.

How did the Sandinistas go wrong?

When a government has to face a situation like you had in Nicaragua, they become isolated. I often traveled to Nicaragua to speak against repressive policies by the Sandinista government, such as the imprisonment of members of COSEP [members of the private sector who publicly opposed their policies] and their attacks on the press, particularly the closing of *La Prensa*. Some members of the National Directorate regarded me with suspicion, notwithstanding my vocal opposition to the Contra War in the United States, because I spoke against those policies. When you have an embargo and a Contra War, you put moderate voices in an untenable position. I could not allow the Reagan and Bush [senior] administrations to use me as a tool. They offered me residency in the United States if I was prepared to apply as an exile. Of course I declined. If I had accepted, I would have become the most prominent Contra.

I could bring my criticisms to the Sandinistas, but I could not use the criticism to fuel the actions of the Contra revolution. I know there were a lot of other people in my situation who disagreed with some of the policies of the Sandinistas, but at the same time they couldn't let themselves be manipulated by imperialistic forces. I was distrusted by some of the Sandinista leaders because I spoke plainly to them about their mistakes, I was trying to make them see what the stakes were. The Sandinista government couldn't deal with criticisms. In the last years, they were incapable of accepting even constructive criticism and that contributed to their failure.

VERY SAD. DIDN'T YOU HAVE AN ESPECIALLY DRAMATIC EXPERIENCE IN HONDURAS IN 1981?

In 1981, I was asked to visit a refugee camp in Honduran territory. At the time, the U.S. government was providing economic and military aid to a Salvador government that was engaged [as the saying goes] in killing its own people. They were bombing wide areas of Morazán in the northern countryside. People were trying to cross the border to reach Honduras. A river divides the border between El Salvador and Honduras, and many drowned attempting to cross it. Thousands of people came to Honduras seeking refuge, and the UN set up refugee camps all along the border. I traveled to Honduras as part of a fact-finding mission with a U.S. congressional staff. Salvadoran death squads and the Salvadoran army were crossing the border with the Honduran army's blessing, entering the refugee camp, abducting young male refugees, taking them

back to El Salvador to be killed. I traveled to Colomoncagua, situated in
quite a remote area, quite an inaccessible area in the mountains [about
20 kilometers from the Salvadoran border] with a five-person delegation. When I arrived, I first went to the village. A few minutes later, I
was urgently called back because the death squads had entered the
refugee camp. I rushed back and saw approximately thirty-five death
squad members, some wearing military clothes and all of them carrying
M16s and wearing bandannas. They had tied thirty to forty male
refugees by their thumbs and started marching them out of the camp.
We, the members of the delegation and the relief workers, had only a
few minutes to make up our minds. We had nothing to defend ourselves
with. We decided to run behind them. Along with us came the mothers,
wives, and the children of these refugees. We ran along a dry river bed
for about half an hour. Some of us had cameras, and we were screaming
that we had evidence that we were going to present to the world. At one
point, we got close to them, and the death squad members turned
around and pointed their M16s [at us]. They were near enough for us to
hear them [swearing] "*Estos hijos de puta ya nos estan controlando*
[These sons of bitches are going to catch us]." They pointed their guns
at us, and we yelled that they would have to kill us all. They talked
among themselves. At that moment, I thought we would be killed. A few
seconds later, which seemed like hours, they turned around and let
everyone go. I realized how a small act of courage can save lives. The
mere fact of an American being present, or someone perceived to be an
American, could help save the lives of innocent people. That's why I believe in the importance of bearing witness, to become a voice for the
voiceless.

WAS THAT THE END OF THE EPISODE?

When I came back to Colomoncagua, the press was saying I had been
killed along with everyone else. We went back to the capital, where a
very strange incident occurred. When I first arrived in Honduras, I was
a day later than the rest of the delegation. There was no room in their
hotel, and I had to go another one. After we returned to Tegucigalpa, we
first went to my friend's hotel and I waited in the car. At the reception
desk, members of the Honduran Army were looking for me, and since
they didn't believe the hotel receptionist, they proceeded to look though
the guest book. As soon as they left, we made calls to the American and
the British embassies to ask them to meet us at the Honduran airport.

There, the Honduran Army general said that they wanted to interrogate me and didn't want me to leave. So both the U.S. and U.K. representatives objected that they didn't understand why I was prevented from leaving if the other members on the delegation were allowed to go. The other delegation members said that they were not going to leave unless I could leave with them. The Americans stressed to them that it wouldn't be a good public-relations move to hold me for questioning. They finally let me go.

When I arrived in Washington, I was invited to testify before the Congressional Subcommittee on Inter-American Affairs. At the hearing, I spoke about the dangers of widening, of regionalizing, the conflict. At the time, there weren't many people talking about collaboration between the Honduran and Salvadoran armies and the role the Honduran Army was playing in the Contra War in Nicaragua. Many eyebrows were raised in Washington at my statement. However, what I said turned out to be a sad fact in the tragic history of Central America. That began my fact-finding missions, from Honduras to Guatemala to remote rain forests in Brazil to Bosnia, Kosovo, Zambia, Afghanistan, Iraq, Pakistan, and many others.

DID YOU EVER FIND YOURSELF HARASSED IN THE UNITED STATES BY OFFICIALS FOR YOUR ACTIVITIES?

No, I must say no.

ANY OTHER NOTABLE EVENTS IN CENTRAL AMERICA BEFORE I MOVE YOU TO YUGOSLAVIA?

There is an important incident. In the early 1990s, I wrote an op-ed for the *New York Times* about a logging concession Mrs. Chamorro's government was granting to a Taiwanese company. Her government was selling, I think, 280,000 hectares of land. I discovered that Somoza had started it and Antonio Lacayo, Mrs. Chamorro's son-in law, and Pedro Juaquin Chamorro, director of *La Prensa* and a former member of La Contra, became involved in this scheme. I was surprised to discover that General Humberto Ortega, head of the army and an archenemy of Lacayo and Chamorro, also became involved in this shady deal to sell out the territory of Nicaraguan Miskitos. It took me a while to get hold of the contract. I was finally able to break the deal by launching a campaign to inform the international community and foreign-country donors concerned with environmental issues. I found the contract and had it translated and analyzed by an American environmental law professor. I brought it to Congress and launched a campaign of faxes [and e-mails] to Mrs. Chamorro and General Ortega. I lobbied House members in the Appropriations Committee of Congress to stop the aid the U.S. government was going to give to Nicaragua if they went ahead with the deal. There is a clause that stipulates that aid from the United States to developing nations can only be given to nations that pursue sustainable development policies. That enabled members of Congress to threaten to stop the aid.

THE TREATMENT OF THE MISKITOS WAS A GREAT PROPAGANDA PLOY FOR THE UNITED STATES AGAINST THE SANDINISTAS AT THE TIME. DO YOU THINK THERE WAS MISTREATMENT?

The Miskitos have been mistreated by every government in Nicaragua and not just by the Sandinistas. Most governments in Latin America have failed to recognize the rights of indigenous people and their right to their cultures and traditional territories. So although the issue was exploited and exaggerated, the Sandinistas engaged in serious abuses against the Miskito.

DID YOU HAVE MORE SUCCESS IN NORTHEASTERN BRAZIL DEFENDING THE YANOMAMI TRIBE AGAINST THE INVASION OF GOLD-MINERS?

We had only a measure of success in Brazil with our work to demarcate the ancestral lands of the Yanomami people, but their struggle continues. I am concerned at present by a project in Peru called the Camisea Gas Project, which is being developed by five oil companies and has all the makings of a potential disaster. The Inter-American Development Bank [IADB] just approved a loan. After the devastation left behind by Chevron-Texaco in the Ecuadorian Amazon, the Camisea project is set to destroy invaluable rain forests in the heart of the Peruvian Amazon, which contains precious biodiversity, and it will affect the lives of remote and vulnerable indigenous people. This area in Peru has a reserve comparable to that of the Galapagos, and there are plans to build a plant thirty kilometers away to refine gas. Halliburton will be building the plant to liquefy the gas that will be exported to the United States The U.S. abstained from voting at the Inter-American Development Bank because they knew that the political price for voting yes would have focused attention on the connection between George W. Bush's administration and Halliburton and Hunt Oil. Both companies are closely connected to George W. Bush and Dick Cheney. Hunt Oil was one of the biggest financial supporters of George W. Bush, and Dick Cheney was the CEO of Halliburton. I've been told that Vice President Cheney was lobbying for the Camisea project to go through.

HOW DO YOU GET PAST YOUR CELEBRITYHOOD IN GETTING PEOPLE TO LISTEN TO YOU?

Early on when I began my humanitarian work, I understood that in order to gain credibility, I needed patience, commitment, and unwavering perseverance. And I needed to ignore the skeptics. I thought there would come a time when they couldn't deny my accomplishments. I find it disturbing that the media keeps referring to my marriage, since I got divorced in 1979. But the media never wants to let me forget. A man who gets divorced is not forever going to be talked about for it. There are very different standards that we have for women than we have for men.

YOU MAKE APPEARANCES ON MASS MEDIA STATIONS? HOW ARE YOU TREATED AND HOW DO YOU HANDLE THE FLAK FROM THE RIGHT?

I will gladly do debates on television versus doing written interviews because live interviews are more difficult to distort. When I do political debates, I find it challenging but interesting. It doesn't matter to me if my opponents have totally different views, I can deal with it. What I find hard to deal with are journalists that misrepresent or distort my words.

ARE THERE ANY DIFFERENCES IN HOW YOU ARE TREATED BY INTERVIEWERS? WOLF BLITZER, FOR EXAMPLE, VERSUS BILL O'REILLY?

I've enjoyed doing Wolf Blitzer's program, and I even enjoyed having a heated debate with Bill O'Reilly. I will do it any time. I must tell you that just as I don't believe in lobbying only progressives and liberal members of Congress, I don't believe in doing interviews only with those who share my views. I want to reach a wider audience.

HOW DID YOU GET INVOLVED IN THE NEW BALKAN WARS? AND WHAT DID YOU EXPERIENCE?

I first arrived in Bosnia in 1993 to document the mass rape of women in the former Yugoslavia. I had been asked to testify before the Helsinki Commission in the U.S. Congress. During my visit to Bosnia and Croatia, I traveled with UN personnel and I listened to hundreds of shocking testimonies of women who were used as tools of war. I visited refugee camps in both countries. I learned about the horrific conditions people in Srebrenica were living under. That year a UN Security Council resolution had declared the enclave a "safe area," guaranteeing protection by all means necessary and demanding that all military or paramilitary units withdraw from the demilitarized zone or surrender their arms. In February 1995, Srebrenica was placed under the care of a Dutch battalion operating under the UN. Instead of a "safe area," the people in Srebrenica lived under relentless shelling; it became a nightmare zone teeming with refugees, many living on the street. For two years, the Serbs blocked most United Nations convoys to Srebrenica, cutting off food, medical supplies, and clothing. They even confiscated cooking salt from United Nations convoys, replacing it with industrial salt to poison the townspeople.

In July 1995, Srebrenica was overrun by Bosnian Serb troops. Eight thousand civilians, literally the entire male population, were systematically massacred in cold blood in four days—delivered to their executioners by the international community. It was the worst massacre on European soil since the Third Reich. The title "safe area" became an obscenity. It was a legitimized concentration camp. The international community was aware that the Serbs were preparing the extermination of Srebrenica. There was only one voice that refused to be an accomplice to the cover-up: Thaddeus Mazowiecki, former prime minister of Poland, who was the United Nations envoy for human rights. General Ratko Mladic and Radovan Karadzic have been indicted but have never been arrested. Is it because they know too much about the cover-up of the international community and the UN? There were consistent lies, duplicity, cowardice, intrigue, appeasement, and deals like General Janvier's deal at Zvornik. The international community wants to forget Srebrenica and is reluctant to apprehend the war criminals. It knows that to bring to trial those responsible for the massacres will highlight its own liabilities. Governments are mandated by international law to protect people from genocide. The Clinton administration always insisted that they were unaware at the time that tens of thousands were being massacred in cold blood. However, only a few days after the fall of Srebrenica, the United States reportedly presented to the Security Council satellite photographs of men kneeling on the soccer fields before they were killed and of mass graves where they were buried. Human rights organizations have requested those photographs under the Freedom of Information Act and the U.S. government refused to hand the photographs over. One of the shocking aspects of the Srebrenica genocide is that it occurred against a background of warnings and intelligence updates.

HAVE ANY GOVERNMENTS BEHAVED ANY BETTER?

The only government that has done a thorough investigation, and admitted wrongdoing, has been the Dutch. A minister had to resign recently because of the shameful role the Dutch played in the fall of Srebrenica. The French have continued to try to cover up. An investigation took place in the national assembly to find out whether General Bernard Janvier, commander of UNPROFOR in Srebrenica, had struck a deal with Bosnian Serb general [Ratko] Mladic. It is believed that in exchange for the release of 450 French soldiers that had been taken hostage and a promise not to shoot at UN troops, General Janvier promised he would not call for air strikes against the Bosnian Serbs—a promise that is believed to have given the green light for the Bosnian Serbs to go ahead in Srebrenica. Eight thousand Bosnian males, almost the entire male population, were killed. The massacre and subsequent cover-up has probably been the most shameful passage in European history since the Holocaust.

WHAT DID YOU DO ABOUT IT?

For many years, I lobbied UN Secretary-General Kofi Annan and various UN under-secretaries to establish a commission of inquiry to investigate Srebrenica and determine whether UN personnel should be held accountable for crimes against humanity. When that failed, I began to urge members of the General Assembly to pass a resolution urging the Secretary-General to establish a commission of inquiry. I went to the General Assembly because I knew it would never be approved in the Security Council, because most of the members were involved in the cover-up. When a number of states agreed to support the effort, I was told that Bosnia needed to make the official request. I went to see the Bosnian ambassador to ask if he was prepared to make the request. He said, "It will cost me my job, it may ruin my career, but I will do it." He did it, and to my great surprise, in November 1998 the resolution passed by consensus, and today he is in jail in the United States Once the resolution was approved, Kofi Annan had two options: one, to call for an independent commission of inquiry by a panel of independent experts, or two, to call for a UN internal commission of inquiry. He did the second. He appointed two people to prepare the report. When the report was ready to be published, I got a call from one of the two people involved. He told me that the UN wanted to scratch the report or do a whitewash. In the end, all the names were taken out of the report. The irony is that Kofi Annan took credit for the report, although for years he was adamant against calling for an investigation or establishing a commission of inquiry. When the report was published, he gave the impression that the report was done under his initiative because of his commitment to reform the UN. Furthermore, he gave the appearance that the UN was prepared to admit mistakes when what he did was to eliminate names from the report in order to make those guilty of collaboration with the culprits immune from prosecution. I believe that the people in Srebrenica need to know and have the right to know what happened and who the culprits are and why the international community failed them, allowing this terrible genocide to happen. We need to know in order to prevent it from ever happening again.

SO DID YOU FIND YOURSELF ON THE SIDE OF THE NATO BOMBING IN 1995 AND AGAIN IN 1999?

I was against bombing Serbia. I called for the use of ground troops. I must add to that that if the international community had responded to earlier signs that genocidal activities were under way in Bosnia and later Kosovo, there wouldn't have been the need for military intervention. What are we human rights campaigners supposed to do in the face of genocide? The international community simply procrastinated, pretended it was not happening, turned their backs and closed their eyes in the face of the atrocities. There was a big debate among human rights organizations, who until then believed that their role was to monitor human rights violations. The question was whether they should continue to monitor atrocities and count the bodies or should they call for intervention? I felt that one simply cannot watch genocide unfold without calling for intervention. But I am against indiscriminate bombing. The bombing of Serbia was wrong; the killing of innocent people is always wrong.

IN IRAQ IN JANUARY 2003, YOU WERE IN THE DELICATE POSITION OF OPPOSING AN INVASION OF IRAQ WHILE ALSO TRYING NOT TO PRESENT YOURSELF AS A PROP FOR THE SADDAM HUSSEIN REGIME. THAT WAS A PRECARIOUS TIGHTROPE WALK. HOW DID YOU FEEL WHILE DOING IT?

I felt it was important for those who opposed the war not to accept the status quo. I believed we needed to put pressure on Saddam Hussein. I urged the Iraqi government to pass a law allowing political pluralism. I called for freedom of expression and dissent, for a proactive approach with regard to weapons inspection and for allowing opposition factions like the Kurds, Shias, and others to participate in new UN-supervised parliamentary elections. I made that clear in meetings I held with Iraqi officials, such as the Foreign Minister [Nagi Sabri], member of the Regional Command Council [Hoda Ammash], Speaker of the House [Saadoon Hammadi], and Minister of Health [Omeid M.

Mebarak]. I brought a request from Amnesty International to allow human rights monitors inside Iraq. I said, "I am here to oppose the war. However, I am here to urge you to start a process of democratization. Your government needs to engage in significant changes if you want to avoid the war." I was very conscious from the moment I landed that I was facing the danger of being used by the Iraqi government. I informed them that I was not going to talk to the Iraqi media and would do no interviews. I urged them not to try to use me as a propaganda tool.

IT'S VERY TRICKY, ISN'T IT?

Definitely. I am always conscious of that. During the Contra War in Nicaragua, I found myself in a very difficult position. On one hand, I publicly opposed the Contra War, and on the other, I wanted the Sandinistas to know that I opposed their crackdown on freedom of the press and on freedom of expression. I walked a very difficult and fine line. In Nicaragua, campesinos found themselves caught between both sides. I understood that many joined the Contras because they were upset by mistaken policies of the Sandinistas. You had innocent people on both sides that were used as tools in the war. I went back to Nicaragua and spoke on behalf of the Contras for redistribution of land, and I spoke for them when the United States tried to force them out after they had incited them to leave the country to fight against the Sandinistas. When they were of no use anymore, the U.S. government wanted to repatriate them to Nicaragua.

WEREN'T THE CONTRAS JUST A BIT BEWILDERED TO HAVE YOU AS THEIR ADVOCATE?

Maybe some were, but others accepted me. I have always been willing to admit when I make a mistake. I made a mistake in my understanding of the composition of the Contras, not in my opposition to the Contra War. I went back to Nicaragua to film a documentary just after the Sandinista defeat in the elections against Violeta Chamorro, during the repatriation and disarmament of the Contras. I came to the sad realization that many Nicaraguans who died in the war on both sides, particularly among the campesinos, had been tools of either the United States and Contra leaders or leaders of the Sandinista government. I am still profoundly troubled by the war in Nicaragua. The United States, a superpower, launched a covert war against another nation in violation of international law, a war that was wrong and immoral.

BUSH RAMPAGED RIGHT INTO IRAQ DESPITE MASSIVE INTERNATIONAL
OPPOSITION AND IS NOW CAUGHT IN A VERY DIRTY WAR.

Why was this war so wrong? The war in Iraq was not about weapons of
mass destruction, not about noncompliance with weapons inspectors, not
about the connection between Saddam Hussein and September 11th, and
certainly not about the liberation of the Iraqi people. It was about oil and
world dominance. George W. Bush and Tony Blair had to convince the
world that Hussein represented an imminent threat. That is why Tony
Blair lied when he claimed in the September 2003 dossier that Iraq could
launch a chemical or biological attack within forty-five minutes. And
George W. Bush lied when he mentioned the Iraq-Niger uranium connection. What he failed to say is that the British were relying on their intelligence white paper based on the same false information that Joseph
Wilson [former ambassador to Niger] had already refuted. The [Interna-
tional Atomic Energy Agency's] Mohamed ElBaradei told the UN Security Council that the allegations were unfounded and a crude forgery. Despite this, Bush and his administration claimed that they had proof that
Saddam Hussein was reconstituting his weapons program when clearly
they did not. Since by now it is evident that there were no WMD, George
W. Bush and Tony Bush are desperately trying to find new arguments for
going to war in Iraq. I was surprised to read in an interview of Paul Wolfowitz that he said that the decision to highlight weapons of mass destruction as the main reason for invading Iraq was only a "bureaucratic"
choice. For George W. Bush to invoke human rights as a justification for
war is cynical, opportunistic, and laughable. When he appeared shocked
by crimes by Saddam Hussein against the Kurds and Iranians, he failed to
tell us that when those crimes were committed during the eighties, the
U.S. and the U.K. supported Saddam Hussein and were selling the
weapons that gave him the ability to annihilate them. There is that famous
photograph of Rumsfeld shaking hands with Saddam Hussein in [1983].
Bush and Blair combined their efforts to deceive both nations, both peoples, in a carefully coordinated manner, more so than anyone is willing to
point out in the media. Did Tony Blair release his famous dossier to support George W. Bush when he was going through a thorny patch? The
media in the United States let Bush and his administration get away with
lies and deceptions. The bottom line is that the decision to overthrow Saddam Hussein was clearly defined in the documents published in 1997 by
a small clique of neoconservatives, members of a think tank, the Project
for a New American Century. The members of this cabal are now in the

inner circles in the Bush administration [Dick Cheney, Donald Rumsfeld, Richard Perle, Paul Wolfowitz, Douglas Feith, Lewis Libby, Elliot Abrams, Jeb Bush, and many others]. The project was concerned with world dominance and particularly with getting hold of Middle East oil. For someone born in Nicaragua who has seen the U.S. government at work overthrowing governments in Latin America, now I see a similar pattern of deceptions used by George W. Bush to overthrow Saddam Hussein. Bush invoked the threat to national security and WMD. The only difference between now and then is that now the threat is terrorism instead of communism. The media continue to accept some of these arguments [and the concept of preemptive strikes appears to have become an acceptable argument to attack another state].

How do you see the Iraqi situation playing out?

In order to try to salvage this experiment, George W. Bush will have to come to the UN and admit that he was wrong, which he has not done.

Now that would be a sight.

There is a need for some admission of wrongdoing. What I cannot understand is why George W. Bush and his administration are not being more pragmatic in their approach to what's happening in Iraq. It's not a question of whether he likes or dislikes the UN or whether the UN is a perfect institution. His political future is at stake unless he's prepared to admit that he was wrong in going to war against Iraq in violation of international law and the UN Charter. The only hope we have for the experiment in Iraq to succeed is for the UN to be in charge of nation-building.

Do you ever feel that you perhaps have dispersed your energies among too many causes—AIDS, the death penalty, and so on?

The work that I do is all related to issues of social and economic justice. It might not seem so to an outsider, but they are all intricately connected. It's all to do with issues of justice: the debate between developed nations and developing world, the oppressed and the oppressors, crimes committed by Chevron-Texaco against indigenous populations in the Ecuadorian Amazon, or speaking about AIDS, the massacre in Srebrenica, the war in Iraq, inequalities of resources, or the death penalty. I am always talking about justice.

(9)

MARCEL OPHULS

documentary filmmaker

Marcel Ophuls really would rather be making musicals. "People always laugh when I say that. But people are quite wrong who think they can patronize *Top Hat* or Fred Astaire or the people who made it." He protests that he never craved the role of Minicam-toting conscience. After all, the pay is lousy, the hours are infinite, and one never runs out of injustices or the multitudes of small complicities that enable those injustices to take root. Officially sanctioned injustice is his lifelong topic; exposing complicity in all its forms is his métier.

Ophuls has been likened to TV's Columbo, a sly rumpled detective who deftly succeeds through deceptively simple queries to pin his smug prey squirming to the nearest wall. No one can surpass him at peeling away the protective devices by which hideous behavior is rationalized by criminals, collaborators, and cowed people who are only being "realistic" by adjusting to thuggish regimes. Dissecting the reasons why people shut their eyes to historical horrors—from the deportation of Jews in occupied France to ethnic cleansing in Bosnia—might prod us to open ours.

Ophuls seems fated from birth to be cosmopolitan, a filmmaker, and a thorn in the side of authorities. He was born in Germany in 1927, the only child of director Max Ophuls and wife Hilde. In 1932, as the Nazis were on the brink of power, his family fled to Paris. When France fell in 1940, they slipped into Switzerland, and in 1941 they emigrated to the

United States. Ophuls attended Hollywood High and the University of California at Berkeley. He served with occupation forces in Japan and in 1950 became an American citizen. In 1951, he returned to Europe to work in many directorial and writing capacities for French and German television. In the early 1960s, he directed two small features: an episode of *Love at Twenty* (1961) and a comedy, *Banana Peel* (1964). But his striking works in that decade began as projects for the French state television station ORTF. In 1967, ORTF screened his caustic documentary of the diplomatic maneuvers behind the 1938 Munich Agreement. A companion study of France under the occupation, focusing on the town of Clermont-Ferrand in the Vichy zone, was under way when Ophuls took part in a directors' strike protesting state censorship during the May 1968 upheavals. He was fired and moved to Germany, where he scraped together the funds to complete his masterpiece in demystification.

The *Sorrow and the Pity* dispelled the happy myth of resistance solidarity, highlighted homegrown anti-Semitism, and examined the virtual civil war and vicious class conflict rending France long before the Panzers ever rolled in. An ORTF official objected that the film "destroys myths that the people of France need." Memorable interviewees included a French Waffen SS officer, a shopkeeper who placed a newspaper ad in 1942 denying he was Jewish, and a resistance fighter and Buchenwald survivor who somehow lived peacefully beside the fellow who had turned him in. The government refused to screen *The Sorrow and the Pity*, but the documentary played for years in a French cinema. A fair-minded critique leveled by Stanley Hoffman is that Ophuls's film, while it ignited a much-needed reappraisal, was perhaps too harsh insofar as it characterized all French behavior on the basis of a single town. Robert Paxton's book *Vichy France* and Henry Rousso's book *The Vichy Syndrome* cite exceptions and extenuating circumstances but in no way refute Ophuls's treatment. Only when François Mitterand came to power in 1981 was *The Sorrow and the Pity* at last shown on French TV.

Ophuls next ventured into Northern Ireland in *A Sense of Loss* (1972), where he concentrated on grim sectarian oppression. In *The Memory of Justice* (1976), he examined the Nuremberg trials and mused mordantly on their legacy in this new age of napalm and the My Lai massacre. The Oscar-winning *Hotel Terminus* (1988) spilled out a sinister saga of nasty collaboration among American and other "free world" intelligence agencies who made ample use of the likes of Klaus Barbie, former chief of the German secret service in Lyons in 1942–1944, whose valued skills were oriented exclusively to keeping the proles in line. Intelligence professionals, it became clear, had more in common with unapologetic ex-Nazis than with the democratic institutions they were supposedly defending. The meanings and implications of the fall of the Berlin Wall was the subject of *November Days* (1990). His documentary *The Troubles We've Seen* centered on war correspondents in Sarajevo but sifted through the whole dubious history of war reporting. Can reporters only or ever be dispassionate analysts? His investigation spans the Spanish Civil War—including an interview with Martha Gellhorn (who still relishes the romance of "la causa") and an inquiry into quibbles over Robert Capa's photograph of a Republican soldier at the instant of death—and extends to observations about coverage of the press-pooled 1991 Gulf War. (A French journalist recalls informing his editors that in liberated Kuwait, the man-in-the-street interview they wanted could consist of nothing more than the esteemed correspondent dangling a microphone beside a highway to pick up the sound of fleets of Mercedes whizzing by.) At one point, Ophuls, the impish provocateur, pads in a bathrobe around a nude woman in a Vienna hotel room for no purpose other than to rile oversensitive feminists. BBC executive Paul Hayman, who worked with Ophuls on *November Days*, attests that Ophuls, "like any great talent," is "a nightmare to work with" but is well worth the trouble. The interview was conducted in Chicago Film Festival offices in the fall of 1995.

YOU SAID IT IS NOT YOUR BUSINESS TO PROVIDE SOLUTIONS. YET *THE TROUBLES WE'VE SEEN* URGES A POLITICAL SOLUTION—YOU WANTED THE WEST TO INTERVENE IN BOSNIA. THAT STANCE IS NEW.

Yes. That is new for me. But I think that part of a documentary filmmaker's business is not to have any absolute principles, otherwise he closes too many doors in advance. So you must always be prepared not only to surprise other people but to surprise yourself. Something might happen to you in the course of events that changes your mind about previous statements in previous interviews.

ARE YOU CONSCIOUS OF ANY DIFFERENCE THAT ADVOCACY MAKES IN YOUR WORK?

Oh, I still refrain from voice-of-God commentary. I still don't identify with André Malraux, and I still try to avoid propaganda.[1] I think the question is very good. But as a matter of fact, I started out advocating. *The Sorrow and the Pity* is certainly not a relativistic or neutral film. It comes down very squarely on the side of the resistance. The film is realistic enough to assume—even before being told—that the majority of people by nature and by circumstance are not resistance fighters. But that doesn't mean that the film was philosophically or politically neutral. It was not. In this film, frankly, I can't understand how anyone could get involved, whether on the ground or as a journalist, in what is happening to these people [in Sarajevo] without choosing sides. I can't imagine how that would happen. And certainly the very few journalists I have met who tried to maintain a neutral stance or came out on the Serbian side seemed to me to be agents provocateurs. They're probably paid by the enemy. It's that clear-cut.

WHY USE CORRESPONDENTS AS YOUR FOCUS?

It's their role as mediators. It's because whether reporting a fire in Chicago or as White House correspondents or as Woodward and Bernstein or whether it's what happening to Mitterand in France, the role of journalists as mediators is one of the most fascinating subjects of our time. It's not a new discovery. It's based on Phillip Knightley's book *The First Casualty*.[2] It was not a new discovery when he wrote it. I think it's simply that problems of censorship, pressure, schooling, competition, sensationalism, jingoism—all of these problems become more acute and dramatic in a time of crisis and so obviously make the filmmaker's job easier. In a time of violent crisis, it's more interesting to see a man or a woman on camera with bullets flying around than to find them just at the city desk. That doesn't mean you shouldn't make the connection between the city desk and what is happening in Sarajevo. As a matter of fact, I hope I made the connection with the city desk, and if I ever get the chance to make the third part of the film, the connection will be even stronger.

THERE IS A TENSION BETWEEN AN INTERVENTIONIST STANCE, VOICED BY JOHN BURNS, AND THE REST OF THE FILM THAT DISPLAYS HOW FALLIBLE REPORTERS ARE.

I am not using John Burns.[3] I think John and I just happen to have the same ideas on this, and he does make that point in the film. He says in the film that in other places this might not be a healthy thing that we all agree with one another. Yet I chose to showcase that statement. But it is his statement. I happen to agree with it.

YOU PRESENT EVIDENCE FROM MARTHA GELLHORN ON THE SPANISH
CIVIL WAR THAT GIVES AUDIENCES PAUSE TO THINK SKEPTICALLY ABOUT
CORRESPONDENTS WHO GET SO CAUGHT UP IN A CAUSE THAT THEY LOSE
CRITICAL DISTANCE.[4] THAT IS NOT TO SAY ONE CANNOT, LIKE ORWELL, BE
FOR A REPUBLIC AND YET REFUSE TO IGNORE TERRIBLE THINGS GOING ON
WITHIN IT.

And not fake it. Yes. Why is Orwell's book the only one we get out of
the civil war that still has meaning and value to us? As opposed to Malraux or some of the other propaganda writing? Because he saw through
the bullshit. But that's also what this film is about.

YOU USE FRIVOLOUS CLIPS AND REFERENCES TO CAGNEY, ROSALIND
RUSSELL, AND OTHER OLD FILMS, INCLUDING YOUR FATHER'S FILM SET IN
SARAJEVO.

I think a general sign of maturity is that as we get older—by "we," I
mean people who are paid to make personal statements in writing, painting, or whatever—that usually as we get older we become more interested in form than in content. It's quite natural that people should feel
that that fault is somewhat shocking in a documentary about death and
violence and victimization. A filmmaker who says he is more interested
in form than in subject matter seems to be saying he is getting bored with
victimization and oppression. So I'm leaving myself open to that. But it
is true that trying to make connections between *His Girl Friday* and
James Cagney and to connect these dramatically with Sarajevo and what
is happening there may seem repellent to some people. I chose to assume that risk. I chose to try to convince people that it is not frivolous.

WOMEN IN [HOWARD] HAWKS'S FILMS ARE FORMIDABLE. ONE CAN'T
HELP NOTICING, HOWEVER, IN ONE SCENE THAT YOU GO OUT OF YOUR WAY
TO NEEDLE FEMINISTS.

I would quarrel with some modern women on their repressiveness,
their terrorism, their narrow-mindedness, their puritanism. But I would
not quarrel with feminists who know about movies, as Molly Haskel does,
who would explain to us that Hawks's basic attitude toward women was
patronizing. I would not quarrel with that. I think it was. But that would
not change the fact that he was one of the great directors of all time.
Certainly Angie Dickinson in *Rio Bravo* and Jean Arthur in *Only Angels Have Wings* and you name it, they are being made members of a

club on an exceptional basis in the way that some Jews got into a Harvard fraternity if they had the right credentials—but only on tolerance. Certainly from that point of view, Hawks's attitude can be criticized. But it was coherent, it was intelligent, and, for the time he lived, it was generous. One thing we should always do is use a time perspective. I hope that audiences will not misunderstand. They are more likely—from the first femifascist reaction I've been getting, from the bad vibes I've been getting in this country—they are likely to resent the presence of the call girl in the hotel room. They seem totally hung up on that.

BUT YOU ARE PUTTING OUT THE BAIT.

Yes, I'm putting out the bait, and I will continue putting out the bait. If they ever want to get anything done, they will have to stop that kind of shit.

WHO ARE THE FEMIFASCISTS? I SHUDDER AT YOU AND RUSH LIMBAUGH AGREEING ABOUT ANYTHING.

These women are using victimization. Particularly in America, victimization is used as a form of collective identity to oppress and victimize others. We should fight that.

YOU DEAL WITH INDISPUTABLE VICTIMS—PEOPLE WHO WERE TURNED INTO THE NAZIS IN THE DAYS OF THE RESISTANCE, PEOPLE WHO WERE TORTURED BY KLAUS BARBIE. I SUPPOSE WHAT YOU ARE COMPLAINING ABOUT IS THE DEBASING OF THE ROLE OF VICTIM. A LACK OF PROPORTION. YOU WANT TO COMMENT?

No. You just said it. I think you have to make choices, and choices imply hierarchies that are based not only on looking at your own navel but on a sense of proportion. I am not a Holocaust celebrationist and I don't say only Jews were victims of genocide. But until people are willing to face the fact that the gas chambers are the ultimate form—for the time being; it may get worse—of willful victimization. This is not excluding other forms of genocide. Not at all. There's a good argument to be made that during decolonization there were many crimes against humanity committed. And that there were many people who should have been brought to trial and condemned.

But unless you are willing to face the idea that it is not just a matter of whose ox is being gored, unless you are willing to relativize your own suffering to what you know about history, I don't think you will be able to face any kind of reality. And reality will continue to fade into the background amidst all the violence and shit and frivolity. It will all become spectacle—all of it: narcissistic spectacle.

CAN YOU RECONCILE GOOD FILMMAKING WITH GOOD REPORTING?

One of the characters in the film says that one of the worst things that can happen "when I get back to Paris is that people will say to me that they saw me in this film because this makes it look as if I were only making a movie and I am ashamed of that." I think what I am ultimately trying to convey in this film is that we have to lick the problem of *l'information spectacle*. We have to face the fact that we are in show business and then try to deal with it in a decent and humane way and try to lick the problem. We're not licking the problem. We're getting licked by it. Not only the journalism [films] but many feature films we've seen are just escalations of indecency. There's a virus around us that makes more and more people less and less able to discriminate between what is legitimate show business and what is perverted show business.

ARE YOU TALKING ABOUT REALITY SHOWS?

Yes, but not only the reality shows. Also some shows are extremely successful that display arrested development, a refusal to grow up, a tendency to blame our parents for everything. Here's a hierarchy of people who feel victimized accusing those whom they feel are responsible for their victimization. All of this escalation of anger leaves the people in Sarajevo more helpless and more alone because they are facing real genocide. People who make movies about justifying murder and mayhem because their parents weren't nice enough to them are not facing that kind of reality.

WHO DO YOU THINK WAS TO BLAME FOR THE WAR?

The Europeans are. Bush refused to do anything, but it's more interesting to respond about the Clinton administration because Clinton made promises to the Bosnians that he hasn't kept. We all know why he hasn't kept them. He hasn't kept them because Mitterand and, in a minor way, John Major influenced him and prevented him. But perhaps it's like the movie's barroom fight where a fellow says, "Hold my coat because otherwise I'll get into it." It's a bad situation, and I think we'll all be paying for it.

WHAT ABOUT FINANCING THE FILM?

It's mainly due to friendship that's been going on for the last ten years with Bertrand Tavernier, who is just about the only Frenchman who worries about my getting employment in France and who made tremendous efforts so that I could get enough money to make it.[5] It hasn't been easy. Then good old Beeb [the BBC] came in with 80,000 pounds, I think. And the French subsidy system. Again, I happened to be lucky because Jeanne Moreau happens to be president of it right now. If not, maybe I wouldn't have gotten it.

YOU HAD A DIFFERENT EXPERIENCE WITH THE BBC OVER A SENSE OF LOSS, WHICH IS SET IN WAR-TORN ULSTER IN 1972.

At that time, I was on very good terms with the BBC because they had shown The Sorrow and the Pity. They were very much interested in the next film, and the head of purchasing programs wanted to have an option. They were very anxious to see A Sense of Loss because it was about their problem—and when they saw it, they didn't want it. It was the only one of these marathon documentaries that never made it onto the BBC. All the others did.

HERE WE ARE TWENTY YEARS LATER AND WE HAVE A FRAGILE PEACE PROCESS IN PLACE. BUT UP UNTIL 1994, YOUR FILM WAS JUST AS RELEVANT AS IN 1972.

I think you are right. I think, unfortunately, that until [very recently], the shape and the contents of my film on Northern Ireland would have looked like A Current Affair. But that could happen to any one of that series of films. In some ways it happened to November Days, which was a much more recent film about the joy of the fall of the Berlin Wall. But then the only excuse for either film is that I am not a political prophet. Matter of fact, I'm not very good at politics anyway. I'm certainly not very good at predicting the course of human events. I don't want to sound apologetic about it.

I think A Sense of Loss was a fairly good film. I think the BBC may have been right because it was not the best work I've done because I felt uncomfortable with the very idea of the American sponsors who backed me. Of doing the Irish Republican movement with the same kind of awe, respect, and sympathy that you would feel for the French resistance. This is why I was commissioned to do it. I never felt very comfortable with that idea. So I concentrated mainly in this film on the North on the mayhem and the violence and what it means to people to be casualties in that kind of civil strife, which I suppose is an easy way out.

HOW DID YOUR SPONSORS REACT?

I think the sponsors were not terribly happy because the film did not make any money. Possibly one of the reasons it did not make any money in the United States is that the original intention was to please the Irish-American community, and of course it didn't do that. In fact, it was quite sarcastic in this respect, showing the contrast between the St. Patrick's Day parade in New York and the business of collecting money for the IRA—this distance between all the folklore and what actually happens on the ground.

That's how the film starts. So I'm trying to make elbow room against pressures on both sides, between what the sponsors originally want and what they get. Trying to make elbow room sometimes pays off—and sometimes it doesn't. It is certainly one of my main activities in life to try to make that effort pay off.

IS MAKING EVERYONE UNHAPPY A SORT OF VICTORY?

At the Edinburgh Film Festival, the response was just that—that it made everyone unhappy. But I don't think a film should just do that. It may be a sign of some sort of filmmaker's independence or stubbornness or whatever to make everyone unhappy, but it is not a moral victory.

WERE YOU UNHAPPY?

Not terribly, no. Because I think sympathizing with the oppressed and sympathizing with the victim is one of the easiest thing a documentary filmmaker can do. It is part of correct political thinking and I have never been a correct political thinker, even before the term was coined. I am against it.

TOO FEW PEOPLE WERE INTERESTED. THAT SEEMS TO BE YOUR TASK—TO INDUCE OTHER PEOPLE TO GO AND DIG OUT THE FACTS IN OR-DER TO UNDERSTAND WHY THE WORLD IS LESS CIVILIZED THAN IT OUGHT TO BE.

Well, don't cast me into the role of Atlas, because it is too heavy for me. I don't know the mythology. Does he still continue to carry it on his shoulders?

AFTER A BRIEF RELIEF BY HERCULES, YES.

Well, that's a very flattering portrait. What your question implies, if I
have correctly understood it, is that other people are not doing that kind
of job. That the world waits for me to come along and do it in the place
of the other people. That's why I talk about Greek mythology, because I
can't take that heavy a compliment.

THERE ARE VERY FEW MAVERICKS AROUND LIKE YOURSELF OR, SAY, PE-
TER DAVIS.[6]

Peter is a friend of mine, and I think *Hearts and Minds* is a very important film. Luckily for both of us—and you can add Claude Lanzmann
[director of *Shoah*] and others—we are not alone. There are historians
and there are investigative journalists who come out with important
work all the time. The fact that we try to put it together audiovisually is
just a temporary phenomenon. Again, we get into this business of *l'information spectacle*. We may tend to overvalue right now the impact
that nonfiction filmmaking has on people. I think it is going to have less
and less impact because of television, because there is so much
crammed onto the evening news that I don't think we can adapt to and
deal with.

WHY ARE YOU TALKING ABOUT QUITTING FILMS?

I think my way of dealing with it—long films, long interviews—is not
going to bring home the bacon any more. It's one of the reasons why I
am retiring. After all, the only commercial success I ever had with these
films is *The Sorrow and the Pity*. I haven't had one since. There are reasons for that. It has to do with people who no longer are able to afford
the attention span that is necessary. So you have to find something else.
Peter Davis and I are obsolete. We really are.

IS YOUR WORK SPURRED ON BY CONTRASTS? THERE YOU ARE—A EURO-
PEAN JEWISH ÉMIGRÉ AT HOLLYWOOD HIGH, OF ALL PLACES, WITH THE NAZI
MENACE A VERY VIVID MEMORY. YOUR PARENTS FILL YOUR LIFE WITH HIGH
CULTURE AND A SENSE OF PURPOSE OUT THERE IN LA-LA LAND. AM I WARM?

You romanticize it. First of all, we were very privileged and we got out
much earlier than other people did. It did not at the time have all that
profound an influence on me. We did not get near a concentration

camp. We were in unoccupied France in various dangerous situations. Most of them were kept from me because my parents were very good parents. They were very intelligent, very cultured, very knowing, very sophisticated. As you say. Wonderful parents. So they tried to soften or cushion both the Hollywood experience and the Vichy experiences.

They didn't entirely succeed, otherwise I wouldn't have become the fucked-up person that I've become. Parents never entirely succeed. But that doesn't mean they should be blamed. My response to that culture shock was very simple. I became a French snob. I retreated into book-wormish, wallflowerish behavior because I couldn't cope with the dating system. So I never met Marilyn Monroe—but then she couldn't cope with the dating system there, either. I only ceased being a French snob when I went into the American army, which was a very happy experience.

WHAT YEARS?

In 1946–1947. Before I went to college, I went to Japan as an occu-pier. I didn't drop the atom bomb, so I refuse to be blamed for it—all those clichés. Anyway, I was very happy. I had a very good time both in basic training and in Tokyo. I discovered American movies before I ever came to America. But jazz and Brooklyn and Tennessee and all these things that are closer to the American reality than Hollywood High School are things I discovered in the American army and that make me very fond of this country. I'm very fond of this country. So by the time I got out of the army, I was no longer the snob. But Hollywood High School was pretty bad. Yes.

YOUR FATHER'S REPUTATION DEEPENED OVER THE YEARS IN PART BE-CAUSE PEOPLE HAD THE CHANCE TO SEE RESTORED VERSIONS.

But why do they get that chance? Certainly not because of the distrib-utors and the money people. There is one very simple answer for the posthumous revival and fame of my father [Max Ophuls], which he cer-tainly deserves. François Truffaut did it—and a few friends in Paris. As in so many other things, François was the leader because he had the talent and was interested enough, he was crazy enough, he was fanatic enough.

SPEAKING OF TRUFFAUT, IN THE SIXTIES, YOU MADE A *LOVE AT TWENTY* EPISODE AND *BANANA PEEL*. WHY DID YOU MOVE TO NONFICTION? THE OBVIOUS GUESS IS LACK OF MONEY.

That's right. I was married. I was a family man. There was no work. I just happened to be spending an evening with friends and a woman who worked for French television. We got to talking. What would I want to do if I worked for French television? I said, "I don't want to work on cheap fiction stuff because the directors are working under terrible conditions and you can't possibly do any good work there. So if I were to work on French television it would be reportage, a magazine piece." She said, "Well, do you have anybody special in mind?" I said, "Yes. I see some anti-Gaullist stuff that I rather like. There seems to be a small group of good people there who are doing good work, and if I could work with them that would be OK." She said, "We'll set up an appointment for you." I left the country. I didn't believe anything would happen.

But when I came back, I found messages from this woman for three different appointments. So for two years, thanks to her having me meet these television producers and journalists, I very happily and for very little money would do 20-minute pieces for something like America's *60 Minutes*. That's what got me into it. Then one day a producer said to me, "Would you like to do Munich? We are going to do historical evenings on Channel 2, and we would like you to start off because you are our senior director." I was middle-aged by that time. I remember saying "Munich the town or Munich the agreement?" He replied, "The agreement, of course." And that became a three-and-a-half-hour film of interviews and archives. That basically is what I have been doing ever since. There is no explanation [for my career] except anecdote and circumstance.

DID YOU START OUT WANTING TO TACKLE THESE DEEP AND THORNY MORAL SUBJECTS?

No. I would have much preferred to do musicals. People always laugh when I say that. People like John Simon in New York have written about this; that here I am such a profound thinker of our time and I actually like *Top Hat*. Well, I like John Simon, but I think he is quite wrong when he thinks he can patronize *Top Hat* or Fred Astaire or the people who made it. No, the great artists of the twentieth century in filmmaking— God knows there have been some, including my father—are [in fictional films]. I've always thought that. So it's mostly groceries now. That doesn't mean I patronize myself. It doesn't mean I think that I've been doing unimportant work. Circumstance, the groceries, and pressures have brought me time and again into situations of filmmaking where I think am a good one. But that is not for me to say.

THERE IS ENORMOUS FICKLENESS IN THE RISE AND FALL OF DIRECTORS' REPUTATIONS. BUT THAT OF YOUR FATHER SEEMS TO HAVE STOOD VERY WELL.

A great deal of it has to do with fashion. And a great deal of it has to do with people's ways of making a living. In other words, for film critics, it has become more and more important not only to their own ego but also to the size of their bank account to be seen at the source of a rediscovery. That's why you get all this business about restored versions when in fact, as in the case of my father's *La Ronde*, I had to fight off these art historians because they disregarded my father's right to the final cut. "Ah," they say, "but he was pressured into shortening the film."

Then somebody had come up for very suspect reasons with a restored version of *La Ronde*. I had to defend my dead father's rights against this being restored because he is no longer around to be asked whether he was pressured. We have to be careful not to fall prey to this kind of vicious circle of fanatic film buffery. Reevaluation is good and is necessary. But one of the things I think we discover is that posterity is no judge of art, either. Shaw, I think, said people who write for posterity are pompous asses.

ARE YOU TEMPTED TO PLAY INVESTIGATOR AGAIN?

The BBC wants me to do a thing on the revival of fascism. But fascism is always with us. It is not being revived. Anyway, I don't want to spend another two years living these nightmares. For one thing, my memory is fading. I have to rely too much on other people. Fortunately, I have found very good people to help me. But the business of keeping one hundred to two hundred hours of rushes in my head is something that is becoming too difficult and too strenuous to deal with. So I said, "If you want me to interview that creep in Russia or if you want me to interview Berlusconi, I'll do it if the BBC pays me well and I can add another room or two to my retirement home." But I will not otherwise spend two years dealing again with the nightmare of the problems that these people—the neofascists—are banking on. I've already done it.

WHAT ARE THE PROSPECTS?

I don't think it's going to work out. I wish it would.

NOTES

1. André Malraux, 1901–1976, French author (*Man's Fate, Man's Hope, Man's Estate*) and radical political figure, minister of cultural affairs from 1959 to 1969.

2. Phillip Knightley, *The First Casualty—from Crimea to Vietnam: The War Correspondent as Hero, Propagandist and Myth Maker* (New York: Harcourt Brace Jovanovich, 1975).

3. *New York Times* staff reporter.

4. Martha Gellhorn was a legendary foreign and war correspondent, a former wife of Ernest Hemingway, and author of *The Trouble I've Seen* (New York: Morrow, 1936), *The Face of War* (New York: Simon & Schuster, 1959), *The Weather in Africa* (New York: Dodd, Mead, 1978), and several works of fiction.

5. French film director of *Clean Slate* (1981), *Round Midnight* (1986), *Life and Nothing But* (1989), *Revenge of the Musketeers* (1999), and *Laissez-Passer* (2002).

6. Peter Davis is the director and producer, among other works, of the Oscar-winning documentary *Hearts and Minds* (1975), a powerful cultural and political critique of America's involvement in Vietnam, in which Daniel Ellsberg made an impressive cameo appearance.

10

WOODY ALLEN

film director

Woody Allen hardly needs an introduction: stand-up comic, playwright, screenwriter, author, and director of dozens of films, including *Play It Again, Sam* (1972), *A Walk with Love and Death* (1975), *Annie Hall* (1977), *Interiors* (1978), *Manhattan* (1979), *Stardust Memories* (1980), *Zelig* (1983), *The Purple Rose of Cairo* (1985), *Hannah and Her Sisters* (1986), *September* (1987), *Crimes and Misdemeanors* (1989), *Husbands and Wives* (1992), *Manhattan Murder Mystery* (1993), *Bullets over Broadway* (1994), *Mighty Aphrodite* (1995), and *Deconstructing Harry* (2001). His books include *Getting Even* (1978) and *Without Feathers* (1986). The interview below occurred in Chicago during his promotional tour for *Small Time Crooks* in the spring of 2000.

Who could possibly resist reminding readers that in his Oscar-winning film *Annie Hall*, the Allen character forever is doggedly trying to drag his girlfriend, and anyone else in reach, to watch Marcel Ophuls's *The Sorrow and the Pity* again and again—until all its lessons sink indelibly in?

WHY THIS RETURN TO WHAT FOR YOU IS OLD-FASHIONED COMEDY IN *SMALL TIME CROOKS*?

I liked it that the notion that people want to rob a bank and that their cookie business, which they use to rob the bank, takes off and makes them rich had an element of wit in it. It may not be the profoundest point. That's what attracted me to it, whereas many contemporary comedies have gone in a different direction because audiences have encouraged it. Comedies come out with relentless toilet jokes in them is because there is a big market for it. People don't line up for my films at the box office as they do for these others. There's a reason for why they line up for what I call the Neanderthal style.

SOME CRITICS WILL SAY THAT THAT IS BECAUSE THE MASS AUDIENCE IS BECOMING DUMBER AND DUMBER.

I never believed in the dumbing down of the country. It can't be that—because every generation has got to feel that their generation was the bright one and the cultivated one and the sensitive one and the new generation is pragmatic and philistine and they don't get it. I don't think it's true.

SO WHAT DO YOU THINK IS GOING ON?

I think culture has gotten more informal and more relaxed. For example, at the time I first saw *Streetcar Named Desire*, it was very clear that Blanche was the heroine and Stanley was the nefarious, sinister, unruly brute. But after you look at it over the years you start to feel that, you know, she's crazy. She comes into his house and she's stiff and she's formal—and the world has gotten more informal and so now we understand Stanley's position more. So when [Ernst] Lubitsch was making films there was an Old World element to the immigrants in this country because the war forced a huge influx of very urbane European actors, filmmakers, and writers who came over.

THAT'S PRETTY MUCH GONE.

Now you don't have that. You have a more American sensibility. More relaxed, more easygoing, less formal, less elegant. That's expressed in clothing or sexual mores. It's a general loosening up of the culture, and it is reflected in films. No one has come along, really—except in period films like [Martin] Scorsese, say—that [emulate] European openness and sophistication, which is a thing I grew up with that American films never had before. Which was a positive step forward. In comedy, they got more—I don't know—infantile. There are no comic talents around at the moment who can fuse the sensibility of the culture with a real inspired comic view.

WHY DO YOU SO OFTEN TAKE CRACKS AT DRAMA?

I wish that I had been born with the talent to be serious. I envy—my favorite artists have all been serious artists: Chekhov, Tennessee Williams, Ibsen, Eugene O'Neill, Arthur Miller. These are the people I idolized. Ingmar Bergman in film. I just don't have what it takes to be that kind of artist. So I struggle. I try to make that work every now and then. But I sweat and I huff and I puff and maybe sometimes it's okay or it embarrasses me. Whereas when I'm working in comedy, it comes very gracefully for me. It's just an accidental fate that I was born with that kind of gift.

HOW DID YOUR COMIC STYLE EMERGE, AND WHO WERE YOUR MODELS?

My comic style was innocent to begin with. We had a great group of gifted comedians on stage in the United States in the early and late fifties. Mort Sahl, Jonathan Winters, Shelley Berman, Lenny Bruce. They were very original and different. There are no comedians today that are comparable to those ones that I have named. I think there are many funny people. When I flash through the cable channels, I see a million comedians and occasionally I see some that are funny, but often not. There is that same labored style—walk up and back and start being gratuitously filthy and try to be socially relevant in a heavy-handed way that isn't really relevant. I do think that it's hard to find people today who are as good as Nichols and May were or Lenny Bruce or Mort Sahl or Jonathan Winters. I don't know anybody now that is on that level. I've probably gotten to be a tougher judge. Maybe if I was younger and these people came to me fresh, I would think differently.

WHO DO YOU LIKE AMONG CURRENT FILMMAKERS?

I like the director who did *Magnolia* and *Boogie Nights*. While I don't think either of those pictures was perfect by any means, they showed enormous amounts of style and originality and were not factory-made films. They were works by someone with clear-cut talent for theatricality and for movie-making. I liked *Wonderboys*. That was not one of these factory-made formula films that was put out just because they get a couple of high-powered stars. There's a film called *East-West*, a very interesting film. I always enjoy Scorsese's films. I feel I am in the hands of a first-class filmmaker, an original filmmaker. I feel that way about Coppola too. There are a number of people out there.

FILM IS THE QUINTESSENTIAL COLLABORATIVE ART FORM—WHEN IT IS ART. HOW MUCH DO YOU DEPEND ON OTHER PERSONNEL ON SET OR IN THE EDITING ROOM TO SPUR ON THE CREATIVE DECISIONS?

I always make that decision myself. I'm not out there to please the audience or to please the film studio. If I write something and I like it, I make it. If I don't, I throw it away and no one ever sees it. I write in a notebook some idea that strikes or that I read in the newspaper or it hits me. Or I don't have the idea and I sit in a room for as long as it takes—it could be weeks—and just sweat it out until something comes eventually. It's arduous and it's exhausting and no fun. Then comes the big test for me: Does the film go anyplace? I, and all the writers I know, have a million good ideas that don't go places. They're very funny ideas. When I wrote *Purple Rose of Cairo*, when the guy comes off the screen was a funny idea but it didn't go anywhere. I got fifty pages out of it, and the thing drops dead and I put it in the drawer. But six months later, it occurs to me that if the actor in Hollywood comes into a small town and the guy comes off the screen and falls in love with the girl, who has to choose between fantasy and reality and she chooses reality and it hurts her—I knew I had something. Then I wrote it, and it became one of the movies of mine that I was prouder of.

IS THIS WHAT HAPPENED, FOR EXAMPLE, IN *BULLETS OVER BROADWAY*?

Same thing with *Bullets over Broadway*. The idea of the gangster as a playwright and he really did have talent was a funny idea. But it dropped dead halfway through. Only when the idea occurs to me that the gangster realizes that the actress is screwing up his dialogue and he kills her did I realize I had someplace to go with the movie. The same with dismal small-time crooks in the fact that they rent this store next to the bank and the cookie store hits it big, that's a nice idea. Only development occurred when I had the idea that money changes them. And once they start putting on airs and becoming pretentious did I then really have it. Comic ideas are cheap, but ideas that flower into something, that develop, are not so easy to find. Until you feel you have the result of the idea, it doesn't pay to sit down and write it.

It's laborious to plot out things. When you get that idea, you tend to rush ahead too rapidly and you force the ending and the ending is prefabricated and ill thought out. There is no shortage of film companies that will want to make those films. They'll see an idea that's funny and they won't care that it doesn't go anyplace. They recognize [that it] doesn't go anyplace and they give it to a movie star and he or she will want to do it because it will see a lot of laughs but never realize it isn't going anyplace and they find it is a disaster. It happens all the time.

WAS FILMMAKING YOUR AMBITION ALL ALONG?

I wanted to be in law enforcement [laughter]. I really did. And I toyed for a while with being criminal. I started out as an amateur magician with card and dice tricks. I gradually learned to cheat at cards, and then it was short step to being a confidence man and then a short step—I didn't want to work in an office and I thought maybe I could be a jewel thief. Anything but a nine-to-five job. Then at a young age, I found I could write jokes. I took off in that direction and eventually got a chance to write a film script.

I went to Europe and they made that film. It was a great opportunity for me and they just mangled the script. *What's New Pussycat?* I stood there with no clout whatever because it was my first job. There were huge stars in it—Peter O'Toole and Peter Sellers. They were nice people, but no one knew what he was doing. It was a film that was motor-powered by studios. So I decided I would never work in film again if I could not be the director and writer.

When I wrote *Take the Money and Run*, I knew I could make that film. It never occurred to me for a second that I couldn't do it, that anyone could make it better than me. No one else could make what I know this joke is supposed to be. This guy does this and that guy says that. It was full of flaws. We reedited it six million times, but somehow it managed to eke by. So it was in protection of myself as a writer that I came to directing.

WHY DO YOU LIKE TO PLAY DIM-WITTED ROLES?

There are two things that I can play—apart from a sperm and an ant. I can play an intellectual. I'm not an intellectual, but I can play one. I get credit for appearing to be an intellectual because I wear big dark glasses. But I'm not. I'm closer to the dimwit in this movie. You should see me at home. I'm not hunched over a copy of Heidegger making marginal notes. I'm sitting with a beer in my hand watching the Knicks and the Bulls.

I can play intellectuals because of the way I look and I can play dim-witted characters because that's who I grew up around. I can play *Broadway Danny Rose* and the character in *Take the Money and Run* and I can play this character. I just have an affinity for them.

CAN YOU STILL BE WOODY ALLEN WITHOUT THOSE TRADEMARK SPEC-TACLES?

Every time I take them off I don't look like me. I don't have the same impact. Nothing looks the same. I always make the pretentious compar-ison that it's like Groucho Marx without the mustache.

MANY CRITICS HAVE LOOKED AT YOUR FILMS AS NOSTALGIC PIECES OF A WHITE ETHNIC IMMIGRANT WORLD.

I write about things that I am capable of writing about. I can't write about black families with that verisimilitude. I just don't have the knowl-edge or the nuance or the detail. I can write about some Jewish families that I knew and maybe some Italian and some Irish families. That's what I feel familiar with and what I know. I also have a weak spot for New York City, and I fantasized about it as I grew up. It was never a New York that really existed anywhere except on film. But it was a New York of open houses and white telephones and limousines. But I really do my own background.

YOU STILL RETURN TO STAGE OCCASIONALLY.

I wanted to be a playwright originally. When I was a young man, the theater was much more significant than film—and the best films were foreign films and the only good work a writer could do was in the the-ater, like Arthur Miller and Tennessee Williams. What happened was the influx of these great foreign movies by great European filmmakers who got to Hollywood and started to wake American filmmakers up. Suddenly American movies started to improve and got more mature. Films grew up a little bit. And in comparison, American theater got more and more into these factory-made spectacles and got away from the great things it had. I wish the theater was thriving as I knew it in New York when I grew up. Unfortunately, it's not.

THE MAIN CHARACTERS DO SEEM EMPHATICALLY TO BE WOODY ALLEN, EVEN WHEN YOU ARE NOT PRESENT ON SCREEN, OR WAS KENNETH BRANAGH PUTTING YOU AS WELL AS THE REST OF US ON IN *CELEBRITY*?

It's probably my fault as a director. I don't direct my actors sufficiently. I sometimes tell the actors how I want the scene to go and in some subliminal way I communicate to them that they should be doing it that way and so they do it that way. In *Bullets over Broadway*, it was no problem because John Cusack had a small role in an ensemble. In *Celebrity*, it was largely held against the picture and against Kenneth Branagh that he was doing me. It didn't bother me at all. But the part had to be done by a man of forty—I'm nearly sixty-five—so I couldn't have played that. I guess I could have said to him more frequently "You're doing me. Stop it or I'll fire you."

But he's a great actor and I'm lucky to get him and I'm not the most forceful director. If Sean Penn hadn't done that role on *Sweet and Lowdown*, it would have been a different picture—Johnny Depp had passed; then I would have placed a completely different cast on the picture. It would have been more comic but less forceful. But Sean Penn did it and he is an actor of great genius and complete self-confidence and wouldn't for a moment think of imitating me or being influenced by me. I'm lucky that he listened to me at all.

WHAT IS THE PRICE YOU PAY FOR FINAL CUT?

I had the power of final cut. They let me alone; they let me work. My films were financed in advance. So when I pull it out of the typewriter, I'm in business. I call up my production manager and we start budgeting it and casting, whereas somebody else in a less fortunate position finishes a script and then has got to raise the money for it and go through those endless luncheons in Hollywood and talk Jack Nicholson or Robert DeNiro or whoever you want into doing your picture. Six months later or two or three years later, they get their film made if they're lucky. I've always wanted the film to come out and not be a big event and when that is over go make the next one.

HARDLY ANYONE ELSE—EXCEPT MAYBE JIM JARMUSCH—HAS MANAGED TO PULL THIS OFF CONSISTENTLY AND WITHOUT BEING TEMPTED TO "GO HOLLYWOOD."

I'm not technological at all. I don't have a flair for that kind of thing. I have an Olympia portable typewriter that I bought when I was fifteen years old. I know you are not going to believe this. I can't change the ribbon for it to this day. I invite someone to dinner and say "By the way, could you. . . ?" I don't have a word processor. I type it up myself. But I wouldn't want it any other way. You get used to things. Part of my personality is resistant to change. I see change as symbolic of approaching death. I resist change in any form. I write on a yellow pad and I type.

ARE YOU CONSCIOUS OF STRIVING FOR VARIETY EACH TIME YOU TURN OUT ANOTHER SCRIPT?

I'm always seen as doing the same thing. It's like Chinese food—many different dishes, but it's all Chinese food. It's different when you are on the inside looking out. I see no similarities between *Sleeper* and *Everyone Says I Love You*. In a conversation with the *New York Times*, Martin Scorsese said, and he meant it as a compliment, that my whole life I was doing really one film. I just want to knock on doors and tell people that there is no similarity between *Take the Money and Run* and *Interiors*. But the outside world sees it's one of those Woody Allen movies; whether it's the blind spot that I have or the blind spot that the public has, there is something that is rendering them more alike than different in the final analysis to the general public.

HOW DO YOU DEAL WITH CRITICISM?

The best thing is to make the film and not read about it, not read about the film, not read about yourself. Critics will either tell you that you're wonderful and you're a genius or that you are a fool and terrible. It doesn't do you any good. You still go out next time and make the only film that you can make. So it's no help. It's just a distraction. I don't read the critics at all. Being an ostrich, in certain ways, has worked positively for me. You pay a price for it, but it also has its compensations.

❚❚

SPIKE LEE
film director

For a pretty diminutive guy, Spike Lee is not hard to spot even when he is hanging out with basketball players a foot taller and wider than he. Lee is the spunky runt—a self-inflicted image—adorned in a baseball cap, thick eyeglasses, and frayed sweatshirt stamped with his beloved Knicks basketball team logo. So it comes as no surprise that when he was a brash New York University film student and first approached the parents of the four children murdered in the 1963 Birmingham church bombing to appear in a documentary, they took one look and told the squirt to run along. Lee went on to proverbially bigger things, gained the wary parents' trust, and crafted *Four Little Girls*, which may be his finest filmmaking accomplishment.

Four Little Girls, which begins with the only song I know that Joan Baez ever sang soulfully, is an elegiac study of a black community coping with the malignant racism exemplified by four charred children's corpses. Lee recreates the city where police brimmed with KKK members, a white Eagle Scout shoots a black man dead (one is curious about the merit badge for that act), and "Whites only" signs decorated water fountains and washrooms. Civil rights activists knew that they could count on Police Chief Bull Connor to "do something silly," Andrew Young recalls. "If he saw any strength or self-respect in a black person, he went crazy." Not to be missed is George Wallace ("Segregation today, segregation tomorrow, segregation forever.") simpering that a nearby black man is his "best friend" as Lee pans to the attendant, who has the expression of an embarrassed parent watching his child pee on the neighbors' Afghan rug.

If anyone can manage to stay brash well into their forties, Lee has pulled it off. He seems to have perfected the art of gazing at both the beauty and the seamy side of things—even if it means that he struggles publicly with nagging contradictions of his own. Apart from Forty Acres and a Mule Filmworks, Lee runs a record label, shoots music videos, partly owns an advertising agency specializing in the "urban/ethnic market," and at the time of the interview was cranking out commercials for Nike. But true to his gutsy image ever since his breakthrough *She's Gotta Have It*, Lee mouths off, thoughtfully, about any subject. Joe Klein called *Do the Right Thing* (1989) "irresponsible," and *Newsweek* predicted race riots. Why did Mookie toss that rubbish bin through Sal's pizzeria window? (Lee retorts that no black person has ever had to ask that question.)

His book *Best Seat in the House* is an old-fashioned American dream saga of shifting from the cheap seats into the eye-poppingly pricey courtside ones at pro ballgames, where he banters with bemused players. Lee typically can't help jabbing at Karl Malone for wearing an FBI cap or jeering at Boston's slow crawl to integrate pro teams, not to mention the town. He knows what a mirage basketball stardom is and that the dream of upward—or, in the case of Madison Square Garden seats, downward—mobility is only a little less elusive for the ghetto poor than winning the lottery or attending the Ivy League as an affirmative action baby. But Lee, who was raised in mixed working-class neighborhoods in Brooklyn, won't allow any excuses. The interview took place in Chicago in 1999 at a retrospective of his films.

HOW MUCH MORE DIFFICULT IS IT FOR A BLACK ARTIST TO PUT TO-GETHER MOTION PICTURE DEALS?

The struggle is different for different films. I think it depends on what kind of film you want to make and how much it's going to cost. For an Afro-American filmmaker who wants to get a film made, there's work. But with the main studios, if you try to do a film for them, the higher the budget escalates, the harder it is to make the film. We've been trying to make a film on the life of Jackie Robinson for the last three or four years, and we're still unsuccessful in trying to do that film. We just finished a film with Denzel [Washington], and the only way we were able to make that film is that Denzel had to cut his salary. If he had got what he usually gets in any other movie, we would not have been able to do that film. So, you know, he made a big sacrifice.

IS STILL ANOTHER BARRIER THE FACT THAT THERE ARE FEW BLACK BOX OFFICE STARS TO GO AROUND?

You've got to have the name recognition to help the box office. Hollywood is driven by the dollar. You look at actors like Will Smith. He was in the two films that grossed the most money the last two years, *Men in Black* and *Independence Day*. Will Smith was in both of those. Will was not in there from the beginning. He was in there doing films before. It's a process. They invest a lot of money in these films, and they want somebody to bring the audience there in the first few days when the movie opens.

BLACK AUDIENCES DON'T FLOCK TO NONMAINSTREAM FILMS EITHER.

There's no reason why we don't go see *Rosewood* but have to trample one another to see *Booty Call* instead. Not to toot my own horn, but we thought more people would go see *Get on the Bus*, but the next week [another blockbuster] opened and there's another stampede at the box office. So you know we're always crying, "Ahhh, look what Hollywood is doing and what the white people are doing. They got it all locked up."

That self-image is there again and again and again. But at those opportunities where we come out with something good and different, black audiences don't support that in the way we could. Like *Devil in a Blue Dress* with Denzel. Carl Franklin's film. I could keep naming a lot [of other films]. A lot of times when it comes down to it, we're not there. An Afro-American audience is very fickle. I don't know what they want. Therefore, that's even more reason why any artist has to go out and do what's true in your heart, and it's so much more difficult in the film industry because it costs so much money to make a film.

ISN'T THE BOX OFFICE ALWAYS THE BOTTOM—AND THE TOP—LINE IN MAINSTREAM FILMS?

It's not always going to be how much money you can make a film. That should not be your standard all the time. I don't care how many albums the Spice Girls make or how many albums they sell. I don't care if they sell eighteen million albums, I don't buy it. They'll never be better than John Coltrane, I'm sorry. There just has to be a standard.

STANDARDS, ACCORDING TO SOME, HAVE BEEN DECLINING SINCE THE ICE AGE.

Too many people—not just in film—just mess up. All African-Americans have ancestors who put their lives on the line so we could learn how to read. Now we have kids who don't want to do that. Our whole educational system's been turned upside-down so that if you're a black kid in an inner city in the United States of America today and you speak correct English or get all A's, you're considered white. You're considered a white boy or white girl. But if you are standing on the corner drinking a Colt 45 and holding your privates, you're keeping it real. So it's all turned around where ignorance is championed, where ignorance is being black and that's what you aspire to. You try being intelligent and that's equated with white people, and that's something to look down upon.

WHAT'S HAPPENED?

Something's happened since the civil rights movement, when we were all encouraged by family, by relatives, by the neighbors that education was good. That it was an honor to go to college to get a good education and not something to look down upon. I have a two-and-a-half-year-old daughter, and my babysitter likes to watch MTV. So I come in one day, and she and my daughter are watching [a particularly vulgar rap group]. Almost had a fit. She's in front of the TV watching them dance, and she doesn't really know what the lyrics are saying. I'm not trying to condemn all rap lyrics either—but that stuff is crazy. You know, we got to think.

HAS BECOMING A FATHER AFFECTED THE MOVIES YOU MAKE?

It hasn't happened so far.

IN CINEMA, ONE UNHELPFUL MESSAGE MAY BE WHEN A RAPPER, LIKE MEKHI PHIFER IN *SOUL FOOD*, STEPS INTO A FILM WITHOUT ANY ACTING LESSONS. DOES THAT TELL VIEWERS THAT THEY DON'T NEED TRAINING?

I don't think a guy like Mekhi Phifer is a rule, he's an exception. He never acted before. You have to have training. Most people cannot go in front of the camera and be any good. I know he started to take classes after that film. Okay, you can't act and you are just acting as yourself. You could do that once. But that's it. If you want to be versatile or have some technique, you have to go in the woodshed and do that work.

ISN'T IT A SIGN OF MAINSTREAM ACCEPTANCE THAT EVEN SCHLOCKY BLACK FILMS GET MADE?

Yeah. But without what went before [in the civil rights struggle], you wouldn't have *Homeboys from Outer Space* or *Booty Call* or the Wayans brothers being broadcast today on big networks if it weren't for the March on Washington.

YOU LIKED *EVE'S BAYOU*. BUT AREN'T HOKEY FAMILY STORIES STILL STORIES TOO?

Here's three black women, three sisters, who eat Sunday dinner for forty-one years in a row. They never missed a Sunday in forty-one years? I'm sorry, no black family in America hasn't missed a Sunday dinner in forty-one years. Maybe they get together for Thanksgiving and Christmas, but every single Sunday for forty-one years? No interruptions. Not World War II? I can show you black families that meet every Thanksgiving and every Christmas. Not this. And *Love Jones* was a better film than *Soul Food*, I'm sorry.

SO BLACK AUDIENCES LIKE ALL KINDS OF FILMS.

That's one thing we have to fight for. We have to realize that we're not one monolithic group. And so there's going to be an audience for everybody. There's not one black film that everyone in the black audience is going to like.

HOLLYWOOD FILMS MAKE A LOT OF MONEY FROM OVERSEAS. BLACK FILMS REPORTEDLY DON'T GET OVERSEAS DISTRIBUTION BECAUSE THEY SEEM TOO SPECIALIZED.

It's a self-fulfilling prophecy. There have been some cases where Afro-American films were not translated well to the world market. That has happened. But then they say, "We're going to try and cut our losses, so we won't work that hard to make these films [succeed overseas] because they don't believe they can make any money." I've had several films that were not released overseas. *School Daze* wasn't. *Get on the Bus* wasn't.

CAN YOU DO ANYTHING ABOUT IT?

You can talk to them, but I don't control worldwide distribution for my films. You can ask them. So, you know.

CAN BLACK ARTISTS FORM THEIR OWN RIVAL DISTRIBUTION SYSTEM?

But you see, I don't think the distribution thing should be put upon Afro-American filmmakers. It's tough enough to make the film. That's something that the black entrepreneurs that we have ought to do. Don't put that on the artists. So that you not only have to raise the money to make the film, then make the film, and you have to be distributors also? That's too much.

HOW DID YOU APPROACH YOUR FIRST DOCUMENTARY? DID YOU HAVE A ROUGH SORT OF SCRIPT OR AN OUTLINE?

There was no outline. I went to HBO and said I wanted to do something about four girls who were murdered [in Birmingham in 1963]. They said "Fine." That was it. So nothing was written on paper. The Birmingham church bombing made a lot of white America wake up to what was really happening in this country.

DO YOU GET MORE ARTISTIC FREEDOM OPERATING THAT WAY?

It's got nothing to do with freedom. That's just the way it happened. Most documentaries aren't scripted. You just got to go out there and get the material, shoot as much as you can, and then make it in the editing room. But we knew that to get the people in front of the camera, it would be great material, the people you were talking with.

ANY BAD MOMENTS?

I was discouraged at first because I though it was going to happen sooner than it did.

WHAT'S YOUR CRITERIA FOR CHOOSING A SCRIPT?

The criteria really is an interesting story and something I would pay nine dollars and fifty cents to see, which is what it costs in New York. That's a lot of money.

WHAT ATTRACTED TO YOU TO *GET ON THE BUS*?

The reason is I thought it was a good story. These men who are complete strangers making this journey on a bus to DC and see what happens on the way to the Million Man March. For me the film was not actually about the march but about what happens to the men on the way to the march.

HOW DID YOU GET MONEY FOR A FILM THE MAJORS DO NOT SEE AS MASS MARKET?

We decided with the subject matter, and it being a better business deal, that we could try to raise the money ourselves. The budget for *Get on the Bus* was two and a half million dollars. Columbia offered to finance the film 100 percent, but we saw we could make more money on the film by raising it ourselves. So Ruby Cann—one of the producers of the film and who cast the film—and I felt that with all the people we know in the sports, entertainment, and business worlds, if we can't raise two and a half million dollars from all the black folks around here who have some money, then we should be shot. So by raising the money ourselves, we were able to go back to Columbia and sell the film for three and a half million dollars, so we made a million in profit already, but it was difficult to raise that money.

HOW DID IT DO?

It didn't make any money. Nobody went. But at the same time, I don't think you should say black people don't support you. I mean there can be times when they do or not. But that doesn't mean you should throw in the towel and just give up. You look at Van Gogh. He never sold a painting while he was alive, you know? The black audience, you know, we always think we're on top of things, but a lot of young white kids were hip to reggae and Bob Marley long before black people were. When regular black people saw dreadlocks, I don't care what they say about it now, back then when they first saw a picture of Bob Marley, they said, "What the hell is that?" And you still got black people who don't know about the genius of Jimi Hendrix, so we miss a lot of things.

SPIELBERG IS BRINGING OUT *AMISTAD* SOON. DO YOU HAVE AMBITIONS ABOUT BRINGING OUT A SLAVERY-THEME EPIC YOURSELF?

I might one day. I'm still skeptical how Spielberg's film is going to turn out. But I hope it's good. We shall see. Maybe I'll produce one.

YOU'VE LAUNCHED CAREERS OF PEOPLE WHO DON'T SEEM TO COME BACK AND GIVE YOU CREDIT.

So? They're not supposed to pay homage. I don't think because you give somebody a job that somebody owes something to you. That's boring to me. It's not like that at all.

DO YOU HAVE ANY DEVELOPMENT SCHEMES FOR FINDING AND NURTURING GOOD SCREENPLAYS?

We don't develop writers, but we read scripts.

WHAT DO YOU SEE AS YOUR MAIN ROLE AS A FILMMAKER?

My role? Tell a good story. That's what filmmakers are. Storytellers. That's how I feel. I don't just make a film. I tell a story.

IN *HE GOT GAME*, YOU SHOW THAT THINGS AREN'T SO HOT EVEN WHEN PLAYERS REALIZE THEIR HOOP DREAMS AGAINST LONG ODDS.

We just scratched the surface about what goes on. People might think this stuff was wild in the film. But it gets a lot wilder.

YOU TOOK A LOT OF FLAK FOR THE PORTRAYAL OF THE BALLPLAYER'S GIRLFRIEND AS A PRETTY PREDATOR.

Look, we're in the high-rise projects stuck on the edge of Brooklyn facing the ocean. These [young women] see no way out. The guys become a rapper, make it in the NBA, or sell drugs. For the women—I'm gonna hook up with one of these guys for a while. To them that is the perception. That is the only option they have.

YOU HAVE A LONG LOVE AFFAIR WITH KNICKS BASKETBALL AND A MORE AMBIVALENT RELATION WITH MICHAEL JORDAN. IS IT TEMPTING TO MAKE A MICHAEL JORDAN FILM?

I wouldn't know how to make the Michael Jordan movie. There's no movie that can show what Michael Jordan does better than what people see every time they watch Michael play. What actor is going to be able to perform with the supernatural gifts that Michael has? No actor can do that. And, no, Denzel cannot play Michael Jordan.

YOU MADE *FOUR LITTLE GIRLS* AS A DOCUMENTARY. BUT COULD IT HAVE WORKED AS A FEATURE FILM?

I don't think it would work as well. I just felt that this subject needed to be told in documentary form and that we needed the people who were there to tell the story. And I've been very leery of Hollywood doing the story. I've seen both *Ghosts of Mississippi* and *Mississippi Burning*, both done by this producer named Fred Zolo, who definitely has revisionist things happening with them.

I don't know how you make a film about the civil rights movement and have the FBI be the heroes. You know, coming to the defense of the movement. It didn't happen like that. In *Ghosts of Mississippi*, [Whoopi Goldberg's] character was relegated to the role of an extra. That movie is about the Alec Baldwin character, the lawyer. The only time you saw Medgar [Evers] even mentioned in the film is when there is a little clip when he turns on the TV. Medgar Evers does not even exist in that film.

THE ACADEMY AWARDED AN OSCAR TO A COMPETENT BUT ORDINARY TREATMENT OF AN EXTRAORDINARY SUBJECT, THE HOLOCAUST, OVER *FOUR LITTLE GIRLS*, WHICH WAS MUCH THE BETTER FILM.

Well, we didn't make this film for the Academy. You know, it was funny. The best film of 1989, the year that *Do the Right Thing* came out, was *Driving Miss Daisy*. That was voted the best film of the year. To me that told me right away what the sensibilities are at the Academy. So in 1989 we refused to let anybody have to validate our work. So we decided we don't need validation from any group, not just the Academy, to say whether our work has merit, whether it's good or not. So we didn't make this film hoping to get an Academy Award. My greatest fear was that the parents and relatives of the little girls would hate the film. Once we got the stamp of approval from them, that was the validation that was needed. That's what mattered the most.

HOW HARD IS IT TO GET FILMS INTO DISTRIBUTION?

It's a crowded market as it is. So films jockey for position. Not just black films but big Hollywood films. The big ones try to pick a date. I mean, nobody wants to open the same day as *Jurassic Park* or *The Lost*

World. You're going to get wiped out. It's so critical now. Before, there were so many movie theaters and fewer films being made. So theater owners could take a chance and maybe build up an audience in the past.

It's so tight now and so much money is at stake that when that film first opens that Friday, Saturday, Sunday, if you don't have a gross those first two days, you're out. Everything is based upon how you open. Those numbers are all that matter. Do you have the grosses? If you don't have those grosses, the owner is going to bring in the next film. It's just like JFK [Airport]; you get these airplanes lined up on the runway and you get the okay from air traffic control that it's okay to land. There's too many movies nowadays. Too many.

YOU DO A LOT OF COMMERCIALS. ARE THERE TIMES WHEN THE PRODUCT YOU SELL CLASHES WITH THE VALUES YOU HAVE?

I think that's a question each individual artist has to answer. The reason the [commercial ad makers] want you—I mean, don't get fooled by their support—they know the number of people that you reach. So it's not because they're in love with you either. They know that audience that you have, and that's the one they want to buy the malt liquor. That's an individual question.

12

NEIL DAVIES

documentary filmmaker

A pale Welsh ex-paratrooper may not seem an obvious candidate to shoot documentaries about child slavery in Africa or a TV series capturing the sheer communal fun at an amateur variety showcase of black talent in London. But appearances are more deceiving than usual. These excavations and explorations of "working-class cosmopolitan London" were carried off with enormous élan and a sharp eye for people's foibles and fables. This less ritzy side of wildly overpriced London is screen turf that Neil Davies expertly has mined for the camera in a score of outstanding short documentaries.

Raised in a small Welsh village, Davies spent his teens hitching around Europe, hanging around clubs, and casting about for a palatable future. He soon joined the British Parachute Regiment, one of the toughest military outfits anywhere. After service in Aden and Cyprus, Davies made an improbably honorable exit into civilian life. After graduating from York University, he headed to London. Movie stunt work opened doors to film. Davies subsequently carved out a reputation as a tenacious, shrewd, and innovative documentary filmmaker in Britain.

You came to filmmaking through an exceedingly roundabout route.

I was born in Pembrey in Wales, a little mining village. But there were no pits left by then. I had one brother. At fifteen, I hitchhiked across Europe, looking for a Swedish nymphomaniac.

FIND ONE?

No.

WHERE DID YOU FIT IN TEEN CATEGORIES OF THE TIME?

I was a skinhead, a soul boy, or a mod. You don't observe these things the way observers see them. The labels don't fit so well. I saw the Beatles in *The Cavern* in Liverpool, rode motorbikes. They got forty pounds for the gig in our town just before they changed their hairstyle from slick-backed to Beatle mop. We all saw Chuck Berry, Albert King, ska music. It was quite a cultural revolution in 1963–1964. I went to soul clubs. North Wales had lots of them: Little Millie, Little Richard, Chuck Berry, the Supremes. The whole circuit was there from Liverpool to Manchester.

WHAT THEN?

Then I joined the Paras.

WHY?

Otherwise, it was either the pits or the steelworks or the odd job.

DID YOU HAVE ANY LARGER AMBITIONS?

I thought I was unemployable. But I had already been all over Europe and I saw people were getting married in Pembrey at sixteen. I had to get away from that. I didn't have much of an education. So I joined the Paras in the spring of 1965. My cousin was in the Falcons RAF parachute team. He was a top rugby player, and I used to idolize him. I guess it was an impetuous decision that you make because you are fed up and just want to get out. The military pay, anyway, was three times what I earned as a teenager on building sites.

WHAT WAS TRAINING LIKE?

There was seven months of training with a lot of Irish, Scottish, and Welsh lads—the Celtic fringe—along with a couple of Indians and West

Indian blacks. There were a handful of blacks in the Paras. They fit in better with the Celtic fringe, and they were protected. The Paras had a 75 percent failure rate in training, but I had to get those wings because I had to succeed at something important and so I went through the worst winter of my life.

SO YOU WERE A WELSH SOCIALIST IN THE PARAS, OF ALL OUTFITS.

When we were drilled to disperse trade union demonstrations. I said, "We are professional soldiers and we shouldn't be doing this." I was definitely in the minority. But there was a higher level [than that] where you bonded to survive. We closed ranks. I responded to that and became a good soldier.

AFTERWARD YOU WERE STATIONED IN ADEN?

May to December 1967. We were the last ones out of there. We Paras were dumped into Aden. We were playing games—war games. I loved it at first. But I saw the worst poverty there that I'd seen in my life, which was pretty impressive for someone who grew up a barefoot Welsh lad where leather shoes were tucked away for Sundays.

IT SURE WAS A LOUSY A CLIMATE.

It was 140 degrees. We were fighting guerrillas one day and government troops the next day. I remember the interrogations, the brutality, the smell, the cruelty, the shambles of architecture. It was Lawrence of Arabia country where soldiers sang "Green, Green Grass of Home," "Jumpin' Jack Flash," and Vietnam-era tunes. I saw a lot of inhumanity, a lot of firefights. The South Aden army rebelled, and we were under fire. We were not supposed to return fire from them, and our discipline was absolutely amazing. We knew that we were cannon fodder. They could shoot us with impunity for those few days.

The local factions there were angling for the advantage to fill the gap when we left. The civil war grew more intense as well as the fight they made against us. I knew it was all a question of who are we going to give power to as we departed. When we were leaving, we had refrigerators and blankets that we gave to the people there, who were in a bad way. I remember we had regular discussions with a former Yemeni soldier in the British army, and I learned a lot from him about what was going on there. It was working-class lads in my regiment—even some people who could be psychopaths—who were giving these things away to the local people.[1]

WHERE DID YOU GO AFTER ADEN?

In 1968, we parachuted into Cyprus in a show of force and wound up in Turkish whorehouses in Famagusta picking fights with Swedish UN peacekeeping units. Other Paras attacked the RAF hall. We were just out of control after Yemen. Eventually, the unit was dispatched to Aldershot. By then I knew I had to get out of the army.

HOW DID YOU MANAGE THAT?

I was alternatively in charge of a section or a section was in charge of me. As a noncom I just squeaked out. Above my [bed] I put up a poster of Tommy Smith in the Olympics with his black fist salute held high. That didn't work. But a friend helpfully advised "Pin this guy with the beard up and you'll be out." I hadn't a clue who Karl Marx was. In Welsh socialism he didn't figure, although we knew Lenin.

YOU MEAN IT WORKED?

It worked. Honorable discharge.

WHAT NEXT?

In 1969, I went to the steelworks for a year and led a wildcat strike over safety conditions. Then I went to Italy and sniffed around the Maoist movement. In 1970, I headed to York University, which had a bunch of mature students, including a few American Vietnam vets. I had a glorious time reading and talking: history, politics, literature. You name it. I read every book I could get my hands on. I was encouraged by a Welsh professor. I also organized a cross-country team. Rode motorbikes. I wrote poetry for *The Dragon*, a Welsh literary magazine. I was always into film. After graduation in 1973, you could walk into a job quite easily.

YOU MOVED TO LONDON IN THE MID-1970S.

I thought it was brilliant. Everybody's here. Barbadians, Irish, Pakistanis, Indians, all live on the same street in 1975 in Cricklewood and Willesden. I'd go to a West Indian dance near the White City tube station one night. You'd go to a *ceili* [dance] evening another night. You tasted all the different cultures. Different nationalities in working-class communities mixed pretty easily. The West Indian blacks had a Welsh notion of life—we are more impulsive and passionate. The extended family takes up people who are not blood relatives. That's the way you were brought up. You had to be reliable, and you had to keep your word.

WHEN DOES STAND-UP COMEDY POP UP?

Stand-up comedy became "another way of agitating," to make points and make you think. That's what you did in the Welsh evenings before TV, and in the army too. If the story wasn't funny, it had to be really tragic—and it had to be funny too.

WHEN DOES FILM TRAINING BEGIN?

In the 1980s I decided to write and went to work as a supply [substitute] teacher. I wrote scripts. I also started Red Rope—a socialist mountaineering organization for weekends in the mountains for trade unionists and such. In 1985 I decided on film or TV as a medium. I was doing stunt work for the BBC and by getting to know the people, I learned the camera. Cameramen are very generous and love to tell you about their jobs. Then I went off to China in 1986 and filed reports for the Australian News Agency, once while on a ferry with 3,000 coolies on a three-day journey, with a jazz band too. I was turned away at the Tibet border. Then it was pop promos, lots of sport programs for Sky television and cable, short documentaries, and freelance work.

YOU EVEN FILMED YOUR DAD'S CHOIR IN WALES, THE SORT OF SCENE CELEBRATED IN *BRASSED OFF*.

It was called *The Choir, the Passion, and the Song* and was done for Channel 4 in the summer of 1993 with the male-voice choir in my hometown of pit closures. They were raising money for charities. The choir was led by people who led the 1984 miners' strike. I became a minor celebrity in Wales because of it. And it was my father's choir. Then I did a 30-minute film, *Desperate Dan*, for BBC, recording wheelchair civil rights protests with a small Hi8 camera. I'd crawl under the train and film them like that, from that angle, as the authorities brought their bar cutters to cut loose the chained protesters. I got all this lovely intimate footage because I was using a Hi8 camera and using no narrator or reporter in the final cut.

THAT'S YOUR TRADEMARK STYLE: NO NARRATION. IT'S ALL IN THE EDITING.

I make documentaries without monologues and let the images be their own headlines. I did *Auf Wiedersehn, Pet*—which is not the same as the comedy series—which initially went into an *Undercover Britain* slot in the autumn of 1995. I went with two mates (or so I thought they were at the time) to Berlin building sites where a Dutch mafia was ripping off British workers and providing nonexistent safety measures. I spent five weeks on the building sites and was talking into this covert camera in a toolbag, which looked kind of funny to other guys, but it worked.

SO YOU PRACTICALLY PIONEERED A STYLE THAT IS ALL TOO FAMILIAR TODAY.

Oh, don't blame me.

APART FROM THAT, YOU SHUN COMMENTARY OF ANY KIND IN YOUR WORK. WHEN I ACCOMPANIED YOU A FEW YEARS AGO, I WATCHED YOU MOVE THROUGH RIDLEY MARKET IN LONDON WITH A DIGITAL 6 PANA-SONIC VIDEO MINICAMERA WITH A 500 RESOLUTION—VERSUS, AS YOU IN-FORMED ME, A 650 RESOLUTION FOR THE SHOULDER KIND—WHICH AL-LOWED YOU TO MOVE AROUND PRETTY INCONSPICUOUSLY.

It's indispensable.

DIDN'T YOU TAP INTO YOUR PARATROOPER BACKGROUND IN THE MAKING OF A NORTHERN IRELAND DOCUMENTARY?

I worked on a Bloody Sunday [in Londonderry] documentary in 1990, and I came to the conclusion that it was snipers on the walls that started it.[2] I talked to former members of my Para outfit in a mortar platoon. I was convinced there were guys on the walls firing down. The soldiers thought that they were being shot at by the IRA. The people were be-ing shot at by the soldiers when they were all being shot at by the guys up on the wall. But I was unable to squeeze it into the final version be-cause it was regarded as anecdotal. For Praxis Films with John Godard, and for Channel 4, I worked as a researcher and producer and did everything, shot *Dispatches* pieces of women in prison, eccentrics in Yorkshire, and tributes to computer hackers' ingenuity. I went to Zim-babwe to investigate killings of former hero guerrillas by Mugabe. They were run over by trucks.

In 1997, *Nights at the Empire*, a series on Channel 4, was a breakout for you, showing the black community celebrating its talented offspring and itself.

I wanted to show the way the community is defining itself. Their faces are glowing because they are cheering for a member of their own community to succeed and that affirms their culture. Here is variety reinvented by the black community, the extended family, the grannies cheering for their nephews. It was like watching a South Wales singsong. It was great.

This is something the Irish and Jewish people had done in eras before this. This is what TV should be about—taking them for a ride through the stage, the back stage, the band, and letting the audience think about what they see. I wanted to show all the action in the wings with all the cultural significance and meaning and all the tremendous warmth of the audience. And they didn't mind if a white boy from Essex or an Irish boy came on. It wasn't meant to be exclusively black. They can see past the color of your skin.

What was your favorite moment?

There were 1,000 people in the theater on Saturday and a sixteen-year-old girl was shaking and trying to sing. It was the moment that touched the audience the most. This young girl made the biggest impact. Entertainment is not only or always the slickness but connecting at the human level. It was amateur variety night at the theater.

They had showed four of the original four programs because Lady Di had died at that time. It was a hard battle to sell. Yasmine Anwar, commissioning editor of multicultural programming at Channel 4, fought for it and gave it to a Welsh ex-soldier. It became cult viewing in Ireland and Wales. It had Richard Blackwood, Roger Dee, Lorraine Benloss, Rudy Lickwood, Junior Simpson, and Marcus Powell, and then Terry Alderton, a white guy from Essex and the Paul Morocco Band and a white juggler too. The blacks are just not getting a chance to grow.

You did a flurry of pungent shorts too.

I went out to the Montserrat volcano in October 1996 to film British citizens on British Island, who were neglected by Tory governments in ten-minute interview production. And in March 1997 on BBC I had a fifteen-minute short documentary of a black skiing club of thirty-some

Afro-Caribbean blacks from London arriving in a small town in Italy where the chromatically impaired hotel manager declares, "You're Africans, not English." They had rung him for reservations and he went on their voices, which of course were English. So these people, who are more English than I, are suddenly facing this resistance. They decided to occupy the hotel, and I recorded divisions among the other tourists over their case. They split in their attitude toward the ski club members and their right to be there.

YOU CAME UP WITH A WACKY BUT REVEALING TV SERIES, PAIRING CELEBRITIES WITH THEIR MOMS FOR A NIGHT OF COOKING.

It gets under the skin and offers a peep behind the curtain of celebrity. We've had Olympic athlete Colin Jackson; Falklands War veteran Simon Weston; news presenter Lucy Cohen; rock musician Mal Pope, who played and wrote for Elton John; and world champion super-middleweight boxer Joe Calzaghe dining at home as his father cooks. One talks about his mother's cooking making him fart. We filmed two hours and edited the best thirty minutes, expressly banished the presenter. No narration ever. We offer the keyhole without the paraphernalia of presenting.

We film in their own homes and domain where they feel confident and they are in charge and therefore we get the real them; once they're in the swing, they let it go. The idea is to make them feel really comfortable so they forget you're there, and a lot of the time they do. You get real tips about cooking as well as the people themselves. Never use a whole onion, mash the tomatoes. Getting Sardinian cookery hints from Joe Calzaghe's grandfather, chatting. And they're talking about how brutal and barbaric boxing is and how the bank balance is all that makes it matter. It takes more courage when you are crap to step in the ring.

YOU ARE FILMING A YOUNG CONTENDER FROM START OF CAREER TO, HOPEFULLY, THE CHAMPIONSHIP.

I began by shooting boys in this Welsh valley who won't move out of it, who are training in a clapped-out cardboard kind of hut of a gym. Windows missing, held together with bailing string, and a thirty-year-old punch bag. Later I met Faisal Muhammed, who, as we speak, has twenty-four KOs in twenty-seven fights, and began shooting *Contender* for Channel 4, following him from his home in Irish Kilburn as he tries to become heavyweight champion.

IT IS RUMORED THAT YOU USED YOUR PARA TRAINING TO TRAIN COMICS.

I took a band of comedians on a mock-up but intense Para-style week-long training course in Devon where these very individualist stand-up artists bonded brilliantly. You need something like this to cooperate, and then you catch the bantering amid the battering. I think eventually we'll get some good ideas for films and series about living in multicultural London.

YOU'VE SETTLED IN WALES WITH YOUR JAZZ-SINGER WIFE PAULINE AND YOUR KIDS.

We love it. My wife Pauline [Swaby], a Jamaican Londoner, wowed them. I think she's Welsh. She fit right in in this Welsh town and sang one memorable night in the male-voice choir with a crew of fifty-to-ninety-year-old Welsh miners doing backup. It was an extraordinary evening.

NOTES

1. In Aden (later South Yemen), British soldiers suffered 57 killed and 651 wounded from 1963 until their withdrawal in November 1967.
2. Bloody Sunday occurred in Derry on January 30, 1972, when a British Para regiment fired upon a crowd of Catholic community demonstrators, killing fourteen and wounding many others.

⓭

DUSAN MAKAVEJEV

film director

Dusan Makavejev, born in Belgrade, is a burly bearded man in his sixties. After taking a degree in psychology at Belgrade University, he gravitated to amateur filmmaking. Makavejev diligently honed his craft on shoestring budgets until he managed to direct the features *Man Is Not a Bird* (1965), *Loves of a Switchboard Operator* (1967), and *Innocence Unprotected* (1968). His classic sexual-political romp *WR: Mysteries of the Organism* (1971)—a film unsurpassable in its fierce anti-authoritarian thrust—was duly denounced by the Tito regime as "ideologically harmful." It remained banned in Yugoslavia for sixteen years. Under duress, Makavejev left Yugoslavia and settled, more or less, in Paris.

Since that highly dramatic juncture, he has made *Sweet Movie* (1974), which for ostensibly nonpolitical reasons managed to get banned in Britain, Canada, and South Africa; *Montenegro* (1981); *The Coca Cola Kid* (1985); *Manifesto* (1988); and *Hole in the Soul* (1994). The interview took place in 1995 after a screening of *Gorilla Bathes at Noon*, a satire about the fall of the Berlin Wall, shot in Belgrade and Berlin in 1993. Negotiations were going on over the new round of Balkan wars. Makavejev's insightful comments then still seem to apply in the region, despite the post-1999 NATO intervention. We also discussed the politics of film, the protectionism controversy in Europe, and the fate of his ravaged homeland, which was once upon a time just called Yugoslavia.

YOU GREW UP IN WHAT IS NOW SERBIA?

I was raised in Belgrade. My mother was the first woman veterinarian there, and she worked in the production of serums. She was divorced. I never knew my father. I think he was lost in the war. I can remember as a child how we Serbs were proud that Belgrade was burned on Hitler's personal order because we had told him "Fuck you" [in 1941] when Prince Paul signed a deal that Yugoslavia would not join the Axis [while Hungary and Romania did] but would let the Nazi trains come through. The next day, everything German in Belgrade was burned because we could not stand having anybody telling us what to do. Our degree of pride not only borders on the totally irrational but, as you see now with the civil war, it gets into psychosis, an absolutely disproportionate understanding of your own importance versus that of other people.

I started elementary school when the war started. I remember this proud city half burned down and the black market and all kinds of illegal activity. You'd have five families in one apartment. Three of every four schools were taken over as German army barracks, so we had about fifteen minutes per class. There were so many surreal things. Similar things are in *Hope and Glory*, a film I really like: kids being happy about Hitler bombing their school; parachutists coming from the skies. In nice weather, you'd see the Allied bombers going over Belgrade to bomb the Ploesti oilfields [in Romania].

On Easter in 1944, we were walking all nicely dressed to church and we were waving at the planes—and bombs started falling. People cursed, but some people went on waving because it meant freedom was coming. It was a sign of the end of the war. These are paradoxical things I remember from childhood. After the war, there was nationalization of everything, but mostly the industry was destroyed. This meant there was a renovation of the whole country, and everybody was in it, or almost everybody.

THESE DAYS TITO LOOKS RATHER GOOD.

Many people really loved him, especially poor people. He was a great master of imagery; it was almost on the order of kitsch. I became a member of the League of Communists in 1949 when we were building antitank trenches. It was kind of funny to be a member of communist organization that was anti-Soviet. But I remember thinking at the time that something is wrong with me because I cannot love this man. My first understanding of how Tito operates was when I was thrown out of the Party in 1953. I was an editor on the student paper at Belgrade University that would not change their editorial policy, which was pro-[Milovan] Djilas, who at the time was leader of the hope that we could get a democratic socialism.

The editors of many pro-Djilas newspapers were replaced. Hard-liners would come in and write more of the front-page articles, but the rest of the staff would stay. I came to an editorial meeting one day, and there was a new editor. So I went home and wrote a film review, which I submitted and published. I continued writing reviews and started making amateur and experimental films, and I removed myself from mainstream political activity.

All Yugoslavia was like that. Everybody learned to create his own niche. In Tito's system, there was space for everybody. If you speak of politics having grains of truth—not really carrying the truth—Tito perhaps had more grains of truth than others. He was maneuvering against Russians, creating a new kind of Third World formation. He became a kind of popular king. People were happy having him being kissed by Kenyatta or whoever. It was like a Viennese operetta. It had this kind of [Ernst] Lubitsch quality, you know?

But Tito banned *Mysteries of the Organism*.

We were under the heavy shadow of the Soviet Union. Brezhnev was mad at the film. Tito banned the film because of it. There was nothing in it against Tito personally. But he left me to cook in my own juices.

How was the temperature turned up?

While I was still mixing *Mysteries in Munich* in May 1972, a Belgrade paper got a picture not approved by me. In it is a naked actress and in the room is a poster of Lenin. They called me first, and so I managed to cover the poster. So the picture came out without Lenin. A month later, a new girlie magazine came on the market and there was a center spread with this picture with Lenin on the wall. The next morning the Soviet Embassy wrote a letter to our Ministry of Information saying "This is a disgrace." I later learned that the girlie magazine was printed by the same company that translated the main Soviet magazine. It was a Soviet Embassy operation, a disinformation campaign. Within a week, the people who allowed this film to be produced were replaced.

The film was banned. Obviously I was not the target. I was used. The main target was Tito because he was not happy about the Russians invading Czechoslovakia. Reviewers would say that this movie was betraying socialist ideals. You always got these fundamentalist ideas here and there, but 1973 was a watershed year when the hard-liners become more important. Tito let witch-hunts happen to feed his hard-liners. You felt the fingers around your neck. We got a minute sum for development of *Sweet Movie*. We tried to do a short documentary about the city of Belgrade building apartments for workers. It was a good cause for poor people, but all doors were closed. The main attack on *Mysteries* was that it was used by the Western press to show how horrible communism is. But the foreign ministry people were happy with me because my films were playing everywhere and ambassadors were getting praise.

Then the whole liberal leadership of Yugoslavia was wiped out in December 1972. Art, you know, is a good playground for hard-liners against liberals because they can talk about morals, not art. One day I start driving my Volkswagen and I heard a strange sound. I went to the right front wheel and opened the hubcap, and of four bolts, three were unscrewed. This was the government whispering to me in a very strong whisper. I got out a few days later.

GORILLA BATHES AT NOON HAS THE LEAD, A SOVIET OFFICER, WHO IS IN BERLIN WHEN HIS REGIMENT DEPARTS. HE FENDS FOR HIMSELF AND TURNS OUT TO BE AN AMIABLE GUY, WHILE IN MYSTERIES, THE LEAD, A SOVIET SKATER AND ALSO A MILITARY OFFICER, IS A RIGID FOOL AND A MURDERER.

Yes, and he doesn't understand why. I like exploring what is beneath the uniform. Soldiers are recruited to kill, so when they are not killing, they are in a kind of suspended state. If they don't start killing at a certain point, what is the point of having the army? Then you can use firemen to keep order. In *Gorilla*, soldiers who lose their uniform are like snails without their shell. The body of a snail looks so frail and a shell is so important. In most professions, you can choose to be professional and a private person and the difference is not necessarily great. But with soldiers, the difference is enormous. You are omnipotent, and then you come home and put on your slippers or have children crawling over you. There is this incredible discrepancy.

DO YOU SYMPATHIZE WITH YOUR SOVIET OFFICER IN GORILLA WHO TRIES TO CLEAN A STATUE OF LENIN?

No. He is just a crazy guy who does something he believes in. My quarrel with Russia was with the Leninist or Stalinist part of Russian culture. Russian culture is part of our culture. We had brilliant translations not only of Dostoyevsky but of the great Russian writers of the 1920s. After the Russian Revolution and before Stalin suppressed it, there were ten years of a flourishing of arts. My generation believed we had to continue what was done in Russia in 1920s.

ARE YOU A DEMOCRATIC SOCIALIST?

Yes—with a substantial anarchic streak. I felt okay with everything that was democratic and socialist. But I also felt okay about things that were democratic and not necessarily socialist, because the world is multifaceted and there are so many meanings in it. I like the idea of the market. But the American idea of free market is really not normal; there is a psychotic ingredient in it.

BECAUSE IT OPPOSES ANY REGULATION—THIS IDEA THAT THE MARKET IS MAGIC?

Yeah.

DOES WILHELM REICH STILL MATTER TODAY?

Partially, yes. Reich was dealing with the animal side of people, which is why I like to use animals in my films. This is a good side of us, because animals control this basic energy. Most animals are not birds of prey or beasts. Most are more like horses, cows, and dogs. There is this psychological-ecological game going on in the world that Reich was very well aware of.

DO YOU SPEAK OF REICH ONLY THROUGH THE 1930s—WHICH EVEN CRITICS TEND TO AGREE WAS A PERIOD OF PERSONAL BRILLIANCE?

I speak of Reich through the end of his life. He was this very sensitive man who had an incredible awareness of energies. People who knew him speak of him as incredibly perceptive. So he was a healer—even before being educated by Freud. He was a healer who detects where your tragedy is—if it is in your shoulder, in your jaw. I was fascinated by him. My film was a kind of homage. I just tried to learn as much about him as you can. But I tried not to be fascinated with things about him that were unreal.

LIKE THE ORGONE BOX?

I think the Orgone Box was done by an ex-communist who believed you could put someone in a box and he comes out an angel—this magic idea that you can make a new man.

WHEN DID YOU DISCOVER REICH?

As a student in 1951.The first writing by Reich I read—*Marxism and Psychoanalysis*—was translated by a man who fought in the Spanish Civil War and became one of our top commandants [in World War II] and was foreign affairs minister at a time of a most progressive policy of Yugoslavia being friendly to everybody. A lot of leftist romantics were like him. Much of the war in Yugoslavia was commanded by people who had fought in Spain. None of them was pro-Soviet because they knew what the Soviets did in Spain.

So if there were independent communists in postwar Europe it was these people who did not trust Russians but were strong antifascists. I remember in my youth speaking with many of these people—and if I was ever romantic, I was romantic in this sense. I read Jack London and the American socialist tradition too. In my political views I was closest to British Labour [in the 1940s]. It was all one world. People fought the war so you would have no more wars anymore. The Cold War was something artificial.

DOES THE PSYCHOLOGY OF TOTALITARIANISM EXPLORED IN *MYSTERIES* APPLY TO SERBIA TODAY?

Absolutely. It's a totalitarianism that is not able to control itself.

AND MICRONATIONALISM RUNS AMOK TOO.

Under the Nazi occupation, Serbia and quisling Croatia were similar—with a lot of nobodies doing all this chest-thumping and claiming that their country is great Croatia or great Serbia. And they were absolutely fake people who were very dangerous, which is very similar to this totally artificial nationalism today. We have here nations who are not actually distinct as nations because we speak the same language. The cultural distances between Serbs, Croats, and Muslims are really small distances. You have people who don't know how to cross themselves speaking about the great role of the Church in Serbia. They were nonbelievers yesterday and they will be nonbelievers tomorrow if somebody else comes along and they can profit.

They are total chameleons. Paramilitary leaders don't know how to fight except to throw bombs to get everybody running and then they rob the villages. They are thieves pretending to be soldiers. When you go with twenty tanks against people who have twenty rifles, what kind of war is it? If armed people are attacking women, children, and old people, this should be stopped with harshest measures. It was not done. The military knows how to stop the fighting. You can neutralize heavy weapons with simple tactics; it is no big deal. So there is this understanding in Serbia that there is an unwritten agreement between the West and [Serb leader] Milosevic that he should clean the West of all Muslims. And that is what's happening.

WHAT DO YOU THINK OF THE NEGOTIATORS?

[Cyrus] Vance and [David] Owen and [Lord] Carrington can't understand the realities when Greek Orthodox, Muslims, and Catholics share the same, very refined language in this multicultural society where everybody understands everybody else with half a word. Carrington drops the federal government, which is weak but still had some clout and knowledge about what could be done, and he starts discussing peace with six presidents. You have him talking to these guys who were some of the worst that our nation can produce.

THE WEST HASN'T BEHAVED AS IF IT WANTS TO END IT.

We don't know how much the West has a vested interest in the situation as it is. I understand even America is selling weapons to these arsenals and selling like crazy to Greece and Turkey too. The American weapons industry is hoping for a new Balkan war and is supported by Congress. It's unbelievable. Getting two NATO countries ready for war among themselves! Greeks and Turks, you know, have no other enemies but Greeks and Turks.

DOES TERRITORIAL DIVISION MAKE ANY SENSE?

The territorial division is crazy. You get one nation with electricity and another with factories and another with water supplies. In Bosnia, they cut all the roads. So each side has to build everything they need. Communities that once shared a post office or school will have to have one each. You'd have to have border control every five miles. Someone said if they apply the maps there would be 100,000 kilometers of borders. It's impossible. Owen is sent there to keep talks going any way he can. So if they like maps he will give them maps. He is doing something totally insincere. He has already said the West will do nothing. The West sends food, but a lot gets stolen and wasted and most of it is going to be given to people who will just die a month later.

You have old people in Belgrade holding hands and jumping from buildings because they cannot buy a few potatoes. I've seen people eating from garbage cans, respectable people who worked all their lives and now go begging. But why is it more important to bring food than to create communication between Belgrade and Zagreb? During the World War, trains were going between the cities every day and the road was never cut or only cut for a little while because of partisans. On any given day, if the whole world decides this communication will be open, it will be open.

How do you get them to talk in good faith if Serbs—and everyone else—are so stubborn?

Pressure Serbs and they get more spiteful. I was in Belgrade the day when they announced the bombing [threat]. Nobody was afraid. Instead, they give more and more power to this fake socialist party of Milosevic and never want to talk to the opposition. But I remember a moment in Geneva when it looked like the West would go in and stop it. A friend told me that the soldiers commanding Serbian, Croatian, and Bosnian units all sat together so that if the war stops they can quickly establish communications and coordinate things. They are all Tito's officers. Because they all know each other personally, they could turn from hostile to peaceful partners overnight if the constellation is not as it is—and this constellation is largely determined by the outside world, not only inside the borders.

Would military intervention do any good?

I am against more fighting. The pressure should really be put on the leaders who run the war and now are free to fly to Geneva or wherever. And you cannot apply sanctions on Serbia and not apply them to Croatia—both sides are killing Muslims. In Serbia, the understanding is that the sanctions are applied unjustly and unequally. The feeling is that Croats are privileged because they are pets of Germany. Obviously it is much more complex. But popular feelings in crazy times are kitschy feelings. It is B movie–type thinking. Serbs believe the pope is our eternal enemy and is talking every day to England and that England is a Catholic country.

They don't even know Protestants exist. For them, this idea of the pope in England is sane. To them, Muslims are the same as Turks or Gadhafi or Iran. So you have these different ethnic groups thrown into the worst possible thinking and you have the most stupid Muslims, most stupid Catholics, and most stupid Orthodox leading their so-called nations. To me, it's not clear whether these are tribes or nations. I don't want to sound as if I'm on this side or that. I really don't believe I am on any side. I'm against everything that's happening.

BACK TO FILM. WHERE DO YOU STAND ON THE FUSS THE FRENCH RAISED ABOUT AMERICAN DOMINATION OF EUROPEAN CINEMA?

I think defense against America is absolutely healthy because it is trying to protect America from the great danger of becoming a monopoly. So in this sense there is no conflict because America is based on competition. But I do not think we can raise barriers and sit behind them. I know when you make something that is not expensive, you have to get it into 50 to 200 theaters to get money back. So we have to have space for small products that could easily be competitive in their own fields if the venues are not closed. But when you get art cinemas playing Spielberg movies—and this is happening all over the world—this is horrible. Not that I am against Spielberg. He is today what Walt Disney was for my generation. I've seen *Raging Bull*—a movie that has to be seen on a big screen—in a multiplex. Here is a film with a great soundtrack—and Scorsese is great with sound and with images—in a small theater of fifty seats and we hear the soundtrack of two other films because the walls were so thin. It was a shame. It seems to me that we are caught in several processes of huge industrial changes.

SUCH AS THE INFORMATION SUPERHIGHWAY?

It seems we are living in one world with instant information. We learn about an earthquake in Armenia and we are watching at same moment as Armenians are watching.

AREN'T WE GETTING JUST ONE MONOTONOUS VERSION?

Sure, we can't live on CNN. They are so dull in what they did with the Gulf War. Having reporters in four capital cities each in his own hotel room and showing maps and saying they hear the sound of rockets. It was totally ridiculous. CNN doesn't know how to be different, how not to behave as nonmonopolists. They forget to listen to the other side because they don't need to. Somebody with the proper instinct would do it.

We have to come up with new ways of making competitive commercial products so we don't get all flooded by this electronic river that is going to turn us all into numbers. They turn a piece of film into numbers and then reconstruct it—and they believe they can do the same thing to people. They get our genetic code and recompose us. Like in [David] Cronenberg's *The Fly*, a film I really like. But even more dangerous than the dinosaur dominance of Hollywood, I think, is the omnipresence of television. People forget to go and see movies.

THE FEW BRITISH FILMS COMING OUT ARE OFTEN MADE WITH TELEVISION BACKING, AND THEY ARE USUALLY GOOD.

I think it is very specifically British. I think it must come from Anglo-Saxon puritan morality. If you have to do a job and people give you money and leave you alone, you will produce high quality. The BBC charter is quite unique. You have a public company that is crafting products that look in every way like they are made by a private craftsman. You don't have many cultures that have that. As soon as you start working for government, it is sloppy. In France or Germany, when they produce serious work it is very boring and unwatchable.

In England you have even these low genres that are done so well. It's a pity that you can't export it. Even in this horrible crisis in English production—having just little more than a dozen films a year—you find that almost everything is good. In France, probably 35 percent are good, in England it is closer to 60 to 70 percent. In America, humor is very vulgar. Without sex they have no humor. In England you get this sense of the absurd, an unbelievably high-quality humor, that Monty Python trademark. The sex is well disguised because all humor is probably sexual—I'm probably quoting Freud—and it goes all the way back to fairytales. They are perverse, but at same time you see humor. What can be more perverse than selling dead parrots?

Look at Hitchcock, who takes monstrous stories and makes beautiful tales of them. I don't know exactly what the difference is between a story and a tale, but there is one. When you see his films they are so full of grace. It's like getting on a flying carpet. Take any Hitchcock film—*The Birds*, *Vertigo*, *Psycho*—and it's like a children's story: the basic story of life as something dangerous and beautiful.

AND YOUR NEXT PROJECT?

No idea. The first one that seems right, I'll do.

14

BRUNO BETTELHEIM

psychologist: another look

World-renowned child psychologist Bruno Bettelheim (1903–1990) was an incorrigible maverick who questioned everything, including psychoanalysis. Even—perhaps especially—eminent mavericks often are made to pay for their independent ways once they obligingly shuffle off this mortal coil. Bettelheim's suicide in March 1990 triggered an astonishing avalanche of odium from half a dozen former patients (called "residents" at his Orthogenic School treatment center at the University of Chicago) and staff, who clearly reveled in accusing this illustrious Viennese émigré of almost every imaginable wickedness. His many defenders were ignored or distorted in the ensuing media frenzy. Bettelheim, almost overnight, became reviled as a fraud who mugged his patients, intimidated his staff, blamed mothers for autism, plagiarized freely, and fabricated his credentials.

Bettelheim published a quartet of books based on immensely detailed case studies at the Orthogenic School, which he directed from 1944 until 1973: *Love Is Not Enough* (1950), *Truants from Life* (1955), *The Empty Fortress* (1967), and *A Home for the Heart* (1974). He analyzed, and meditated upon, his grueling concentration camp experiences in *The Informed Heart* (1960) and *Surviving and Other Essays* (1980). In 1977, he won a National Book Award for his psychoanalytic foray into fairytales, *The Uses of Enchantment*. Although himself a savvy critic of the limits of psychoanalytic method, he penned a short but scathing critique of the excessively technical fashion in which American psychiatry insistently has construed

Viennese psychoanalysis, *Freud and Man's Soul* (1982). He became professor of education and psychiatry at the austerely intellectual University of Chicago but nevertheless was a sought-after contributor to popular periodicals. All these and many other career achievements were thoroughly impugned as the pseudo-scandal remorselessly played out.

Yet the nagging mystery remains as to how the highly dubious "revelations" squared with the impressive lifelong record of a passionate man who wrote more than a dozen undeniably insightful books and helped heal many deeply disturbed youngsters. Bettelheim fearlessly tangled with authorities over controversial issues ranging from the behavior of inmates in Dachau and Buchenwald concentration camps (where he spent nearly a year) to the causes of infantile autism to the legacy of Anne Frank. Phonies don't jump into fraught frays where they are easily exposed. It simply didn't add up, and the reason it didn't add up is that hardly any accusations turned out upon investigation to have a basis in fact. Those that did—such as slapping children—were wildly exaggerated.

Several biographers, in the midst of this tense scandal-mongering atmosphere, sallied forth to interrogate Bettelheim's friends, foes, and alleged victims in order to get to the bottom of the mystery. One writer produced a seamless hatchet job, artfully crafted to accentuate (or, in some instances, invent) the negative; another biographer, despite indulging in parlor-analysis guesswork and her tactical need to prove that Bettelheim was no angel, showed some warranted awe at his work and was even compelled to take staff members seriously about how wild and preposterous the charges of abuse were.[1] What neither biographer could bring themselves to say was what became obvious to anyone who really sifted through the evidence: that Bruno Bettelheim was the real thing. Since then, Bettelheim's former literary agent has added a predictably more favorable book to the debate but has by no means cleared up the controversy or reversed the tide of opprobrium.[2]

In advance of a lengthier volume under way, and as a representative sample of the gist of numerous interviews, I present four conversations about Bettelheim's life and work and about the grotesquely trumped-up scandal with a psychiatrist who worked at the school, a child care worker who not only worked there but knew Bettelheim for much of his life, a former patient who since has published a pseudonymous memoir of his Orthogenic School experiences, and an appreciation by Pulitzer Prize–winning psychiatrist Robert Coles, an eminent maverick himself.[3]

ROBERT BERGMAN, PSYCHIATRIST

Bergman trained in psychiatry at the University of Chicago. After the Orthogenic School experiences described below, he would go on to become chief of the U.S. Public Health Service on the Navajo Reservation in Arizona.

HOW DID YOU FIRST KNOW OF BETTELHEIM?

My first contact was when he did group supervision with us [medical] residents and I presented to him. He had a reputation for being a sort of frightening guy, hard to get along with. But he was very helpful and brilliant and made an enormous impression on me. So the attitude that I went to the Orthogenic School with—which I think was shared—was that he was a great genius, an outstanding person who was doing wonderful things with these disturbed children.

I was a psychiatric resident in the last days of psychoanalytic domination of American psychiatry. At that time at the University of Chicago and at most of the highly regarded [medical schools], a residency in psychiatry was to a psychoanalytic institute what a college football team was to the National Football League. If you were good, you made it, and if you didn't, you were sorry. So it was a very psychoanalytic department and one that was proud to have the association with Bettelheim. The child psychiatrists certainly had a high regard for him.

SO YOU VISITED THE SCHOOL AS A PSYCHIATRIC RESIDENT.

I left town for an internship year, but then I came back as a psychiatric resident, and just by luck I entered my child psychiatry rotation relatively early. A standard feature of that was to spend, I think, a half a day a week at the school. I started going more because I was so interested. I sort of fell in love with the place.

HOW LONG DID THAT TAKE?

About five minutes. It was a beautiful place. There was a contributing élan [among the staff]. There was a whole chemistry; you could count on the level [of commitment and enthusiasm]. Bruno was definitely "big daddy." It was a great privilege to work with him. I never knew anyone else who was as smart about psychoanalysis as Bettelheim. Just when we thought we had him figured out, we found we didn't.

WHAT YEAR WAS THAT?

That would be the spring of 1964. So I did that and then I continued to visit. I had a six-months' elective in my residency, and I arranged to be a counselor there for [that period]. It made an impression on me. The association became stronger—or more ambivalent [laughs]—at the end of my six months of working full-time the way any counselor did. I suppose what attracted me to him and the school was that of all the things I had high expectations of, he and the school were the least disappointing, and maybe the most overfulfilling. He was even smarter than I thought he would be and even scarier than I thought he would be. I had read *Love Is Not Enough* and *Truants from Life*. The school was exactly as described. That was one of the things I loved about it.

While I was at the Orthogenic School, I visited an adolescent unit at Elgin State Hospital. It made me stop and think. The kids at Elgin celebrated the Fourth of July on the 30th of June and Christmas on the 20th of December because the staff wanted those days off. The O. School celebrated Christmas on Christmas.

DO YOU KNOW ANYTHING ABOUT HIS RELATIONSHIPS WITH PSYCHOANALYSTS?

The relationship with the psychoanalytic community was uneasy. He was a friend to a number of them. My analyst, Paul Kramer, was a good friend of his. Bettelheim was pretty close to Heinz Kohut, and certainly with Al Flarsheim. He had an odd relationship with the psychoanalytic community. They didn't recognize him as an analyst. I don't think he had completed his training in Vienna when they put him in the concentration camps. He wasn't an MD.

I remember attending a talk on autism at the Chicago Institute of Psychoanalysis by Margaret Mahler. Bettelheim was being gracious. He praised the paper. Then he said, "I have just one small question. I don't think that kid looks all that autistic." The room exploded. I remember Mahler angrily countered that he wasn't "even an analyst."

I HEAR HE HAD BETTER RELATIONS WITH ERIK ERIKSON.

I met Erikson at the Orthogenic School and also met him later at the
Indian [Public] Health Service. They'd known each other a long time.
You saw the two of them together and they seemed to agree. Erikson was
good at kidding him. Bettelheim was late to a staff meeting one night. We
knew that he was with a visitor but didn't know who he was. Then he
came into the staff meeting with a very distinguished-looking gentleman
and said: "This is the staff of the school, and please meet Erik Erikson."
My first thought was: "That guy has that same name as Erik Erikson."
Years later I told that to him. Then Bettelheim went into one of his modesty fits. He said he was just the janitor and we did all the hard work. And
Erikson said, "Yes, but you keep the furnace well stoked, don't you,
Bruno?" That was probably the summer of 1965. I was never there when
[Fritz] Redl was there, but I certainly heard about the Redl visits.

THIS RAISES THE TOUCHY QUESTION OF EXTERNAL MONITORING OF THE
SCHOOL.

The staff itself was aware of the 24-hour operation of the school.
There were visiting analysts. [Psychiatrist George Perkins] was there
when I was at the school. The idea of that was to have an outside observer monitoring progress. But I should think the main monitoring was
us. It was a big staff. People like me came and went all the time. Among
the people who came and went, some didn't like Bettelheim at all. But
for years and years, anyone who was in child psychiatry or was a child
fellow at the University of Chicago visited the school.

In my day, it was six a year and later I think it was a greater number.
Not all of them are admirers. [I recall a woman] who was a resident a
couple years ahead of me. She was someone who by turns would ideal-
ize and denigrate people. She initially enormously idealized Bettelheim
and then turned on him. The specific thing she complained about was
that he hit kids, which was true. He did hit kids. He didn't hit them very
much. But he regarded that as an important thing to do, and he did it.
[She] was shocked and suggested that he was sadistic and brutal and was
a terrible guy. No one was restraining [her] from saying those things
publicly. I think there were a number of other people who had a bad
feeling about his hitting kids. I got kind of won over to it myself [instead
of applying restraints, quiet rooms, or drugs].

WHAT WAS YOUR RESPONSE WHEN YOU FIRST SAW IT? IT'S THE ONE
THING THAT IS NOT IN THE BOOKS.

I was quite shocked. That was not in the books. I was very surprised. Bettelheim said that it was utterly necessary that the kids feel secure in the school and that to feel secure from one another, which was the hardest thing to arrange, there had to be absolutely enforced rules about their not hurting one another. So there had to be a fearsome authority that the kids would obey and be afraid of so they wouldn't bully each other and take each other's stuff and what not. He didn't want them to be afraid of their counselors. We were comforting to them. He was supposed to provide structure and security, and the simplest and most direct way to do that was with quick, immediate, and effective punishment, if it was called for. It was threatened more often than it happened, and it happened only occasionally. Certainly when I was there I don't think Charlie [Pekow, one of the most vociferous complainants] ever got hit. I don't suppose I saw [slapping] happen more than four or five times, if that.

THIS HITTING WAS ALWAYS SLAPS TO THE FACE?

Yes.

DID YOU THINK IT WAS JUSTIFIED?

I think it was justified. When they went nuts, it was to him they ran. When the smoke cleared, no one was hurt. I think that for the kids, Bettelheim's hitting them [seemed] frequent because they were frequently so scared he was going to.

WHAT DO YOU MAKE OF THE ANGRY ACCUSATIONS TODAY?

For some of the kids, Bettelheim was more important than an ordinary father. If you are carrying him around as a horrible introject, then you are going to spit him out. If it was so terrible and terrifying, why aren't more people possessed with a consuming hatred? Most are living [well enough]. It is a cottage industry for these people, accusing Bettelheim.

HE THOUGHT OF YOU AS A SUCCESSOR FOR HIS JOB, DIDN'T HE?

Every weekday the routine was that when the kids got out of class, there was an overlap when the teachers and the counselors were on duty at the same time. As a transition between school and dormitories, the kids would tell a story, lead a song, lead a discussion on something. One day a week, it was Bettelheim's turn. He would always get up in front of the group and say, "Are there any questions?" There always were questions. One day someone asked him about any building plans he had. He talked about the adolescent unit, which was just then being planned. He said, "Maybe when Bob gets done taking care of the Indians in two years he can come back and supervise constructing it."

That was the first he said to me about coming back in any capacity. I was too surprised and didn't quite know what to make of it or believe what I had heard. Then he said something about my coming back as supervisor of psychotherapy. And again I did nothing about it except be surprised and pleased and excited and perturbed by it. So prior to my leaving Chicago for the Indian Heath Service, people kept saying to me, "Are you going to be Bettelheim's successor?"

You had no clue that he thought so well of you?

One of the worst things you could do was tell him you did something good because he was utterly unsatisfiable. Nothing was ever good enough. He didn't want us to feel satisfied. He always wanted us to be trying harder. So he would take particular pains to point out what was wrong with anything anyone would say was good. There were little things, though. He would imply that he knew that I got along well with the kids. I remember one time when the kids got all upset because a sub teacher was reading them a story that I ordinarily read at bedtime, and they said, "That's Bob's story." He said something about it being special because it was me, or something like that. I think that was the most fulsome praise I ever got from him. Bettelheim was just awful with good-byes too. My last shift ended at one in the morning and some of us went out to have something to eat and drink and I turned to Bettelheim to say something and he was gone. He didn't like to say goodbye to people.

What then?

I think then I got a call from some Jewish children's agency and they asked if I wanted to apply to be director of the Pritzker Center. I was very surprised. I had at this point been six months in the Indian Health Service. They said, "You come very highly recommended. Why don't you come to Chicago for an interview?" I asked who recommended me. They said, "Danny Freedman [chair of the Department of Psychiatry of the University of Chicago]." I knew him very well. I called and asked him what was going on. He said, "You're good, and this is a way to get you back here to talk with you." So I was interviewed by a board of directors. I said, yes, I was interested in residential treatment of children and that I had a meager amount of experience at the Orthogenic School and that I didn't think I was ready for a job like that. They said, okay.

THEN WHAT?

I talked with Danny and he allowed that the real reason all this had happened was that he and Bettelheim wanted me to go back to the Orthogenic School. Freedman figured I should finish my training in another year and then be at the school. Bettelheim did this time say he wanted me to come back and be assistant director for a couple of years and then he would retire and I would become director. I mean, I was one of a succession of [candidates as] successors.

This must have been early 1967. I had a year in the IHS [Indian Health Service] at that time. In the meantime, Danny came out and spent some time with me in the IHS. He was interested in the Zuni religion, which I was too. Everything soon began to unravel. Danny made a very good offer financially and every other way. I was supposed to be a child psychiatry fellow for a year and was gonna get a nice salary and they'd help us finance a house and all sorts of stuff like that. I was getting overstimulated and anxious. But Danny figured out that I didn't see eye to eye with him at all. What he wanted to do was change the Orthogenic School after Bettelheim retired, and he saw me as the way to do it. I was to change the school into an institution for doing research on the biology of autism. And I said that was a terrible idea and all of a sudden the offer began to vanish.

BUT WHAT ABOUT BETTELHEIM'S OFFER?

The offer from Bettelheim stood. One of my most memorable conversations with Danny was about the fact that he didn't believe the results. He said nobody can reproduce it. And I said no one can reproduce walking on a tightrope unless you know how to do it. I said, you know, there's a lot of data. I told him about kids being evaluated by an outside analyst every six months and a whole lot of day-to-day notes on what happened with every kid. I said, "Why don't you go over to the school and read some of this stuff?" He said, "I wouldn't want to because I still wouldn't believe it." This was the beginning of the heyday of biological psychiatry. There weren't control groups, and so on.

SO THE BIOPSYCHIATRISTS HAD STARTED TO PURGE THE FIELD OF ANY-
ONE WHO DIDN'T BUY THEIR OWN BELIEFS.

When I told Bettelheim about this, he nodded sadly and said yeah, or
something like that. I also mentioned the salary I was being offered,
which [with Danny's offer withdrawn] had declined by about 85 percent
[laughs]. Bettelheim said "Well, you know, you don't do this for money."
But the main thing that decided me against it was that I felt I was being
a perfectly decent Bob Bergman in the Indian Health Service and I felt
I would be a fourth-rate Bettelheim in the O. School. I was having a
good time in the IHS and I was very attached to a lot of people and
didn't want to leave.

SO WHAT LASTING LESSONS DID YOU LEARN DURING YOUR TIME WITH
BETTELHEIM?

That self-analysis is the beginning of all analysis; that the customer is always right; that defensiveness is the enemy of therapy; respect for the
symptoms; it's our job to understand what the other person is bringing in
to the encounter. He taught how vital autonomy is; if you don't have that,
you don't have anything. In a word, insight. Using analytical insight to deal
with situations. He showed us how to have a better relationship with our
patients. He really wanted kids to get better. He tore into kids, really, to
get them to do better. He kept trying. He saw them from the inside out.

GAYLE JANOWITZ, CHILD CARE WORKER

Gayle Schulenberger Janowitz worked with Bruno Bettelheim during
the early years at the Orthogenic School, which he converted into a live-
in treatment center for emotionally disturbed youngsters. She later married Morris Janowitz, who became a professor of sociology at the University of Chicago and a co-author of Bettelheim's first book, *The
Dynamics of Prejudice*. Just before she joined the Orthogenic School
staff, Bettelheim had gained permission from the University of Chicago
administration to redefine the mission of a unit originally dealing with a
mélange of neurologically as well as psychologically impaired children,
conducted in what he found to be a cold and utterly ineffective manner.
When Janowitz arrived in the fall of 1944, a few weeks after Bettelheim
took charge, the school was undergoing a tremendous transition in
staffing, methods, and purposes.

WHEN DID YOU START WORKING AT BRUNO BETTELHEIM'S ORTHO-
GENIC SCHOOL IN CHICAGO?

I came about a month or two after Bettelheim [in the fall of 1944]. I
had had a year and a half at the University of North Dakota. Then I came
to the University of Chicago and I asked for a secretarial job, possibly in
a setting that involved children because I wanted to go into social work.
I had an interview. They needed a night nurse. The night nurse was going away for two weeks' vacation. She showed me around. I thought she
was a pruneface, like the wicked witch of the east. She kept complaining
about the [new] director, that he was too good to the kids. I thought,
"Wow, that sounds interesting," because I didn't like her at all.

There was a boy who wouldn't take any food from anybody. So he'd
come and say "I hungry" and stand outside the door. I had a little office.
I'd go down in the basement to the kitchen and make him a sandwich
and get a carton of milk and leave it outside the door of my room. He'd
hear me and come and get it. But he wouldn't take anything from anybody. He'd return the dishes. We did this every night. She said, "This
boy has a full set of keys to the school and the director won't take them
away from him." This made him sound even more interesting. He must
have been on the ball because this nurse wasn't.

IT SOUNDS LIKE IT WAS A TURBULENT TIME FOR EVERYONE.

Oh, the school was the craziest place I'd ever seen in my life. I remember thinking "I'll stick around because it's kind of fascinating. But
this is nuts, this is not the way to take care of children." There were at
least thirty kids [from the previous regime]: epileptic kids, a mix of physically and emotionally disturbed, all kinds of multiple problems. This
boy who had the keys played chess with a man who came in to work
there. He was a fascinating kid, obviously intelligent. I started substitut-
ing and somebody said, "Are you going to the staff meeting?"

So I went, and [Bettelheim] is talking about how he's just come to the
school. He knows everything that's wrong with it. He's going to completely make it over. It going to be only emotionally disturbed children.
He has to place these kids who've become institutionalized from being
there too long. Well, I went out walking on air. It was the most exciting
thing I heard in my life, because I was in on the ground floor. Somebody
knew what to do and was going to do something about it. It was terribly

exciting. It took him a long time to assemble a staff. It took maybe a full year to get out the kids we couldn't help. He had to find a place for each one, the best place he could. We never brought in more than one new kid at a time.

HOW DID BETTELHEIM APPEAR TO THE KIDS AND TO THE STAFF?

He had eyes that could see through you. His eyes saw everything. That's the fantasy the kids had, and the staff sort of did too. There's no use in fudging anything. The main thing that he could not stand was pretense. His favorite saying about people was that "he knows nothing about nothing"; if anybody tried to fake anything, he couldn't stand it. You sort of knew that. You might as well be honest about it. The kids knew it too.

THE SCHOOL PSYCHIATRIST BETTELHEIM BROUGHT IN WAS EMMY SYLVESTER, WHO WAS FROM THE CHICAGO INSTITUTE AND BEFORE THAT FROM VIENNA. WHAT WAS SHE LIKE?

Emmy Sylvester was the first psychiatrist at the school. I heard they had a big falling out later. I'm very fond of her. What was unique about Emmy was that she had this incredible respect for the counselors. She always made it clear that we were the ones, the crucial ones, who helped the children, and that any psychiatrist was just ancillary staff. It was our job night and day to do all the little things for them. She would see the kids and read the records and we would have a meeting with her. It was always an ego trip. She would pick up little things that she thought were important that you'd done. As far as we knew, [Sylvester and Bettelheim] got along beautifully. It was as though the counselor got all the credit for whatever happened to the kids. Sylvester gave the total credit. He did, too. He'd write in reports what was going on with the teacher and the two counselors who are treating your child this month.

WHAT WAS THE SETUP FOR THE NEW KIDS? WAS IT DESCRIBED ACCU-RATELY IN LOVE IS NOT ENOUGH?

It was an old building, but it was bright and clean. We had the living room from the very beginning where all the staff meetings were [held], where parents met their children, where the fund-raisers came. There'd be two counselors for every group. The kids were in groups from the very beginning. They were in dormitories. Before, they took charts of

when the kid had his bottle and that sort of thing. [Bettelheim] ripped
that down the first day. They had a room where EKGs were given. They
ripped it out and put in a pool table, or something like that, the first
week or so. When a child came in, [Bettelheim] decided who got the
kid, who the primary person with responsibility for the kid was going to
be.

So the day came that you met this new kid and you gave him a teddy
bear or some animal. Then you'd take him shopping because many of
the kids arrived without much. I remember [one boy] who arrived with
a long delinquent record and was no more delinquent than I was. He
was kind of a deprived, kind of a needy little guy who responded fantas-
tically. He came in from the Jewish orphanage with [the kind of] cor-
duroy knickers my brothers wore when I was little. So I took him out
[for new clothes]. So you tried to spend time with them individually to
make fudge or something at night. You were responsible for getting
haircuts for them, going to the doctor, and so on.

WHAT AGES WERE THESE NEW KIDS?

The age of new kids was about ten to eleven. It was always about
thirty children.

HOW LONG WERE THEY ALLOWED TO STAY?

Then the kids had to leave at fourteen, sink or swim. That was the fantasy, that we needed two or three years [to help them]. For years, Bruno
went out and visited boarding schools. He went everywhere to find
places for these kids. They weren't good enough. After our kids went
and had a hard time, it was felt they should stay longer. They should go
to high school, stay for years, for these kids who have had too rough a
time.

YOU LIVED INSIDE THE SCHOOL AS A COUNSELOR FOR A WHILE, DIDN'T
YOU?

He asked if I wanted to move in to the school [as a live-in counselor].
It was room and board and a stipend. You're really there. There were six
of us who lived there at any one time. There was a teeny little room with
a Dictaphone [where we made reports]. That was the room you had by
yourself. On either side of it was a room where two counselors lived. A
room for a night nurse and a little office and bed for sick kids.

HOW DID THIS DICTAPHONE REPORTING WORK?

There was a kid named Mickey. The staff told me he was retarded. I stayed behind with him. He played the piano a little bit. I followed him around and I recorded everything he did. Pages and pages showing that Mickey was not retarded. I was so angry. Then Mickey left the school. At some point Bruno said I should turn in reports too. We had a format to go by. He told us what he wanted. Put it in the context of what was going on before [whatever] the kid did. Emphasize what was actually said and done. No theorizing. Just verbatim reports. What went on. Anecdotal reporting is what it was called. Very short anecdotes of what the kids said and did. He came up to me and said, "I like your reports." I said, "Mickey is not retarded." He said, "Of course [Mickey] is not. He'd been institutionalized, had been in a institution too long and he had to leave. Why do you ask?" Because I was so mad and wrote [accounts showing] Mickey wasn't retarded. He said, "Why didn't you give them to me?"

SO HE TOOK YOUR REPORTS VERY SERIOUSLY. NOT MANY PROFESSIONALS ARE IN THE HABIT OF GIVING THEIR FLOOR STAFF MUCH CREDIT FOR ANYTHING.

It was our story. He'd ask continually about things, he was always checking with everybody and asking if you remembered this incident or that. Whenever your child was being presented—he would go to psychoanalytic meetings, if he presented a child with whom you worked, he paid your way to the meetings. This was very exciting and the only way we could have gone.

THE EARLY YEARS WERE DEVOTED TO DISTURBED AND DELINQUENT KIDS. IT WAS BY THE LATE 1950s HE BROUGHT IN AUTISTIC KIDS. IS THAT RIGHT?

We didn't have autistic children then. And we never used those words. Primary behavior disorder was what we talked about. [The difficulties] had to happen before the age of two because it was so very basic. But what it was and how puzzling it was—we all thought it was insoluble. I remember that Emmy Sylvester explained at a staff meeting that some people believe schizophrenia is matter of inheritance, others a matter of nurture. That there is no answer, that it's mixed up. I was so glad [to hear that], because we got all those kids labeled schizophrenic, but with many kids why they should be the way they are didn't make any sense when you knew the parents. There was one little girl [who] I couldn't explain. She had severe learning disabilities. We didn't know about them at that time. We'd see the parents and get to know them and there's nothing.

Although their histories were generally pretty horrible. We had a girl whose mother, I guess, was a prostitute. Every year at Christmas, she'd see the child and have a big bag of wonderful, expensive, and completely inappropriate toys. The social worker would bring them. Once she sent a nude picture of herself to the little girl. At eleven o'clock, the social worker would keep the mother from coming to see the kid by taking her out for a meal. We certainly felt that whatever we did to the children, it couldn't match what had already happened to those kids. You couldn't.

STAFF OFTEN KEPT IN TOUCH WITH THEIR KIDS LONG AFTER LEAVING THE SCHOOL. HOW DID THE KIDS YOU KNEW WORK OUT?

Our kids probably had a lower divorce rate than the general public. They were very determined to stay married and be good parents, and many of them succeeded. When I was think of how we used to sit around and wonder and badger Dr. B. a lot about that—"These kids should probably never marry and have children, should they?"—he'd say, "Maybe not. That's not a decision that we can make." We were dead wrong. We didn't know for sure you could break the cycle, that these kids could make it. We wanted to believe it and staked our lives on it. But at the same time, maybe not. There was so much wrong with them, they had had such a bad time, [so] how could they be good parents? There may be some who failed, but I don't know any.

AUTONOMY IS A BIG THEME IN BETTELHEIM'S BOOKS. HOW MUCH AU-TONOMY DID STAFF HAVE?

When he [took a summer vacation] because of his hay fever, I was put in charge, and we took the children to camp. When I think of it now, it was incredible. So we had a boy who ran away and went to jail. When the [runaway] kids got picked up, the first time they stayed a few hours, the next time, overnight. One severely delinquent kid had to test it out. The [Chicago] police were very good to our kids, took good care of them, spoiled them to death. So I had to go down and get him in this small town. We had a staff meeting beforehand and we always listened to everyone's opinion. Bruno always listened to everyone's opinion. They all agreed that [the boy had] to stay in that jail one day. So I went and saw that he was in jail with adults. I didn't like the appearance of it. I took the responsibility and took him out. I said to [everyone], "I'm very sorry, that's the best I can do." [It worked out okay.] I was craft counselor [and it was decided that the boy] had to shadow me for the whole day. He got bored to death. It was quite sobering for him.

SO THE DIRECTOR WAS NOT A DICTATOR?

Bruno never made unilateral decisions about anything so far as I can remember. There was always a lot of discussion, a lot of argument. He loved to argue too. He'd usually ask what you thought first to see if you had a good idea of what to do. It was a way of life. It was incredible. At night when the kids were asleep, everybody would go down to the kitchen and eat ice cream and sit around the table and talk about their day. Everybody had a story or two to tell Dr. B., and if there was a new child what went on and how he was doing. Or if there was a problem with a kid, he'd want to know how it turned out. It was a continual staff meeting. You were in one all the time.

BY MOST ACCOUNTS, THE STAFF WERE ENGAGED IN SELF-DISCOVERY AND DEVELOPMENT AS MUCH AS THE RESIDENTS WERE.

We all grew up there. There was a great deal of sibling rivalry. We were young men and women, and we were all very competitive. We wanted to be the best. I have no doubt [that Bettelheim] related better to women than to men. It was also considered a woman's job, taking care of children. I was at the university in [the education department], and the men there were not very promising. Now there are very respectable young men there. But it wasn't true at the time. Bruno never had a male assistant. You were always learning things about yourself, and that was an exciting part of working there. [I once told him], "I've just become aware of big problem: Isn't it a danger that we enjoy the children's delinquency too much?" I was thinking of a certain young man on staff who loved to have the kids do everything he never dared to do. You were always discovering things like that.

He was always working at this desk. He was always writing. His door was always open so you could come after work and tell him what you thought he ought to know. I came in and waited for him to finish writing a sentence. Then I announced, "Dr. B., everybody is crazy." He said, "My dear girl, did you just discover that?" I just wanted to tell him that I'm not the only one. You're not the only one.

WAS IT TRUE ABOUT THERE BEING AN UNLOCKED DOOR AT ALL TIMES? A NEWS STORY SAID IT WAS A LIE.

I notice [that a staff member] was quoted in an article. This writer said that Bruno said there was a special door at the school that you could go out but you can't come in. [The staff member] said there was no special door. Well, she's lying. There was a special door. Well, they were all special. You could go out any of the doors. That's absolutely accurate. That was there from day one.

WHEN DID YOU LEAVE THE SCHOOL?

In 1951.

WHATEVER HAPPENED PSYCHOLOGICALLY, THE SCHOOL CHANGED PHYSICALLY OVER THE YEARS. WHAT DID YOU THINK OF IT WHEN YOU VISITED IT YEARS LATER?

It got so elegant, so fancy. Years later, my husband [Professor of Sociology Morris Janowitz], who was very fond of Bruno, saw it and said, "This is Bruno's mausoleum. Isn't it?" [Former staff member and later University of Chicago professor] Ben Wright and I were in the front hall laughing and saying: "Can you imagine the kids sitting out here putting on ice skates here?" We used to go over to the midway and ice skate. Velvet chairs, for God's sake. It was a different place. [When I started work], it was an old comfortable parsonage with old covers on the furniture and stuff. They've made such hoopla about his art as if this doll's house and rocking horse and that stuff had anything to do with therapy for children. It was Bruno; it was his therapy. Being a whole person. That was his thing. He made it famous, and it worked.

YOU KEPT IN CONTACT THROUGHOUT THE YEARS. DID HE CHANGE?

He became more difficult as he got older. He was impossible after [his wife] Trudie died. I think he never forgave her. She wasn't supposed to die first. This man who could tell anyone else how to run their lives or at least make suggestions and be very helpful couldn't hack it at all. He was just angry and miserable.

ANY MENTION OF HIS EXPERIENCES IN DACHAU AND BUCHENWALD?

I was living there and I had this record of songs, like the Spanish "Quatro Generales" and "The Peat Bog Soldiers" [a song written by a camp inmate and sung by inmates in the Nazi era]. I had a record player right by the door, and one day I was playing "The Peat Bog Soldiers" and there was a knock on the door and I opened it and there was Bruno, and he looked so startled when he heard that song. He looked like hell. I went out to talk with him and never played that song again.

I noticed that on his desk he had every book on the camps ever written and he obviously had read them. There'd be two or three, and next week there'd be two other ones. I am convinced that Bruno's walk was unique and that it had something to do with the camps. He walked like this [scrunches her shoulders], very protective of his body. I doubt he walked that way when he was a young man. [Staff member] Betty Pingree would tell me when he came to Rockford College he would sit in a chair and teach. He didn't stand for a long time. He was so much better later when I knew him at the school.

DID YOU KNOW HIS WIFE AND FAMILY?

Trudie would have us over to the apartment. The [family] must have really resented [the school]. At least twice I saw Trudie walk in very upset and practically crying and Bruno took her off to the office. It's because she thought he never came home and he never saw his family. I knew that's what it was about. He would talk to her, and she would calm down. He was there until four in the morning. After everyone was asleep, we'd eat ice cream and sometimes staff would want to talk with him, and after all that was finished he would sit there and write all night. At some point he would go home. He just simply lived there. [Trudie] was in charge of social workers in foster placement at Chicago Child Care. They had a black woman who [helped bring up] the kids.

That was his pattern, these incredible hours. You always felt that he was kind of driven. That he didn't have so much time and he had so much to do. The end of his life was so sad because he felt he outlived it and that life wasn't worth living. He was so terrified, so afraid that he would be helpless. Utterly, utterly helpless. And he was pretty helpless. I was so cross when this dumb girl wrote in this [*Chicago Magazine*] article about his "bizarre" death. It was not a bizarre death. It was a perfectly reasonable, courageous way to go. He was in such bad shape. He couldn't write, couldn't read, couldn't do any of the things that were life to him.

BETTELHEIM WAS ACCUSED OF PSYCHOANALYZING HIS OWN STAFF. DID
HE PLAY THERAPIST WITH YOU?

We talked to him about our kids and about personal things and about
why you reacted this way to this and that sort of thing. I did this. It was
sort of in between. At one point, I began to see him individually after
one or two years there. I considered it preparation for going into therapy. I spoke to a friend in California, and she felt he had loused up her
therapy for her later. I heard a lot of that in later years. Maybe he
shouldn't have, I don't know. But for many of us, it was a way of getting
started. Quite a few of the counselors saw him at some time or other and
then went into therapy.

No, it was not a psychoanalysis at all. Much of it involved the kids and
your work, but then there came a point where if you wanted to talk
about your own problems he was there. It was your choice. If you
wanted it, it was there. He'd make a referral for you. I didn't feel it in-
terfered with [later therapy] in any way. He didn't see all the counselors.
Some he just referred and they went.

DO YOU KNOW ANY OF THE COMPLAINANTS?

I know one of the boys who complained and said a lot of things. We
don't change people basically. He was paranoid as a little boy. We helped
him live with his paranoia, but he is still paranoid.

"STEPHEN ELLIOT," ORTHOGENIC SCHOOL
RESIDENT AND AUTHOR

The name above is the pseudonym for a former resident at the Orthogenic School. We met in the early 1990s. He since has published a
memoir of his experiences at the school, *Not The Thing I Was: Thir-
teen Years at Bruno Bettelheim's Orthogenic School* (New York: St.
Martin's Press, 2003). This is an excerpt from a much longer interview.

THE HALF-DOZEN FORMER RESIDENTS WHO LED THE ASSAULT ON BET-
TELHEIM HAVE PORTRAYED HIM AS A JEKYLL-HYDE CHARACTER. HOW DID
YOU SEE HIM DURING YOUR YEARS THERE?

Jekyll-Hyde is a nice fairy story. Good mother–bad mother, which, you know, Freud would say was a child's first view. Then you integrate those two as you get older and realize they are the same person. What made him who he was was his toughness and his cynicism and his ability to take any situation and use it for whatever advantage it possibly could be used for. [This was] somebody who could be mercurial and brutally frank at times as well as warm and tender at other times. He lived a life of passion. He felt passionately about what he believed in. He felt it was his mission to save kids in any way that he could, and he tried. The fact that he lost his temper and was overzealous and could put people down and be a real shit when he wished was not two sides of him. That's who he was.

HE SLAPPED KIDS, BUT I AM TOLD THAT MUCH MORE OFTEN HE WOULD YELL TO DISCIPLINE THEM. WAS IT FEAR OF PHYSICAL PUNISHMENT OR HIS FORCE OF PERSONALITY THAT KEPT WAYWARD KIDS IN LINE?

I think it was the force of his personality, but clearly he would beat us up when we got out of line. He would slap us on the face five or six times. He was pretty tough about it. It was very much the old European viewpoint of the head of the household. But, you know, it was a time of straitjackets and shock treatments. Then, if you hit a kid a few times, particularly kids who were running around and acting out, it wasn't the end of the world.

The particular instance was over, but the anxiety about getting hit again or the fear of being put down or humiliated in front of everybody continued. That was ever present. There was the sense of being in a concentration camp because really you could get in trouble for whatever trouble he decided was trouble. There was relief when he wasn't around. I thought [the slapping] was arbitrary. But I was pretty much a Dennis the Menace with a real cynical snide twist. I'm no more verbal now than I was when I was at [the age of] six, so you can imagine what sort of a child I must have been.

SHOULD HE HAVE WRITTEN ABOUT THE SLAPPING?

Put yourself in his position. He was once asked if anything were different now that he was world famous. He said, "Yes, now when I think somebody is a horse's ass, I have to keep my mouth shut." Can you imagine what would have happened, given the kind of things that were happening at the time, with straitjackets and lobotomies and electroshocks

and insulin shocks and doping kids up out of their minds with tranquil-
izers—and he said he hit his kids? There would have been a run on kids
getting the shit beat out of them by institution workers, many of whom
who were not trained and were there because there was nothing else
they could do, who were not professionals in any sense of the word. And
now they had a perfect excuse to act out any aggressions they wanted.
Whereas in the school, the acting out by the staff in terms of hitting was
taken very seriously and in fact did not go on. There were a few slips.
But by and large with twenty staff and fifty kids for forty years there
weren't that many. He did not want to serve as a justification for a rash
of attacks on kids being beaten up, and there were not many ways to explain that subtly.

DID YOU EVER TRY TO EXPLAIN IT?

I tried to write a balanced article. The editors turned it down on the
basis that his readers did not understand the school. Bob Gottlieb at
the *New Yorker* said he didn't do profiles about dead people. Subtlety
in the media does not exist. People want sound bites and they want the
spectacular. Which is why when you accuse a famous psychoanalyst after committing suicide of beating you up you get front-page stories in
papers across the country. If you try to explain what he was really trying to do in a decent, well-thought-out way, nobody will run it. He was
aware of how the press was used. He saw how it was used in Nazi Germany. You have to think that yes there was deception, and maybe he
was wrong to do it, but what else could he have done at the time? I can't
really get that angry about it.

WERE YOU SURPRISED BY THE ATTACKS ON HIM AFTER HIS DEATH?

There were always kids who were disgruntled and unhappy. He was
very arrogant, and that stirs animosity. He did that in his career. A lot of
psychoanalysts hated his guts forever.

DIDN'T HE EVER LET UP WITH YOU?

Of course. He had a sense of humor and he would make self-deprecating jokes. We would ask him about his bald spot, and first he would
deny that he was bald, then he would say that it was bald so he could
see. He'd say he had eyes in the back of his head. When *The Sound of
Music* came out with the song "Edelweiss," he knew that we all called

his wife "Edelweiss," and he thought that was funny. Trudie was wonderful. We used to see her all the time. She was really great. She never made you feel uncomfortable. I remember her after all these years as one of the truly great human beings. We would go around the neighborhood. The whole neighborhood knew who we were. We'd go shopping. We'd go to the drugstore. To the bookstore, to the library, to the swimming pool, to the playground, and things like that. So it's just walking around. So we were walking by her house all the time. We'd see her out, you know, with the dogs or talking to the neighbors or whatever, and she'd come over and say hi to us. I remember that someone got yelled at by a counselor and Trudie was there. We were all worried that Trudie would tell Dr. B., but she never did.

WERE THERE ANY AUTISTIC KIDS IN YOUR GROUP?

We were called the Mohawks. There was Peter, a very disturbed autistic kid who was kind of frightening to me because I was aged about twelve.

SO KIDS WITH VERY DIFFERENT PROBLEMS WERE ALL LIVING TOGETHER AND HAD TO GET ALONG?

I think that was what the essence of what the Orthogenic School was about, that people were accepted for who they were and that while they may have irritated and frightened us to some extent—the frightening [side of it] may have been only at the beginning. I think the fact that the symptom was respected, that kids were respected for their differences [was important]. While people might get angry at somebody for holding up the group, for making our lives miserable, for peeing on the rug, and things like that, which used to be a problem with one of the kids when I first got there, you are asking about a lifestyle. When somebody comes to the mores of a new community, you might not like them at first, but over time it becomes second nature—the issue of acceptance of the other, not putting them down and trying to help them.

YOU WERE KIDS, SO THERE HAD TO BE A LOT OF SLIPUPS.

I mean there were times that everybody was nasty and backbiting and things like that, but by and large people were very supportive. The kids were supportive of each other. That's something that never is discussed. It would never have worked if it was just the staff. The older kids helped the younger kids. We'd help each other. Despite all the hassles, when there were problems, we'd pull together. People knew what the limits were, and they had a sense of self-discipline. There may have been one or two kids who were so out of their minds they couldn't do it, but then the other kids banded together. The staff had to help them, but by and large there was a sense of community standards and they were adhered to.

WERE YOU OVERLY RESTRICTED THERE?

I'm not a good person to ask. I don't think I liked restrictions as an adolescent any more than when I first walked in. I chafed at restrictions. Our mail was read, et cetera.

HOW DO YOU RATE THE STAFF?

There were staff there who created lots of problems, who acted out their own things. In the beginning, everybody had problems adjusting. Most of the long-termers, no. Because the really good counselors worked on themselves and were really incredible.

SO, ULTIMATELY, DID HE HELP YOU?

Did I think he helped? I think had he been more wishy-washy about it, the changes might not have occurred. "Do it or don't do it, but don't make any bones about it later on" [was his message]. The school was always about offering choices. The fundamental belief was that the symptom was the highest form of expression for a child, given their view of the world. Nobody was crazy, given their view of the world, for the way they acted. You had to understand their view to understand their way of acting. If what they did was totally logical given the way they saw the world, then you didn't dismiss them as being a nut. You tried to understand them and maybe give them an opportunity for other choices or other ways of resolving things. Basically, [Bettelheim] gave everybody dignity by looking at them that way. And so if the school could give you options for how you live your life, then maybe the whole world wasn't as you first experienced it, maybe there were other possibilities and other outcomes over time. Then that was how you could live your life. I think that was the issue for lot of the kids who were very disturbed. That there were other possibilities. I think that was what they learned.

So what matters is that it all contributed to recovery.

The important thing is that they were cured. Would they have been cured without the severe treatment, without somebody like him? You couldn't have gotten the good that was the Orthogenic School without the bad, which was the price you paid. I think that's what people have to bear in mind. Could the cruelty be done without? Yes. His emotional cruelty is what I'm talking about—when he put people down. But there was an awful lot of shit that went on, an awful lot of nonsense that nobody wanted to deal with that he cleaned up over and over again. To be at the mercy of somebody else totally is a very unpleasant situation. You were at his mercy: he ran the school. And your penalty was ultimately to be thrown out of the school, and everybody knew it. On the other hand, if it were such a bad place, the penalty would have had no meaning. But the fact is, it did have meaning. The kids who wanted out could have gotten out. It was not difficult to get yourself thrown out of there or leave. For a little crazy kid, yes, it was. But for the people who were complaining, [they] could have left.

ROBERT COLES, PSYCHIATRIST AND AUTHOR

Robert Coles, born in 1929, is a prolific and profound author who, like members of an earlier European generation, successfully sought to relate his professional training in child psychiatry to social issues and political reform.[4] As a young psychiatrist stationed at an Air Force base in the Deep South, he became deeply involved in the nascent civil rights movement in the late 1950s. Afterward, he worked closely with legendary psychoanalytic historian Erik Erikson at Harvard University, where Coles has been professor of psychiatry and medical humanities since 1978. He was awarded the Pulitzer Prize in 1973 for his mammoth five-volume study, *Children of Crisis*.

His numerous books include *Dead End School* (1968), *The Wages of Neglect* (with Maria W. Piers, 1969), *The Geography of Faith* (with Daniel Berrigan, 1971), *Farewell to the South* (1972), *Erik Erikson: The Growth of His Work* (1973), *Walker Percy: An American Search* (1978), *Flannery O'Connor's South* (1980), *The Mind's Fate: A Psychiatrist Looks at His Profession* (1985, reprinted 1995), *The Moral Life of Children* (1987), *Dorothy Day: A Radical Devotion* (1987), *Harvard Diary: Reflections on the Sacred and the Secular* (1988), *Anna Freud: The*

Dream of Psychoanalysis (1992), *The Call of Service: Witness to Idealism* (1993), and *Lives of Moral Leadership* (2000).

Our interview took place in the spring of 1997, just after an assiduously negative biography of Bettelheim had hit the bookshelves. A year later, Coles was awarded a Presidential Medal of Freedom. In his acceptance speech, he remarked, "I've been extremely lucky to know and work with children in this and other countries for most of my life. I've tried to focus on those who are isolated from the professional knowledge and experience of people like myself—the poorest and most disadvantaged kids. I urge the pediatricians I know, and the medical students I teach, to do the same."

BRUNO BETTELHEIM'S REPUTATION HAS SUFFERED SEVERELY SINCE HIS SUICIDE IN 1990. BEFORE ADDRESSING IT, I'LL ASK WHEN YOU FIRST KNEW OF BETTELHEIM'S WORK AND WHAT IMPRESSION IT MADE ON YOU.

I knew of him since my residency days reading his books. They were eloquent and well written and cogent. I loved *The Uses of Enchantment*. I loved his writings in the *New Yorker*. I felt this was a man of such unusual capability and the further ability to express in words what he thought. He was a rarity in the field. I place him in the company of [Erik] Erikson, which for me is a pretty high compliment. He appealed to both the professional person and the general public. He was a heroic figure, coming out of the concentration camps and then also as a leading authority on the most troubled and disturbed children, which is also a kind of heroic effort. These are not the children that many of us trained in child psychiatry tended to become concerned with.

YOU MEAN EXTREMELY SCHIZOPHRENIC OR AUTISTIC CHILDREN?

Mainly the autistic children. That work was so enormously taxing and challenging. My experience with autistic children is that they were locked up in the state hospital I saw here in Massachusetts. In my training in child psychiatry, we spent very little time learning how to deal with them because they were not the young people we would have much to do with. They were the hardest to reach. They were [the bottom of] the pail, so to speak, for both society and for us.

DURING YOUR PSYCHIATRIC TRAINING IN THE LATE 1950s, WHAT WAS THE ATTITUDE OF YOUR TEACHERS AND COLLEAGUES TOWARD BETTELHEIM?

Favorable. Very much so. I was trained in child psychiatry in Boston. Those instructors who supervised my work all admired him. I met Fritz Redl [a close friend and colleague of Bettelheim] because I was in the Group for Social Issues and the Group for the Advancement of Psychiatry.[5] He was very lovely, decent person. He was not only knowledgeable but he was a sweet man. Not all people in any field can be relied upon to be kind and nice. He was a very fine person. I met him during the early years of my work in the South when I was studying school desegregation. I was contacted by the GAP [Group for the Advancement of Psychiatry] committee, [who] wanted me to join because of my obvious interest in social issues. I remember him at the time speaking very favorably about Bettelheim and his work. At the time, I don't think I knew that he knew him personally.

REDL WAS A VERY CLOSE FRIEND.

He and the committee were very involved in thinking about the civil rights movement, and I of course was in it. It was a committee of socially active child psychiatrists. Child psychiatry has always been an under-populated subspecialty. Redl was one of these wise older people because he had worked with tough, troubled delinquent kids—again, a population that many of us trained in psychiatry don't always get involved with. Especially when you've got to treat the children of the well-to-do who, relatively speaking, have milder disorders.

YOU WERE IN CHICAGO FOR A YEAR AS AN INTERN. WERE THERE RU-MORS ABOUT ANYTHING AMISS AT BETTELHEIM'S ORTHOGENIC SCHOOL?

No. Never heard that. The major figure in Chicago I attended to was William Carlos Williams. I wrote my thesis on him. He read his poems there at Rockefeller Chapel. And I remember spending time with him. I think at that time he asked me who Bettelheim was.

AND HOW DID YOU BECOME CONNECTED WITH ERIK ERIKSON?

Erikson wrote to me when he read about the work I was doing in the South [on nonviolence] because he was starting to get interested in Gandhi.[6] We established a correspondence. Then I met him. This is the mid-1960s, when he had just moved to Harvard from Austen Riggs. We became very close, and I taught in his course and ultimately would write a profile [of him]. He did mention Bettelheim, and he was the one who used the word "heroic." It was a word he was prone to anyway, since he was always interested in heroic figures, like Martin Luther, Gandhi, and whomever.

He told me that this work is very difficult and that only certain people do it. He pointed out the extraordinary resources of mind and spirit required to take on those toughest of children. Erikson did not always speak highly of people in his own field, so this was unusual. I also knew Grete Bibring, who headed a center of psychoanalytic psychiatry in Boston. She was from Vienna and mentioned Bettelheim to me the same way Erik did, as someone doing the most extraordinary work. I used to hear [Bettelheim] linked with Harold Searles, who worked with schizophrenics in a psychoanalytic way.[7] Later on when I wrote a *New Republic* [review of Bettelheim's book on infantile autism, *The Empty Fortress*], I remember calling him a hero. I took the word on as my own. I don't know if Erik ever visited [Bettelheim's Orthogenic School in Chicago].

HE DID. STAFF MEMBERS TOLD ME THAT ERIKSON AND BETTELHEIM GOT INTO SOME FRIENDLY BANTER. BETTELHEIM WENT INTO WHAT ONE VISITOR CALLED A "MODESTY FIT" AND SAID HE WAS NO MORE THAN A JAN-ITOR. ERIKSON REPLIED, "BUT YOU KEEP THE FURNACES WELL STOKED, BRUNO."

This is the kind of remark that Erikson would make. This is the modesty of very successful people. Erikson was a master—and I say this in no sense as critical or ironic—he was a master of making people feel comfortable through self-criticism or self-effacement, even though at other times he could be very much a grand figure. Do you know if they knew each other in Vienna?

NOT FACE TO FACE. IN AN INTERVIEW IN THE 1970S, ERIKSON SAID THAT IN VIENNA HE KNEW OF BETTELHEIM AT THE TIME AS AN ART HIS-TORIAN, WHICH HE WAS.

Well, look what they had in common—because Erik was an artist then. As Joan [Erikson] would repeatedly say to me—with a bit of mock bitterness because she was really proud of what he did: "You see what psychoanalysis did? It took him away from his art." He was the artist as psychoanalyst, which is the way I saw him. But I never heard anything critical about Bettelheim until years and years later. Maybe even after he died. But you have to remember I was way out of the field.

YOU MEAN, BECAUSE YOU WERE OTHERWISE ENGAGED IN THE SOUTH, YOU WERE NOT BUSY NETWORKING IN THE USUAL PSYCHOANALYTIC CIRCLES.

That's it. Although I trained in child psychiatry, I was out of that too. I did all this work in what I guess you would call social psychiatry. And I was trained in psychoanalysis in New Orleans at the institute there, but that was out of vogue, out of the kind of world [offered in] New York, Boston, Chicago. I know because I had started at the Boston Institute. They were different people there [in New Orleans]. There were practically no émigrés. They were a different breed of individuals.

I had gotten involved in civil rights activities and that was it [for my standard professional affiliations], except for Erikson and the GAP committee. They all held Bettelheim in high esteem. I remember Redl singling Bettelheim out for the nature of the tough struggle against such high odds. I think the reason they were discussing it with me was because I was dealing with children who were facing very high odds [in the South] too, going through mobs to get into schools. That may be responsible for some of these conversations. You are dealing with situations that are difficult because you're not exactly working with your colleagues in a regular setting.

I UNDERSTAND BETTELHEIM WROTE TO YOU AFTER YOU PUBLISHED A REVIEW OF ONE OF HIS BOOKS.

I vividly recall his signature. It was what I would call a strong signature.

IT'S NOT A SHY, RETIRING SIGNATURE, NOT WITH THOSE TWO STRONG B'S.

Yeah. I remember telling Erik about that, and we were laughing because I know [Erik's] signature too. Then he was laughing with me about my own, about which he very politely said, "You have a doctor's signature." But I recall Bettelheim's signature very clearly. And it was nice letter. This was the *New Republic* review. That review came out of my heart. It was called a "Hero of Our Time," and Erik called me afterward and said, "That was good," which I vividly remember because Erik was not one to easily compliment people to their faces. I also got a beautiful letter from Lillian Ross, who wrote for the *New Yorker*. Shortly after that, I started doing reviews and, later, profiles of Erik and Walker Percy and others for them. I got a lot of letters from other people. That review hit home in a favorable way.

SINCE THEN, THERE'S BEEN A TREMENDOUS SHIFT IN THE FIELD TO BIOPSYCHIATRIC EXPLANATIONS. THERE'S A WIDESPREAD BELIEF THAT IT HAS BEEN PROVED THAT ALL AUTISM IS PHYSIOLOGICAL, THAT THE CAUSE IS KNOWN. BUT I ALWAYS FIND RESEARCHERS IN THIS FIELD SAYING THEIR WORK "STRONGLY SUGGESTS," BUT DOES NOT PROVE, THIS OR THAT CONCLUSION. THEY ONLY GIVE THE IMPRESSION THAT THEY HAVE ANSWERS.

I think you're right. No one would claim that they definitively know the cause of autism. The lay audience can read in the papers that we have tracked down the cause of schizophrenia too. There were always some who believed that the biological side is an element, but even today who knows what causes schizophrenia really or definitively? These are speculations. Maybe with some empirical evidence you can begin to emphasize this or emphasize that, but we are nowhere near coming to a causal conclusion.

The [biopsychiatric researchers] may ultimately be proven historically correct and a century, or a half-century, from now someone will isolate [the cause]. [People like Bettelheim, who believed differently,] weren't masquerading. They believed themselves. But when you are thinking of those people, you have to immerse yourself in what was their time, and what their assumptions were, and what the assumptions of their colleagues were. In psychiatry, unlike orthopedic surgery, there is an act of faith involved, since we're not dealing with bones that can be put under a microscope. What we believed then about autism is that this was a very, very intractable behavioral illness caused by the earliest of injuries. The poor mothers and father must have been devastated by this kind of belief. But only the most heroic kind of person would attend such children. In fact, at the children's unit at Metropolitan State Hospital, there were autistic children. You know Boston had per capita the highest population of child psychiatrists to the population of psychiatrically sick children anywhere in the country. It was the capital city of that subspecialty. And yet those children were virtually unattended. They were cared for not by the child psychiatrists but by ward helpers, nurses, et cetera. The reason is that very few people had any interest in working with such children. Practically no one did. And there was Bettelheim devoting his life to those children.

YOU SPEAK OF THOSE "POOR PARENTS." PARENTS GROUPS HAVE MADE BETTELHEIM INTO A CARDBOARD VILLAIN. BUT DID YOU SEE ANYWHERE IN HIS BOOK AN INCLINATION TO BLAME PARENTS FOR AUTISM?

No. You'll see in the current [1995] edition of *The Mind's Fate* an essay I wrote when I was thirty, and you'll see someone who was very sensitive to that [accusatory stance] and who takes on his colleagues. If you look at my book on Anna Freud, you'll see that what I admired in her—and what I admired in Erikson—is an acute sensitivity to the misuse of psychiatry and psychoanalysis as a weapon to bludgeon people, to categorize, to label them, to criticize them. So I think I would have picked that up in Bettelheim, at least as a reader. Now, if he was saying one thing and doing another, that's another matter.

YOUR CO-AUTHOR ON *THE WAGES OF NEGLECT*, DR. MARIA PIERS, WHO WAS ACQUAINTED WITH BETTELHEIM, CRITICIZED HIM AFTER HIS DEATH TOO.

I never knew [Bettelheim] personally. For all the time I worked with Maria Piers, she never brought him up and never criticized him to me. And she had read what I wrote about him. She was quite willing to be critical of two people whom both she and I very much admired, namely Anna Freud and Erik Erikson. Critical the way friends sometimes are. Perhaps he just wasn't on her mind at the moment.

DID YOU KNOW HER HUSBAND, GERHART PIERS, WHO HEADED THE CHICAGO INSTITUTE AND WAS A CLOSER FRIEND OF BETTELHEIM?

Yes. I liked him a lot. I felt comfortable with him. I met him repeatedly because I was asked to speak at the Chicago Institute of Psychoanalysis. I corresponded with him. He was a very sweet man. I enjoyed him. I had fond memories of Gerhart.

GERHART DIED LONG BEFORE. DID MARIA PIERS TALK ABOUT VIENNESE DAYS BEFORE HITLER?

She talked a lot about that and the artistic side of that world, in contrast to now. The same critical thing you'd get from Anna Freud in describing those early people in psychoanalysis versus the kind of organization that's taken over now. You get that flavor in my writing and the reason is that I knew Erikson and Anna Freud. It was also a way for me to give a swift kick at people in my profession who I had second thoughts about once I was finishing up my training. If you read that essay, you'll see where I'm coming from both ideologically and personally.

My hunch is had I met Bettelheim—who can ever know—I would have gotten along with him the way that Alvin [Rosenfeld] did.[8] Alvin and I struck up an immediate friendship. He was a medical student when I was finishing my training and working with Erikson. We had fun. We became fast friends. There was a real friendliness. I didn't get a whole lot of that from people in my field [laughing]. [Rosenfeld] got me to do a seminar on psychiatry when he was a medical student—in essence bringing me back to the kind of work for which I originally had been trained. The same with Erik bringing me back, because I had wandered so far off into that southern work on school desegregation that I had lost all sight of the field for a few years.

It was a detour worth taking.

I felt so, and obviously it was the basis of my whole career.

So what did you make of the astounding attacks against Bettelheim after his death? Piers told me that she believed the stories.

You're entitled to common sense in this matter. If I were Maria Piers in Chicago and I heard all this stuff, I suppose I would absorb that, as was said of Freud, as a whole climate of opinion—and you make it your own. Unfortunately, this is what people do. They gossip and they accept stuff like this and they're not critical. They don't have the time, the energy, the inclination, the personal knowledge, or whatever it is that makes people resist this. This is the tragedy. When Bettelheim killed himself, he gave such stuff a real shot in the arm. Once he did that, [his accusers] could all just go running down the field, some of them just in the innocence of what's been bruited about and others for much more personal reasons, such as the guy who wrote that biography. It's the only time I refused a review. I looked at the book and just said no. This was a hatchet job.

I just don't like books that go after people. It gets my hackles up. Don't you think there is a larger question here about the nature of biographies? Why do people want to do this? People want to write biographies to get even with someone, for a grudge. Then there's biography as a means of uncovering and refuting, not so much as a personal grudge. This is what Jeffrey Meyers does. Every time he writes about someone, he reduces them. He's so mean-spirited. I happen to know this because he tried to interview me about one of the biographies he was writing and just on the phone. I felt, My God, this man wants to murder this person, you know?

Then there are people like me, to be self-critical, who are just the opposite. People say to me that I idolize, that I make them better than they were. So I say, "Okay, that's what I do [because] that's what they meant to me." I omit [very personal] things [from biographies]. I got letters from people who supposedly were friends of Anna Freud saying, "Why didn't you deal with her sexual problems?" I think I *implied* that this was a woman who never had a heterosexual life, so far as I can surmise. But they wanted to know why I didn't deal with lesbianism. People asked if I know about her relationship with Dorothy Burlingham. I told them even if I knew about that, I still wouldn't have written about it. So that's the other side of this. Look, I think Bettelheim was a hero in doing, in the literal sense, extraordinary work against enormous odds, and probably to the detriment of his personal life. I just can't imagine that not being the case.

THAT'S TRUE.

He also was eminently successful as a writer or else there wouldn't be the biographies. What does that generate in people? Envy, rivalry, skepticism, incredulity. Who else would work with autistic children? It was such enormously taxing work psychologically. Bettelheim was also an emotional man. You can tell that by reading him. Like everyone else, he may have had his moments where he quote "had failings," where he lost his cool. Doesn't that go on in the privacy of psychoanalytic offices all the time? We never know about it, though, because we're working alone, and if the patient says it, and only the patient, it is immediately dismissed as a transference reaction. But [Bettelheim] was unprotected. He had people watching, working with him. If he stumbled, that became, as we said in the South, a federal case.

I don't know what would have happened to me if I were doing my work in New Orleans and Atlanta with social workers and psychologists and others around and in SNCC[9] and I heard horrible things, things that really pissed me off, and I in turn argued with my colleagues. If that were a matter of public record, people would say about me: "This guy had mixed feelings about black people" [laughing]. You know what I mean? In a profession that itself is so hazy, is working in the dark and does not have the kind of procedural clarity that other healing branches of what is loosely taught about medicine do, he was just out there. He was just way out there.

MY SENSE OF THE BETTELHEIM SCANDAL IS THAT IT IS A PIECE IN A
LARGER GAME, A CONFLICT GOING ON WITHIN PSYCHIATRY—A TARNISHING
OF ANY HUMANISTIC APPROACH, NOT JUST PSYCHOANALYSIS.

Well, psychoanalysis is the ultimate humanist approach and, when done
correctly, is a huge commitment of time and energy to an individual person day after day. Is it true now? Even at a hospital that used to be psychoanalytic when I was a resident, the whole emphasis is psychobiological,
which is fine to a certain extent. But even if there weren't these stories, the
approach Bettelheim had is going to be shunted aside. What one hears
now is the emphasis on biology and genetics. It may prove to be right. It
may not prove to be right. We don't know. Certainly the culture is not favorable to the kind of approach that Bettelheim [and Erikson] had.

In a sense, I have inherited Erikson's position at Harvard in that I am a
clinician who is a professor there. I teach undergraduates, which is what
he did. And my students have never heard of Erik Erikson! Can you imagine that? It's just a devastation to me that I'm the one who introduces
them to Erikson and who pushes them to get his books. Then they go in
the bookstores and the books aren't there. Even this man who strode
through Harvard Yard here [is shunted aside]. That's what's happened in
twenty years. When he died, Erikson got that incredible obituary in the
New York Times, and so did Bettelheim. They were both on the front
page. It's a different world today. If you had told me twenty years ago this
was going to happen, I would have thought you were out of your mind.

NOTES

1. Respectively, Richard Pollak, The Creation of Dr. B: A Biography of
Bruno Bettelheim (New York: Simon & Schuster, 1997), and Nina Sutton,
Bruno Bettelheim: A Biography (Paris: Stock, 1995).

2. Theron Raines, Rising to the Light: A Portrait of Bruno Bettelheim (New
York: Knopf, 2002).

3. On the multitudinous shortcomings of the previous works, see my articles
"Blaming Bettelheim," Psychoanalytic Review (June 2000) and "'Where There
Is Smoke': Rhetorical Strategies in the Assaults on Sigmund Freud and Bruno
Bettelheim," Free Associations (Spring 2001).

4. See my essay "Escape from the Treadmill: Politics Education, Politics,
and the Mainsprings of Child Analysis," in Vienna: World of Yesterday
1889–1914, edited by Stephen E. Bronner and F. Peter Wagner (Atlantic High-
lands, N.J.: Humanities Press, 1997).

5. Fritz Redl was a Vienna-born psychoanalyst and lifelong friend of Bettelheim who specialized in working with delinquent children and adolescents throughout his career. His books include *Children Who Hate* (New York: Free Press, 1951), *Controls from Within* (New York: Free Press, 1952), and *The Aggressive Child* (New York: Free Press, 1957), all co-authored with David Wineman.

6. Erikson eventually published *Gandhi's Truth: On the Origins of Militant Nonviolence* (New York: Norton, 1969).

7. Searles was the author of *The Nonhuman Environment in Normal Development and Schizophrenia* (New York: International Universities Press, 1960), *My Work with Borderline Patients* (Northvale, N.J.: Jason Aronson, 1986), and *Countertransference and Other Subjects: Selected Papers* (New York: International Universities Press, 1999).

8. An eminent child psychiatrist in New York. Collaborator and also co-author with Bettelheim (posthumously) of *The Art of the Obvious* (London: Thames and Hudson, 1993).

9. Student Non-Violent Coordinating Committee, a driving force in the civil rights movement in the American South.

INDEX

ABOUT KURT JACOBSEN

Kurt Jacobsen is a research associate in political science at the University of Chicago and 2003–2004 visiting lecturer at the Centre for the History of Science, Technology, and Medicine at Imperial College London. He is author or coeditor of four volumes and is book review editor at *Logos: A Journal of Modern Society & Culture*. Apart from professional journals, his articles have appeared in newspapers and periodicals in North America, Europe, South Asia, and South Africa, including *The Observer, The Guardian, The Independent, Irish Times, New Statesman & Society, Sunday Tribune, Sunday Independent, Saturday Star, Le Monde Diplomatique, Lettre Internationale, Chicago Reader, Chicago Tribune, The Progressive, The New Leader, In These Times, The Statesman, Dawn,* and *Economic and Political Weekly.*